machining architecture

NOX

Lars Spuybroek

Thames & Hudson

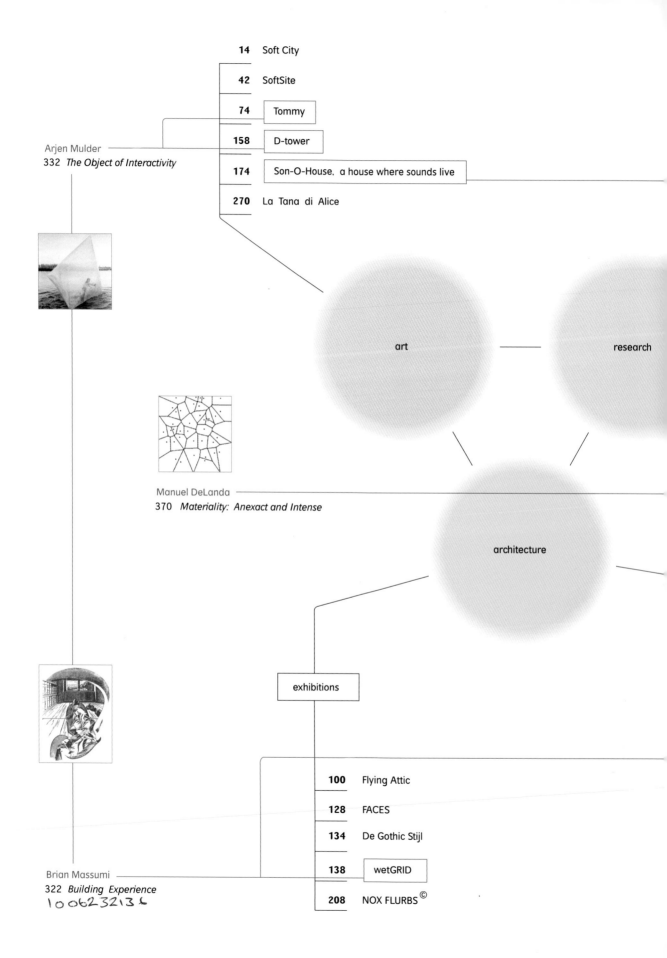

art   research

architecture

exhibitions

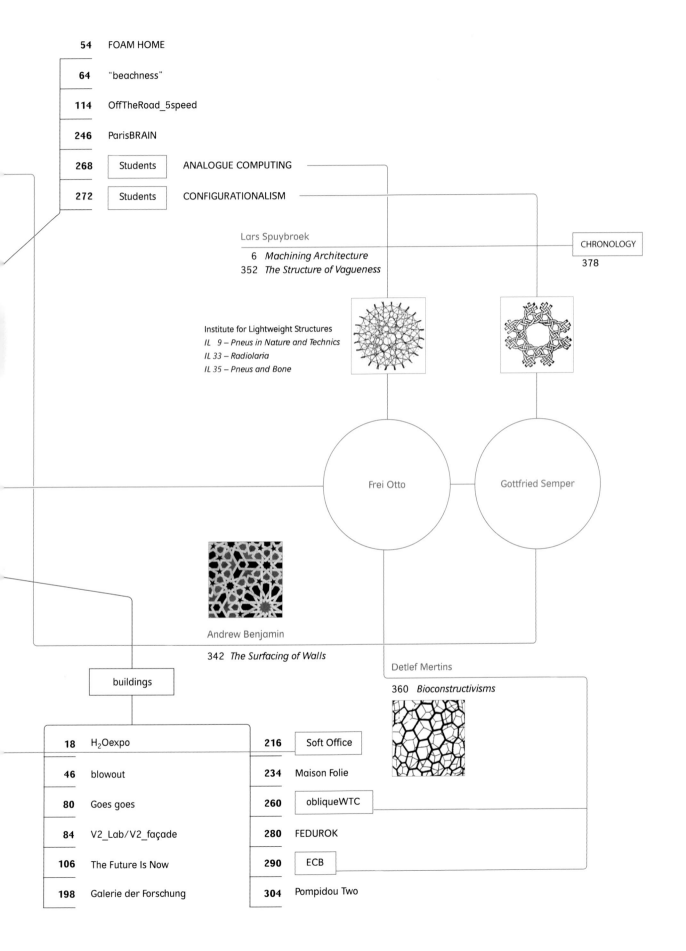

Introduction

The computer has reached a cultural stage, finally. The years that it was used for dreaming of perfect shape grammars and design automation (which seemed capable of producing only snowflake-shaped churches and second-rate Corbu's) or, worse, used for dreaming disembodied dreams of an architecture floating in cyber-space – those years are over. Also finally, and especially important for the architectural profession, computers have outgrown their servile function in the digital drawing room, where the real design was still done far away from the machines, sketched by hand, guided by genius.

A computer is more than anything else a steering device. According to the old rules of cybernetics this simply means two things: direction and flexibility – and this book is about both. An architectural design procedure that follows the rules of strategy and tactics needs both the clarity of determinism and the fuzziness of variability. The architecture of continuous variation is therefore not one of 'free form', but of articulation and structure. Architecture is still an art of the line. This book is a celebration of lines and of tectonics – complex lines and complex tectonics, I hasten to say, since the computer generates and manages complexity. During the second half of the twentieth century science developed fully under the sign of complexity, otherwise known as dynamic systems theory, which seems to have passed architecture by almost unnoticed. Architecture seemed to be caught in the local politics of language.

Machining Architecture aims to be three books in one: a monograph, a how-to book and a treatise. As a monograph it shows the works and projects as they were developed over the last ten years at my office, NOX: art projects, research projects and architectural projects that benefit from each other in such a way that each of them seems to succeed where the others cannot. And naturally they co-exist almost everywhere in the book; the art projects inhabit the architecture and vice versa, research and analysis in general are at the outset of every separate project. As a how-to book *Machining Architecture* tries to be as clear and transparent as possible on the design methodologies of 'machining': stepwise procedures of adding information into a system to generate form. In that sense it can partly be read as a cook-book with techniques and recipes that can be tested, developed or rejected. As a treatise the book operates through my own essays, descriptions, notes and short comments and larger essays by 'embedded authors' interwoven with the projects. These thinkers were invited specifically because of their own research, not to legitimize or criticize NOX's work but literally to connect their own ideas to mine and make them click.

The book tries to develop a clear agenda. It states that an architecture of complex, topological geometry can be pursued only through rigorous means, and though its main theory is of vagueness, its practice is of obsessive precision. It secretly dreams of a systems theory of architecture. Moreover, the topological turn means an innovation at a conceptual level, as well as at a geometrical and a material level. Generally innovation happens at one of these levels only, but not at all three. This makes the type of work quite peculiar. For one there is not enough building, for the other the theory is embarrassingly unacademic. For one the art makes it incomprehensible, while for the other the art is just architecture without doors and toilets. It is not the aim of the book to occupy a glorious middle position, though I am convinced that the middle is more radical than anything.

L.S.

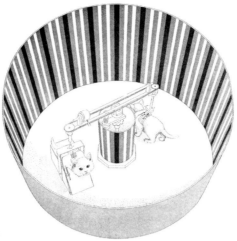

Machining Architecture

Lars Spuybroek

The title of this essay was used before in my *The Weight of the Image* (Rotterdam: NAi Publishers, 2001). That essay followed a slightly similar path, but was fully based on the notion of the diagram – a concept that was highly influential in the 1990s but is now outmoded because of its lack of real precision and instrumentality.

1. Varela, Thompson and Rosch. *The Embodied Mind* (London: MIT Press. 1997): 174–75.

2. Maurice Merleau-Ponty. *Phenomenology of Perception* (London and New York: Routledge. 2003): 127, 165.

Action, Perception, Construction

In 1963 Richard Held and Alan Hein[1] conducted a classic and rather merciless neurological experiment in which two kittens were raised in a carousel under closely controlled conditions. The kittens were connected to each other through a central pivot and could move only in a circle around it. One kitten was able to move freely around a circular track, while the other was strapped in a suspended gondola. As the free cat moved, it pulled the other one round with it. As the young animals' brains developed, their actions and perceptions were integrated into their own individual neurological systems. After a number of weeks, the kittens were released from the carousel. The active cat moved and behaved normally, while the passive cat stumbled and bumped into objects, and was afflicted with agnosia – a condition of *mental* blindness brought on by neurological rather than physiological causes. The free cat was able to link the act of walking to its own perceptions, while for the other, action and vision were severed. It could not coordinate its movements with what it saw because in its experience, action and perception had never existed in the same continuum. This now famous and often quoted experiment proved that these two faculties are inseparable – perception relies on action, and action is possible only through perception.

Naturally the continuity of action and perception can happen only in a body where 'a perception is not followed by a movement, but where both form a system which varies as a whole', as Merleau-Ponty says,[2] that is, through the *Gestalt* of a body-schema or body-image. This system is constantly fed by movements or actions, which it coordinates and consolidates — otherwise it would never be a whole. Furthermore, the system needs to be plastic enough to incorporate new movements. Merleau-Ponty gives the examples of a woman with a feather in her hat (it must be the early 1900s) who automatically bends her head while passing through a doorway, and of the driver of a car who avoids obstacles and takes a bend instinctively, without having to stop the car, take measurements and calculate the degree of curvature in the road. Our body-image allows us not just to create a system of interconnected actions that fit the contours of our bodies but also to extend them into space. Then again, as the stories of Oliver Sacks make clear in

such a terrible way, the opposite also applies: we can shrink into bodies that are smaller, for example when we temporarily lose the use of our legs after they have been confined in plaster for a number of weeks. The body-schema 'is not fixed, as a mechanical, static neurology would suppose; the body-image is dynamic and plastic – it must be remodelled, updated all the time, and can reorganize itself radically with the contingencies of experience.' Sacks adds in an anti-Kantian swipe, 'It is not something fixed *a priori* in the brain, but a process adapting itself all the time to experience.'[3]

It might seem a bit odd to introduce an architecture book with hard-core neurology and neurophilosophy, but these examples – especially the experiment with the cats – have always struck me as fundamental to architecture. What neurologically occupies a continuum is architecturally considered as distinct. Are we architects not trained to plan movement first before extruding it upwards into the image, that is, are we not trained to first draw the plan, the *surface of action*, and then project it upwards into the elevation, the *surface of perception*? Are we not trained to treat walls, floors and columns as distinct elements? Should we not, in parallel to the body-schema, consider architecture as fundamentally plastic, topological and continuous? Should we not consider the continuity between movement and image as the 'original curve' that feeds action into perception and perception into action? Then, when doing so, should we not also realize that this curve is by its nature one of *construction* since it connects the horizontal act with the vertical image?

The Need for Machining

The organization of a machine (or system) does not specify the properties of the components which realize the machine as a concrete system, it only specifies the relations which these must generate to constitute the machine or system as a unity. Therefore, the organization of a machine is independent of the properties of its components which can be any, and a given machine can be realized in many different manners by many different kinds of components. In other words, although a given machine can be realized by many different structures, for it to constitute a concrete entity in a given space its actual components must be defined in that space, and have the properties which allow them to generate the relations which define it. – Humberto Maturana and Francisco Varela[4]

The distinction between an organization and its structure, between a virtual organization and an actual structure is very different from the Platonic idea-and-form or Kantian scheme-and-reality oppositions. What these theories have always failed to explain is how there can be real communication, a physical correspondence instead of a metaphysical one. How can there be discrete organizations (like objects, which they are not): how can they be selected: how do they, when selected, become a structure: and when it is a structure, why is it different from the others that fit the same discrete set? These theories have always needed an external body (God, architects) to activate the process, to enable the shift from the one side to the other, because matter was considered passive and incapable of passing through by itself. But let us begin to consider things as being mobile themselves (and do away with *creationism* in architecture along the way), a notion involving the now well-known concept of self-organization, in which materials are active agents that

3. Oliver Sacks. *A Leg to Stand On* (New York: Touchstone, 1998): 194.

4. Humberto Maturana and Francisco Varela. *Autopoiesis and Cognition: The Realization of the Living* (Dordrecht: D. Reidel, 1980): 80.

RCHITECTURE

seek nothing but agency, that seek an order that is not transcendentally established but emerges from the bottom up. I would add, however, that this emergence is always contained in a framework that is highly historical. The relation between organization and structure exists in all objects, either organic or inorganic, either designed or grown – and it is important to continue to mix them up. Clearly such an ontology (how do things come into existence? Shouldn't we finally consider realism in *architecture*?) needs first to tackle how an organization that is closed and singular can have multiple material structures that must be open or else they cannot vary; or, as they say in biology, 'a variation that is real of a type that is illusory' – we never see the oak, we only see oaks. Somehow, forces in the world are first capable of *converging* into an organizational singularity and, while passing through that point, are then capable of *diverging* into many different actual structures. Such an organization must be a topological structure or it would not be able to change and create variations of itself. A typological structure, for instance, is not capable of transformation (only of deformation) since its components are fixed. The topological schema concentrates on *relations* instead of components, which is also why Maturana and Varela are correct to classify them as 'machines'. Since their transformations happen over a certain time period, they *process* transformations as a formative procedure, as what Varela had earlier called in-formation.[5] Transformation is an intensive process, and all changes are internal changes. Energy and time do not fly about, they happen in material forms and structures, nowhere else (the convergent part), but while it happens, these forms transform and change (the divergent part).

For design, this means that the procedure has a convergent phase of selection and a divergent phase of design.

- Contraction or convergence – a movement of virtualization, where information is gathered, selected, graphed or mapped, then organized into a virtual machine. A movement towards quality, order and organization.
- Expansion or divergence – a movement of actualization, where the organizational diagram germinates and becomes formative. A movement towards quantity, matter and structure.

Though this division clarifies what goes into the system and how it comes out, it does not tell us how exactly the first stage is connected to the second. Though it is evident at this point that it should be a continuous process and that it should be phased, it still means we could take *any* diagram and drop it on *any* type of building to produce *any* form – a horrendous idea. All the phases should be (empirical) machines in themselves. Machines connect only to each other, as molecules, which means *the phases in a process need to be steps in a procedure*. Finding rules. But when we use step-wise procedures does it not mean that the whole procedure is fixed in advance?[6] Generally, 'procedure' is used in a deterministic, mechanical manner, but perhaps we should consider procedures as mechanical blocks that in themselves are straightforward and linear but that when linked can form non-linear strings. The blocks have complex edges, multiple hinges and many ways of connecting to create a complex chain of techniques. It is *path-dependent*, like cooking: it works with techniques and recipes, but what actually comes out is not fully predictable.

Since this theory of form-generation is so dependent on material processes, let us rephrase the procedural techniques within a material framework before we

5. Francisco Varela. *Principles of Biological Autonomy* (New York: Elsevier, 1979).

6. Bart Lootsma. 'The Diagram Debate, or the Schizoid Architect.' *Archilab* (catalogue to the exhibition, Orléans, 2001): 26.

MACHINING A

apply it more exactly to architectural design strategies. Clearly, how organizations transform into structures, how they are extensive and metric first, before becoming topologized and then again form, is rooted in the 'intensive sciences' as Manuel DeLanda[7] calls them, like thermodynamics, topology and dynamic systems theory. Architects might consider form as solid, but this is only a matter of scale and often also of time or temperature, because material form has two major properties: it is flexible and stable. It is flexible enough to be moved out of equilibrium and stable enough to be returned to equilibrium. That means a theory of solids can hardly explain the spontaneous passage from organization to structure. It was Viollet-le-Duc who stated that architecture is an art of crystals, yet this would support only a theory of type, of archives and catalogues but not of self-generative form. What we need are liquid states in the process or at least more viscous states that allow for reconfigurations. The stages of design are thus to:

a. select a *system* and create a configuration for the machine based on this selection
b. *mobilize* the elements and relations in that system
c. *consolidate* to finally have the system
d. result in an architectural *morphology*.

From system to flexibility to rigidity to morphology. In the convergent initial phase there is an acceleration, a topological mobilization that passes through a very narrow channel, after which the process slows and solidifies by diverging towards geometric form. Let us clarify the stages one by one.

> *We never think of transforming a helicoid into an ellipsoid, or a circle into a frequency curve. So it is with the forms of animals. We cannot transform an invertebrate into a vertebrate, nor a coelenterate into a worm, by any simple and legitimate deformation. Nature proceeds from one type to another ... To seek for steppingstones across the gaps between is to seek in vain, forever.* – D'Arcy Wentworth Thompson[8]

All changes are *small* changes, and though they are intensive, they have the power either to individuate or to mutate (one never knows if one has just passed a bifurcation), or, as Bergson would say, produce a difference in degree as well as in kind. Though a transformation can have a large effect, it is always a relatively small step, and the newness of the new can never be appreciated right away. On the other hand, the quote from Thompson makes poignantly clear that type is relevant, not just in biology but also in architecture. When we set out to design a tower, for instance, we are not going to establish a machine with a horizontal configuration. And though we need a topological technique to generate designs, it will always be necessary to *topologize type* (in the case of the tower, topologize verticality), and not just bring in a topological figure or system from any source. There has been too much emphasis on the divergent, proliferative capacities of intensive design techniques and not enough on the initial selective procedures. In what system are we going to mobilize elements and relations? Manuel DeLanda gives us clues about how to operate. First, he advises us to look empirically at real populations of buildings and second, he advises us to rethink type as a 'body plan'.[9] So if one needs to design a tower, look at all the towers, look at their diversity, analyze their differences, map them, organize them, look at their internal relations, look at their body plan.

7. Manuel DeLanda. *Intensive Science & Virtual Philosophy* (New York: Continuum, 2002).

8. D'Arcy Wentworth Thompson. *On Growth and Form* (1917 and 1942). Quoted in Stephen Jay Gould. *The Panda's Thumb* (London: Penguin Books, reprinted 1990): 160.

9. Manuel DeLanda. *Deleuzian Ontology* (published on the Internet). The idea of convergence is strongly defended by Simon Conway Morris. *The Crucible of Creation* (Oxford: Oxford University Press, 1998) and *Life's Solution* (Cambridge: Cambridge University Press, 2003).

RCHITECTURE

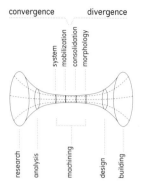

convergence   divergence

system
mobilization
consolidation
morphology

research
analysis
machining
design
building

10. The complexities of these techniques
are explored in 'The Structure of Vagueness',
see p. 352.

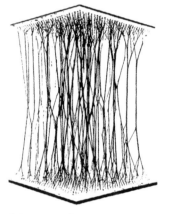

Column system for a tower generated by
wettened wool threads, *IL 35*: 181.

In short, for self-generative design techniques we need empirical research of existing forms. We need to construct body plans out of this research through analysis, then these machines must process information (or difference) through a mobilization of its topologically connected components, which consolidate and take on a form, first as a design and then as a building.

Continuing with the tower design, the phase of the machining procedure (after research and analysis, which are convergent) would start with the configuration of the system, and in this case it might be interesting to highlight the tower-generating machine as it was developed at Frei Otto's Institute for Lightweight Structures[10]. What is relevant in this context is how the machine is configured in relation to the body plan. The tower-machine consists of two grids at a certain distance from each other, one at the top and one at the bottom. Between the grids are lines with a certain amount of flexibility or, in this case, where the lines are materialized as wool threads, a certain amount of slack. After dipping the whole system under water and shaking it horizontally (the mobilization phase), it is taken out of the water and the threads immediately self-organize into complex branching systems (the consolidation phase). This is by no means the only method for tower-generation; it is just one of them, and we have made many variations (see p. 268). What is important to observe is that the transfer from columns to wool threads is not just a topologizing or flexibilization of the structure but an abstraction of a column system into a path system. In this case, a path system for vertical loads. Paths are capable of becoming *single columns* (when single threads become concrete or steel), *thick columns* (when multiple threads have merged), *spatial columns* (where diagonals form nodes), *diagonal columns* (which usually comes later, when bracing the verticals to the horizontal wind forces), *mega-columns* (many diagonals form one large spatial tube), *meta-columns* (like centre lines of cores), and so on. Paths are of a higher order, more abstract but as empirical as the columns themselves. And because they are material (or programmed as material), all movement is transferred in an intensive way, which means the movement dissipates by becoming structure.

Machining Architecture

In this book there are a number of techniques researched and developed that use the mobilization of a system and its consolidation into form. The earlier techniques are based on deformation principles, where a geometric primitive like a sphere, a cylinder or similar is bent and curved through step-wise movements. Though these movements are topological, the technique is fundamentally *indexical*, a kind of 'photographic' freeze-framing. Though there is a considerable accumulation of time during the mobilization, the consolidation phase is but a moment that can become structural only when read through structural members afterwards that are then topologized as if they were part of the mobilization itself. Later techniques, beginning especially with *wetGRID* (p. 138), which started after I met Frei Otto in 1998, are different since they are more *constructivist*; structural members join in and therefore the focus is more on the consolidation. They are based on truly transformational principles, where often the consolidation is directly a self-supporting, self-engineering aspect of the system. The system is not just shaken or deformed under the influence of motion, it actually passes a critical threshold, a point of *self-stopping*, at which it irreducibly transforms. Later projects are of

MACHINING A

a more *configurational* nature: where the movement-phase is replaced by a limited set of variable figures (S-curve, O-curve, L-curve, U-curve, and so on) and the consolidation-phase is replaced by a matching of these figures first in pairs (translation, rotation and reflection) and then in larger configurations. While the indexical technique allowed us to be very exact during the mobilization phase and the constructivist technique gave us more precision for the consolidation stage, the configurational method combines the best of both. Although based on the same notion of broken symmetry, the figure-configuration method allows for a more precise calibration of formal, structural and programmatic information. But before we consider how machining relates to action (programme), perception (form) and construction (structure), we should investigate the fourth phase of the machining procedure, morphologies, which are highly dependent on the described techniques above.

> *How did we ever get the little bones in our inner ear, which directly originate from the jawbone in reptiles? That is unimaginable. The creationists would say that this transformation is impossible because during the transfer of these bones from the hinging position in reptiles to the inner ear of mammals the lower jaw would be hanging loose. This is of course not the case. The transformative shapes have a double maxillary joint, so the functionality is kept when one of them moves to the inner ear position. There is always this huge redundancy. This leads of course to an organic machinery that is everything but optimized, seen from the traditional principles of human design.* – Stephen Jay Gould [11]

Everything but optimized! This is the morphology of the *provisional* not the optimal. Often generative techniques are proposed under a sign of efficiency and optimization,[12] but since the generative relies wholly on the topological and since the topology is real and fully materialized, less determined (and more redundant) in-betweens are included.[13] That means no geometry of complexity, no morphology resulting from an epigenetic process can be fully Euclidean or elementary, because it is the relations that produce the elements, not the other way around. The variability comes before the elementary. All shapes generated through intensive processes are therefore transformative shapes and have a transformative or, better, a *transitive* geometry.[14]

The *systems* discussed in this book are generally line-systems, the *techniques* are almost always line-to-surface operations (though there are exceptions), and almost all the *morphologies* are surface-to-volume geometries. The procedure as a whole follows the classic drawing-to-building transfer, only because the dimensions are not given beforehand and emerge later do they turn out to be continuous instead of discrete. In other words, with a transitive geometry the dimensions of building are not mechanically added up but organically synthesized.[15] In an architectural framework this means that the transformation takes place in the more generic, simpler states of specific body plans (plane façade, plane floor, row-rooms, row-houses, floor-roof, stacked floors) to progress into more complex structures. Four morphologies emerge in the projects here:

> a. *Deep surfaces*. Surfaces either on a flat or curved plane that are deformed generally perpendicular to the direction of that surface. They can be

11. Stephen Jay Gould. Interviewed in *Een schitterend ongeluk* [A Splendid Accident] (Amsterdam: Contact, 1993): 384.

12. Peter J. Bentley, ed. *Evolutionary Design by Computers* (San Francisco: Morgan Kaufman, 1999).

13. See p. 358, 'The Structure of Vagueness'.

14. See p. 328, Brian Massumi, 'Building Experience'.

15. It is *inter-dimensional* – dimensions are nothing but the organization of movement. The procedure of system (lines), techniques (line to surface) and morphologies (surface to volume) should be viewed as a building of movement upon movement.

RCHITECTURE

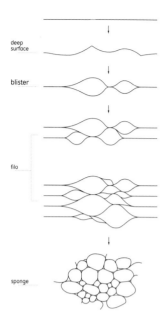

deep
surface

blister

filo

sponge

16. Actually we should consider *three* levels of machining: a. at the passage of organization to structure, b. at the passage of design to building, and c. at the passage of building to experience. The middle level, that of computer-controlled machining techniques, has to be left aside here. The same applies to the differentiation between plastic and electronic interactivity on the third level. However, all of these items are intensely discussed throughout the book.

17. Maurice Merleau-Ponty. *Phenomenology of Perception* (London and New York: Routledge. 2003): 127.

deforming tubes (*H₂Oexpo, blowout, OffTheRoad, Tommy*) or deforming flat planes (*V2_Lab, Maison Folie*). A subset of this category is *porous surfaces*, in which deformations are structurally transformed because of local (*Fedurok*) or global (*SoftSite, ParisBRAIN*) tearings.

b. *Blisters*. Single flat surfaces that are locally transformed to become volumes. It is both deformational, like the bulging effects of the first group, and transformational (*De Gothic Stijl, wetGRID, GDF, D-tower, La Tana di Alice, ECB*).

c. *Filo*. Either double-layered where the pockets lock into each other in such a way they start sharing curvature (*Soft Office, Son-O-House*) or multilayered where stacks are diagonally connected through packed structures of sponge-like morphology (*Pompidou Two*).

d. *Sponges*. Pure multioriented morphology either vertically stretched (*obliqueWTC*) or unstretched (*FOAM HOME, "beachness", The Future Is Now*).

Experiencing the Machine

In the end, these machines are for bodies to experience them. To consider how they relate, we should look at how what comes out of the machine is related to what goes in.[16] We return to Oliver Sacks on the plasticity of the body-schema: 'It is not something fixed *a priori* in the brain, but a process adapting itself all the time to experience.' So what is an experience (in the present)? And how does that relate to experience (from the past)? In architecture we are obsessed by habits, and rightly so, but often we mistake them for mechanical acts, for usage. Habits should not be understood as the sculpting of a passive schema that archives its actions to enable only their repetition. We are not machines, we just *want* to be machines. The schema consists of rhythms and periodic patterns, and it is exactly these that allow variability or change. In *Phenomenology of Perception* Maurice Merleau-Ponty introduces the concept of abstract movement, a movement-tension that is always present in the body, a 'background tension', following the Gestaltists of the 1920s. In fact, this movement becomes available to the body only through the numerous actions performed in everyday life – *movement is made up of movement*, and the abstract and the real feed back and forth continuously. Every act springs from this background tension, a real, actual movement that 'releases itself from neurological anonymity'.[17] In short, it is a formidable critique of the architectural programme as the mechanistic layout of human behaviour within a built system viewed as tasks, routines and habits. With the idea of rhythmicity – 'an internal music', as Sacks calls it – an act is never completely certain, it always differs from itself and is always ready to shift into another act, or even to slide into a 'free' act. When every act is also oriented sideways, a lot of *in-between programme*, undetermined and unprogrammed, could unfold. *Could* unfold, since that depends on the architecture.

This does not mean there is no programme: there is habit and routine, or, to put it more strongly, habit and routine are *at the outset* of all design, but we must consider them as potentially flexible. Because this flexibility is limited to different degrees, it is crucial to set the degrees of freedom beforehand so they are productive in a selected field only. In other words, not every wall-floor connection need be that of a curve, for example. But we must apprehend first that human action feeds the movement during the 'mobilization phase'. Second, movement can be reciprocated in human action *only* when abstracted into structure (during the 'con-

MACHINING A

solidation phase'). Thus, *abstraction of movement is building*, nothing else. There is a fundamental constructivism. All engineers and architects understand this – but they often do not grasp it in the same way. 'Movement' is of a single body, of groups, of multiple groupings and of forces and loads, engulfing schema all happening simultaneously. Bodily *posture* (which coordinates vision and action) is a constructive act by itself, as much in the concrete connection of feet and eyes as in the abstract rebuilding of the schema. But posture in all its variations should be viewed in relation to social groupings, and is as molecular and material, varying between crystallized states and liquid states, states of configuring and reconfiguring. What else can a building be? What other than a permanent actualization of the architecture-schema, and what else can architecture be than a permanent interaction with body-schema and group-schema? All schema are continuously rubbing over each other, *during the design and during the experience when finally built*. Channelled by perception they feed movement and structure into each other; channelled by structure they constantly feed action and vision into each other.

RCHITECTURE

Soft City

video (7'03") broadcast on national television 28 March 1993
and exhibited at several international festivals.
VPRO television, 1992–93

Movement generally is considered to be between the images. In film or in architecture we are always confronted with series of images that are moved or passed by. By using the technique of morphing, movement can be in the image itself. In this video, however, the movement of vehicles is internalized, and becomes related to growth and living form. Ultimately, this genetic experiment is applied to a city that suddenly starts to mutate. In a nutshell, our programme for architecture in the ten years after 1993.

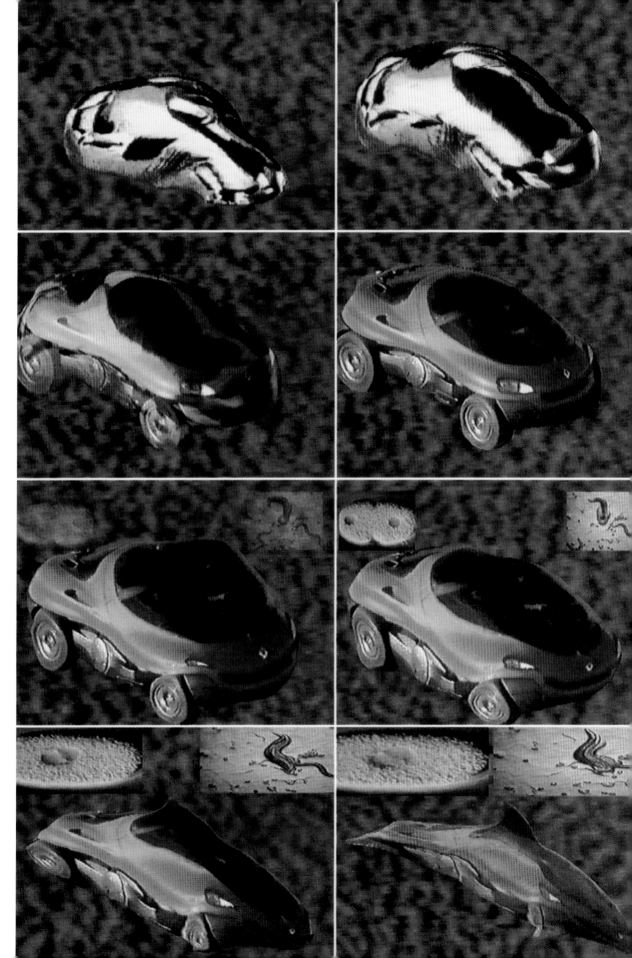

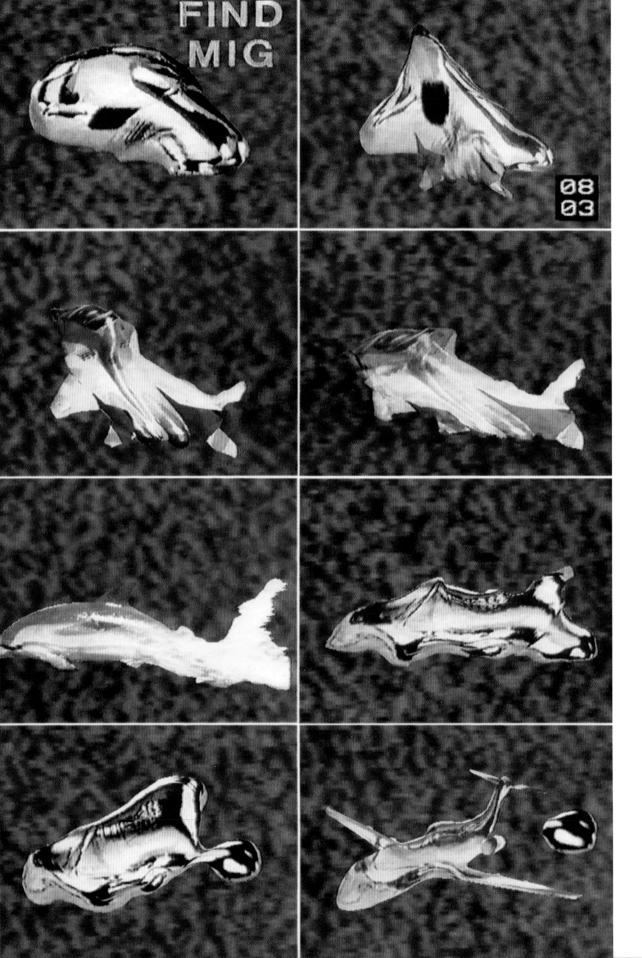

H$_2$0expo

water-experience pavilion and interactive installation for 'WaterLand',
a private-public partnership with the Dutch Ministry of Transport,
Public Works and Water Management,
Neeltje Jans, the Netherlands, 1993–97

The water pavilion is a special building for many reasons: it is the first fully topological structure where curvature is not only in the roof and walls, but also in the floors; no section is horizontal. It is the first fully interactive building in which visitors can transform light and sound in the interior through a wide range of sensors.

The water pavilion, *H$_2$0expo*, is a permanent structure that does not 'contain' an exhibition in the classical sense, as in a museum where moving and seeing are distinct. Here, the images and sounds that emerge depend on the activities of the visitors, while the activities of the visitors depend on constantly changing images and sounds. Beyond the general technological understanding of 'interactivity', here it does not mean merely that the building is an environment of transforming atmospheres through electronic interventions but an architecture of transformation itself.

The building's geometry is generated through iterative transformation. It starts with a simple tube made up of ellipses, which are rescaled according to the programme, then deformed according to site influences, such as wind direction, sand dunes and flows of incoming visitors. The entrance begins with a small ellipse on its vertical axis and ends, some 60 metres further on, with a larger ellipse on its horizontal axis. In between, the building twists and turns. Since the sections are continuous and floor blends into wall and wall into ceiling, the building forces the visitor to rely on his or her own motor system to balance (also there are no windows looking out onto the horizon and informing the body what is level). The visitor must act like water to pass through the building.

The building's first part, which features a three-dimensional door, is constantly flooded with water. Visitors arrive at the 'glacier-tunnel', which is completely frozen with melted water spilling onto the floor. Further into the building are 'springs' spraying mist and water, a 'rain bowl' with stroboscopically illuminated rain and the 'well', which contains 120,000 litres of water, has its own programme of projections and light and is one of the primary

People generally know double curvature only from their car or their cat, which is why this architecture is often confused with the shapes of vehicles or animals. The first refers to the classic motif of streamlining, the second to biomorphism. But because they operate only on the outside of objects, both have become extinct. With streamlining, all movement is projected on the surface and does not result in any internal reconfiguration. The second is pure mimicry that lacks a structural understanding of form. A building is not a car without wheels or a cat without legs.

The first set of operations: elliptical tube, scaling of tube according to programme, twisting according to exterior forces, insertion of ground level, deformation of ground surface.

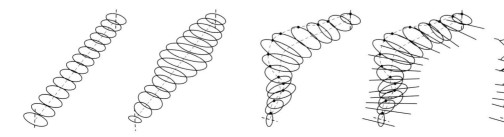

generative forces on the structure. The well becomes another kind of horizon, an inner horizon, not horizontal but vertical, on the axis of vertigo, of falling.

The pavilion's interactivity is continued in the installation of projections, light and sound. Specially designed sensors are connected to three interactive systems that operate together: real-time generated animations connected to LCD projectors; a 60-metre-long spine of some 200 blue lamps placed on the cable duct; and a sound system that can be manipulated and changed.

Sensors are differentiated for crowds (light sensors), groups (pulling sensors) and individuals (touch sensors). Every group of sensors is connected to a projector that shows a simple wire-frame grid, which translates every action of a visitor into real-time movement of (virtual) water. Light sensors are connected to the 'wave'. Every time one walks through an invisible beam of infrared light the projected wire frame undulates. With four of these sensors, the visitors can create any kind of interference of these waves. Touch sensors create 'ripples' in the wire frames, and pulling sensors relate to the 'blob', a wire-frame projection of a sphere that can be manipulated like a drop of water in zero gravity. Interactive projections are scattered around the building, but the effects of the sensors are also integrated on the spine of blue lights. First, without activating any of the sensors, a pulse is produced by these lamps that accelerates every time a light sensor is activated. So the more people inside (and who pass the invisible light sensors), the faster the light courses through the building. The touch sensors likewise create pulses on the light curve: a sudden high level of light splitting and fading in two directions. Finally, the pulling sensors (for the 'blob' projection) are able to slow all this down. When people exert maximum force on the sensors, the light curve is frozen in its last position.

Next to the light and real-time projections is the sound system. All sensors are connected to a CD-ROM with sound samples that can be deformed, bent and/or stretched. But the sound itself can also be electronically pulled out of the well or towards oneself on the spine of light, which serves as the source of the sound system.

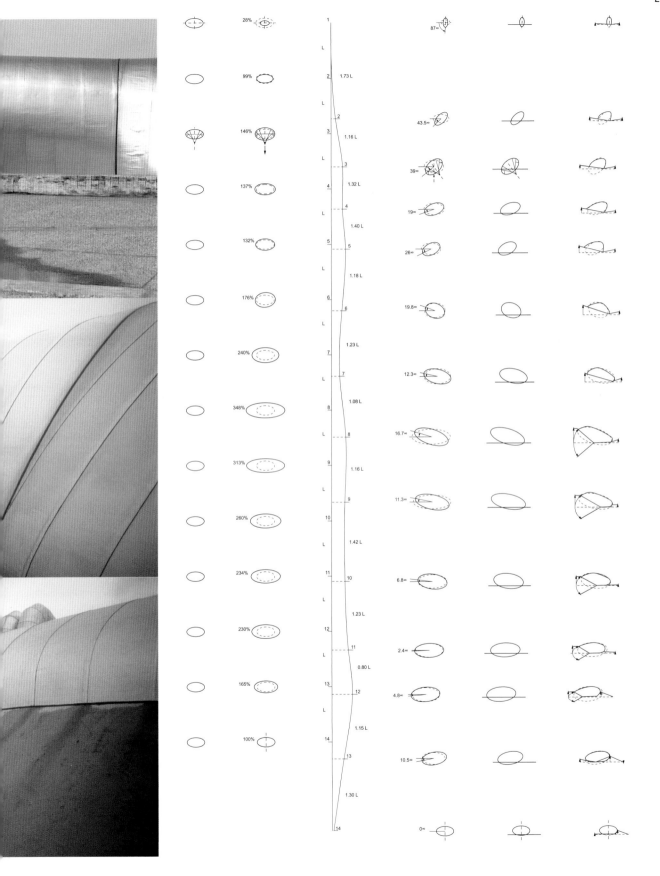

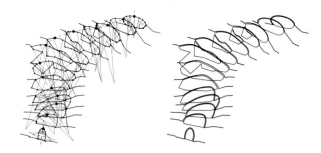

The final step in the procedure is to renegotiate the ground level within the building. Sections also show the circle segments constituting each of the trusses. Each circle segment fits exactly with the adjacent one, making it a smooth curve. We then worked in AutoCAD 11, a program that could only define ellipses by circle segments: completely wrong, but fortunately so, because the machines rolling the steel profiles could work only with circles.

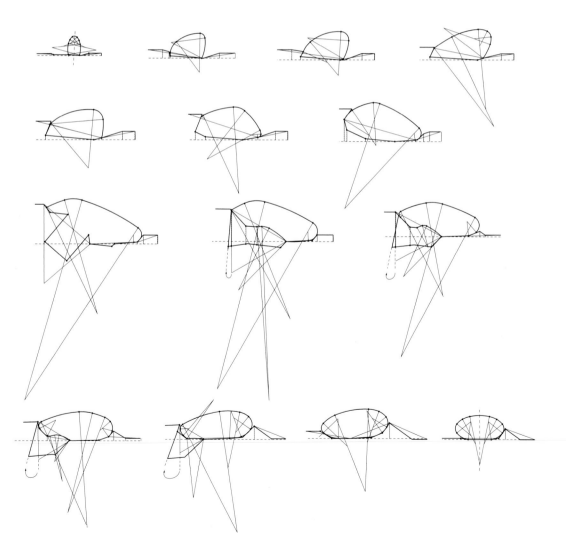

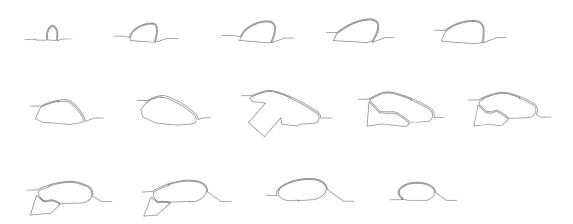

If one 'closes' two curves with straight lines (a 'ruled surface'), these lines appear quickly translated into a secondary structure. But since the tangent on one end of the beam is not the same as the tangent on the other end, one cannot use a normal rigid beam. Our steel contractor pointed out that the beams he used were so cheap (and weak in the lateral direction) that they would simply torque when bolted to the primary, curved trusses. He was right; all the 280 secondary beams are torquing, some up to 50 degrees.

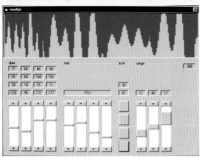
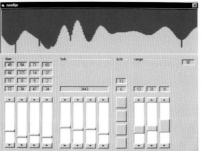

Electrical diagram of connected computers, projectors, loudspeakers and sensors.

The idea behind the interactive system is that it would respond locally and as a whole, and that it would respond to passive visitors as much as to very active ones. Three interactive processes thus operate simultaneously: wire-frame projections, light movement over the central curve and sound. In total there are six wire-frame projections: four ripples, one blob and one wave. The wave is activated by visitors simply passing the invisible infrared sensors; the ripples are activated by groups of touch sensors; and the blob is a game between four players who each have their own pulling sensor. These manual operations have an immediate, real-time effect on the wire frames: waves in line or circle patterns are transferred through the mesh. It is not a film: the ripples are real-time calculated waves dependent on the forces the visitor uses to manipulate the sensor.

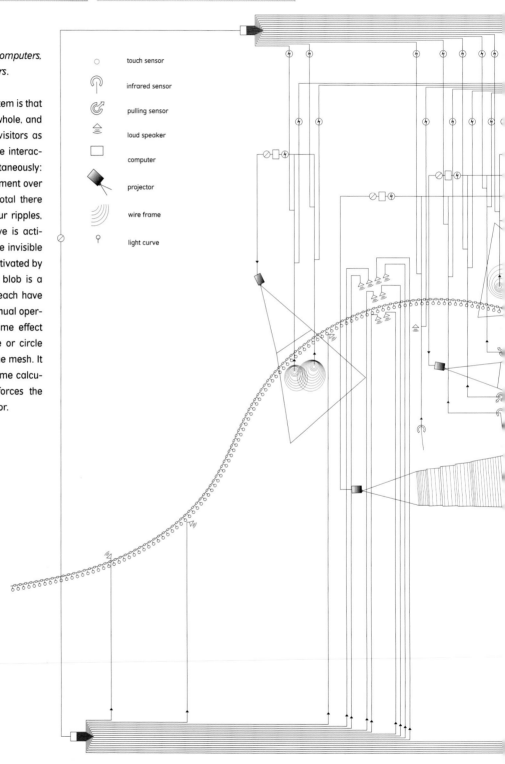

○   touch sensor

◠   infrared sensor

↻   pulling sensor

◈   loud speaker

▭   computer

◆   projector

)))   wire frame

♀   light curve

The ripples are calculated by so-called 'reality engines', graphic cards that allow for incredibly fast image generation. When the sensor is pushed with a certain force, the computer immediately 'drops' a virtual stone of corresponding weight in virtual water. The projector is set up so that the centre of the ripples created by the virtual stone coincides exactly with the position of the sensor, i.e., your foot or hand. We even programmed the force-weight ratio in a non-linear way so that children could create as much of an effect as adults.

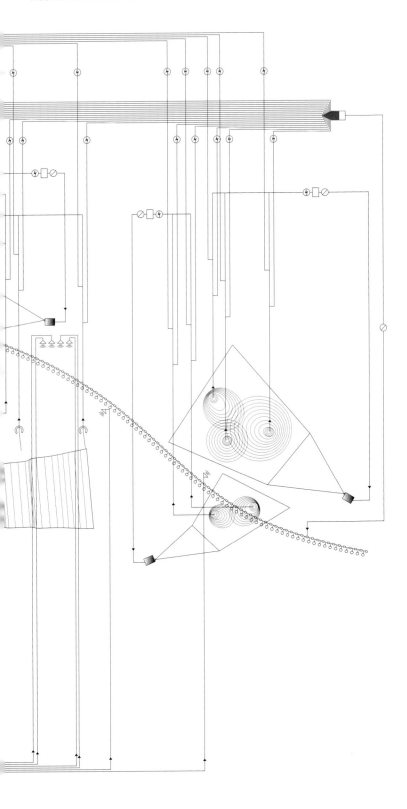

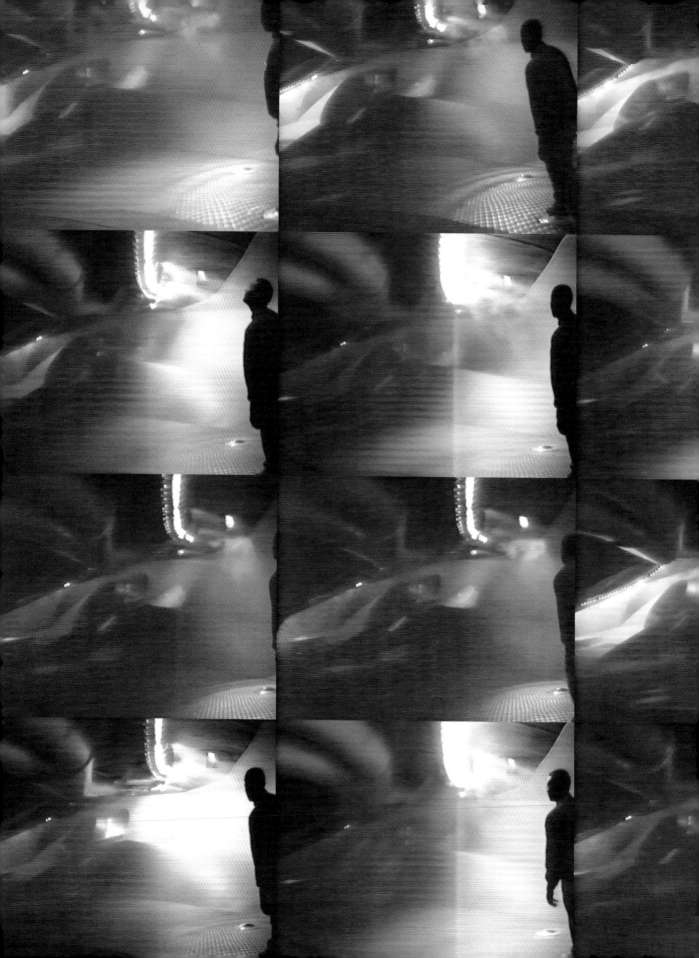

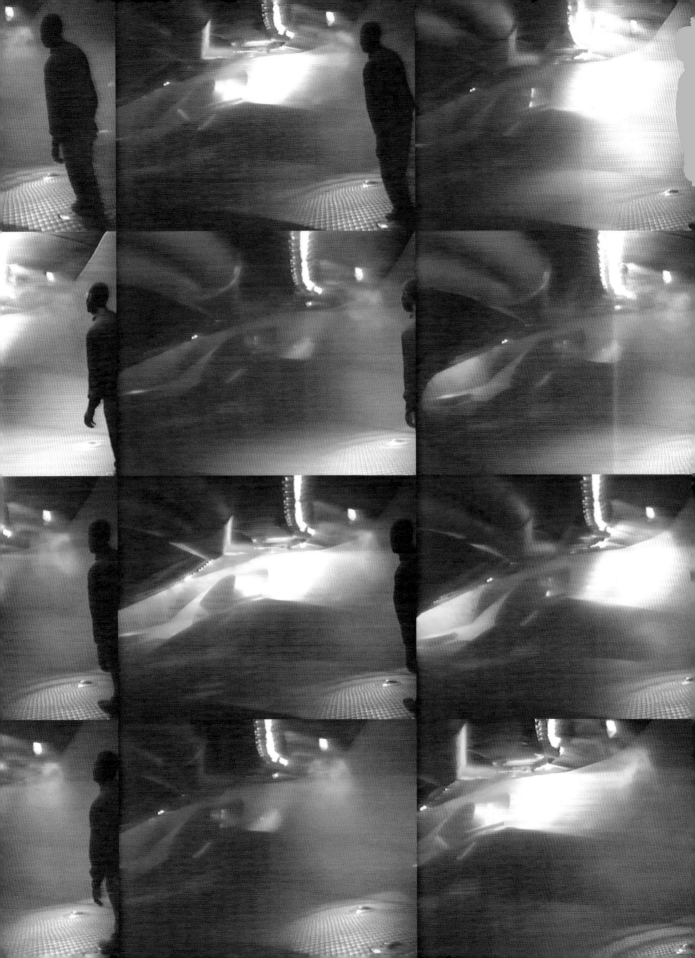

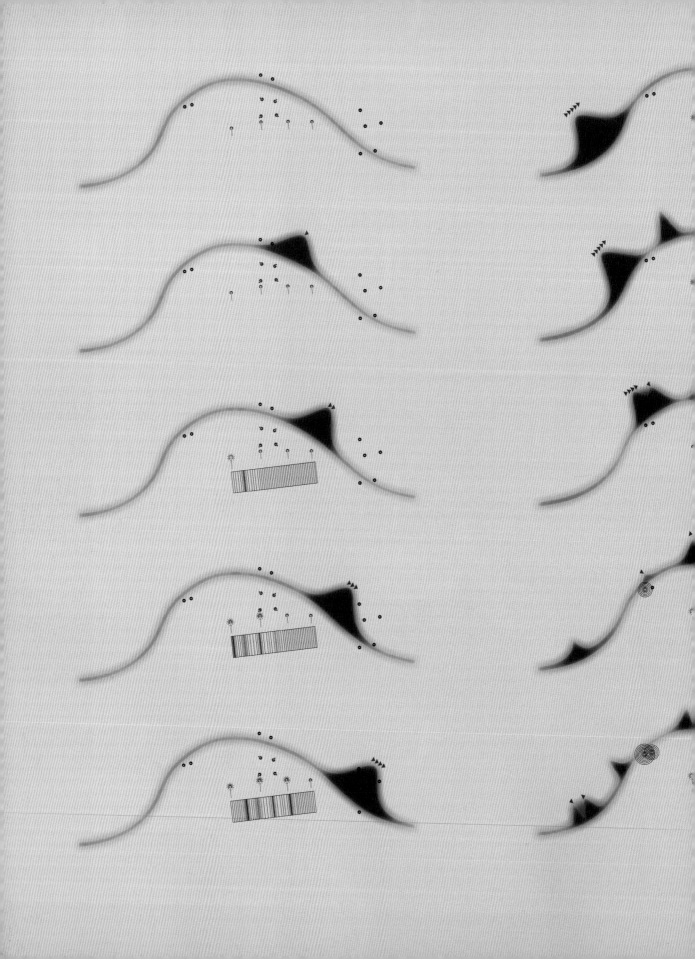

All interactive effects relate to one another. From top left to bottom right: the blue light moves by itself over the light curve hanging from the pavilion's ceiling. When visitors pass the invisible sensors they create an undulation of the wire mesh projected on the floor under their feet and a speeding up of the light pulse. In the middle column one can see an extra manipulation of two sensors that create local ripples in the projections, and simultaneously create more water effects on the light curve. On the right column extra sensor effects are introduced, illustrating a typical day, when many visitors operate the sensors.

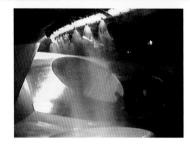

The first third of the freshwater pavilion presents actual water effects: small springs, a jumping water jet and a rain bowl that sprays rain, which, when stroboscopically lit, seems to fall upwards. All the water spills onto the floor, making the visitors jump away with excitement and laughter.

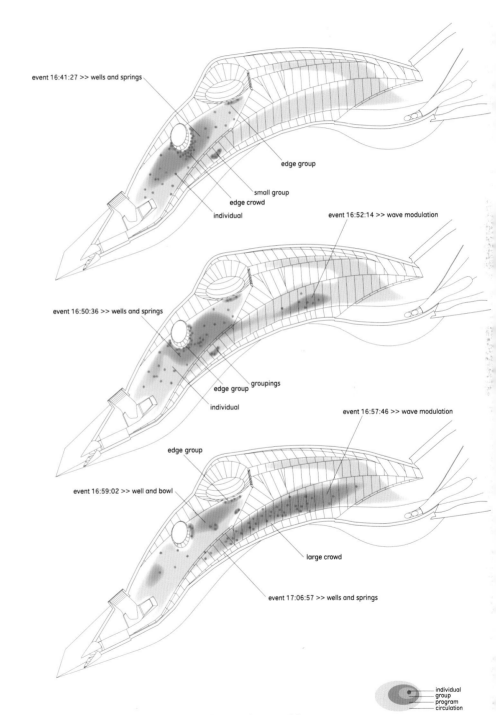

event 16:41:27 >> wells and springs

edge group

small group

edge crowd

individual

event 16:52:14 >> wave modulation

event 16:50:36 >> wells and springs

groupings

edge group

individual

event 16:57:46 >> wave modulation

edge group

event 16:59:02 >> well and bowl

large crowd

event 17:06:57 >> wells and springs

individual
group
program
circulation

The diagram shows that the building hardly has a programme in the classic architectural sense. Visitors are like water molecules, sometimes moving as individuals, sometimes in small groups, in excited packs or passive rows, and sometimes in large crowds.

During the water pavilion's design I became interested in neurophilosophy. Neurology seems to be the only branch of science that by its nature coincides with philosophy. Bergson knew that, as did Merleau-Ponty. With H_2Oexpo it became clear to me that questions of posture, perception and activity are architectural questions. We named this relationship 'motor geometry', the abstract movement in the building, with its transformative geometry, that relates directly to real movement of the body.

p 97
p 139
p 227

The middle area of the freshwater pavilion is dominated by the 'well', a huge structure that contains 120,000 litres of water. The image of a falling drop of water is projected in slow motion at the bottom of the well. In the interactive soundscape it produces a deep sound of extremely low frequency. From the well, the path splits: one part leads down into a dark wet cellar where all natural water is gathered to be filtered, and the other leads to the building's fully interactive section.

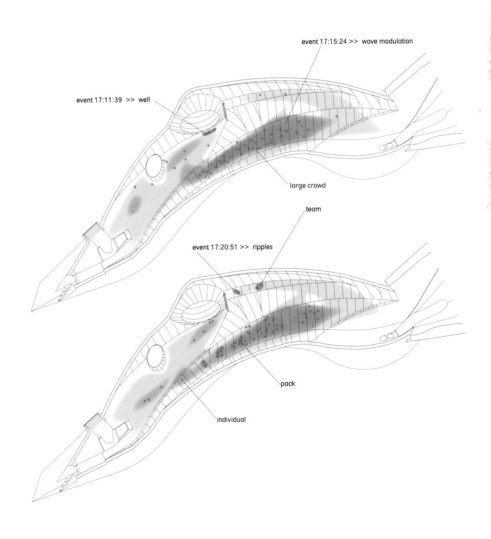

event 17:15:24 >> wave modulation

event 17:11:39 >> well

large crowd

team

event 17:20:51 >> ripples

pack

individual

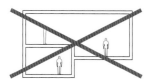

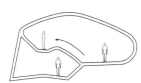

When all architectural elements are connected through geometrical continuity, a number of unexpected social effects emerge. For instance, an elderly man stood in front of the larger bumps, paused a moment and suddenly ran up the slope. This slope was meant for projection, not for walking, demonstrating that the abstract movement of topology intensifies sensations in the body. There is more tension. It creates a larger potential of movement without prescribing specific actions. Events are no longer functions or mechanical actions; they now emerge from the interaction between a less determined architecture and the body.

There is a persistent misunderstanding of the architecture-movement relationship. Through topological vagueness architecture can acquire a language of movement, i.e., 'splitting', 'merging', 'bending', 'twisting', which enables the architecture to move without the actual moving of the building.

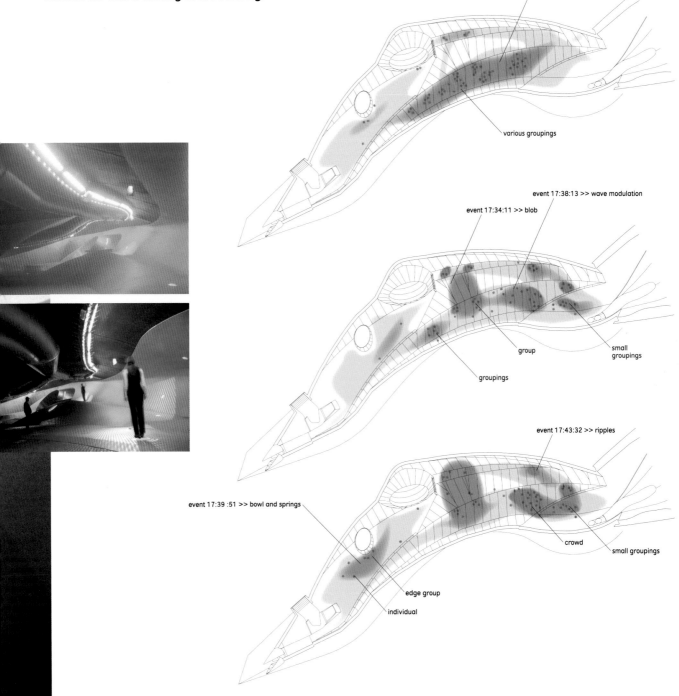

event 17:31:45 >> wave modulation

various groupings

event 17:38:13 >> wave modulation

event 17:34:11 >> blob

group

small groupings

groupings

event 17:43:32 >> ripples

event 17:39 :51 >> bowl and springs

crowd

small groupings

edge group

individual

Topological vagueness is not general, unarticulated free form. In *H₂0expo* there are already many internal edges to the landscape. As in many later projects, the edges are determined objects taken up in a larger field of less determined morphology.

p 18
p 174
p 247

In interactive electronic art, Situationism seems to be fully revived, with the event of the present breaking into the memory structure of the city. Movement-trace versus architecture-track. We should be careful not to misunderstand this opposition as immaterial versus material, since it is not the fact that architecture materializes but that it has always been obsessed by a determinism that makes it disciplinarian. If architecture could resort to vagueness, it would evolve from a determined track-state to a less determined path-state that allows for a wide variety of movement-traces.

SoftSite

interactive installation for DEAF96, the Dutch Electronic Art Festival, organized by the V2_Organisation, displayed on the internet and the façade of the Netherlands Architecture Institute, Rotterdam, the Netherlands, 1996

Why move so much of architecture onto the Internet? All these windows, sites and cafés. Can we envision an environment or information structure that changes and restructures the way it is used? Rather than linger in hierarchized information architectures riddled with road signs, we would find ourselves in constantly changing, fluid environments where the horizon shifts and demands constant reorientation.

The idea of *SoftSite* is to convert the numeric behaviour of changing visitor numbers instantly through a central computer into different shapes that can twist and turn and grow and adapt ever-new geometries, which are then displayed on public media: on the website as an image that functions as a constantly shifting interface and on a building's façade as a projection. Every participating artist or group of artists was given their 'own' so-called 'softscraper' by the website, with its own characteristics. Some twist more easily than others, some only grow longer, while others still are better at cloning themselves.

All this is not exclusively controlled by Internet behaviour. The three-dimensional model also has a behaviour of its own, which enables the softscrapers to establish their own links with other 'artists' on the site, and this is reflected in the interface of the main site by the continuous addition of new windows that give views on new artists.

After two weeks, this activity resulted in a computer file of over 40,000 images, an animation of roughly half an hour. A new city was established in which the behaviour of people instantly created new softscrapers, a city without the distinctions between streets and buildings, form and information, where living, active structures are the result of life.

The behaviour of the 'softscrapers' in the installation directly influences the website's structure. Every time a visitor requests the engine to search for an artist, different windows to other artists are created simultaneously. In so doing, the site gives not only directions but also deviations.

Softscrapers generated through Internet behaviour create a network in virtual Rotterdam.

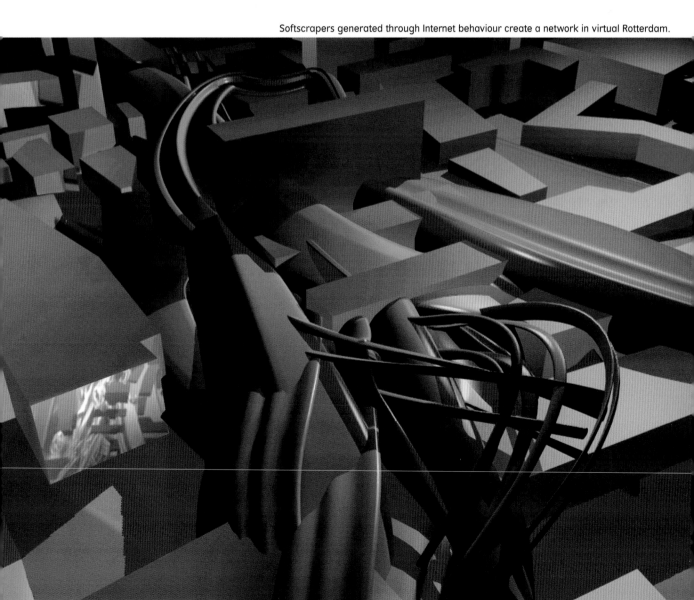

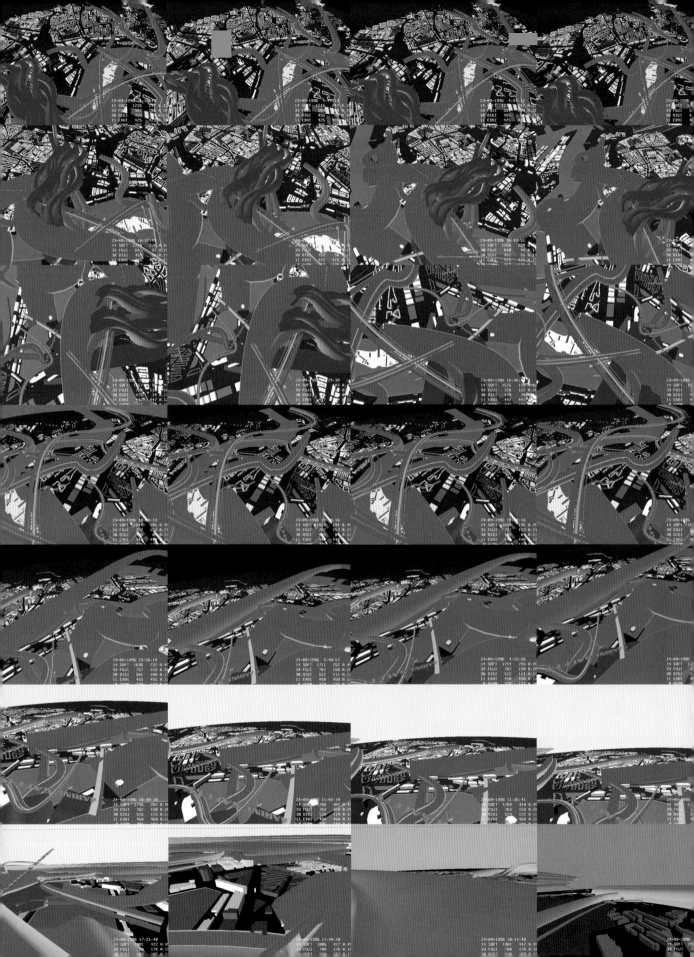

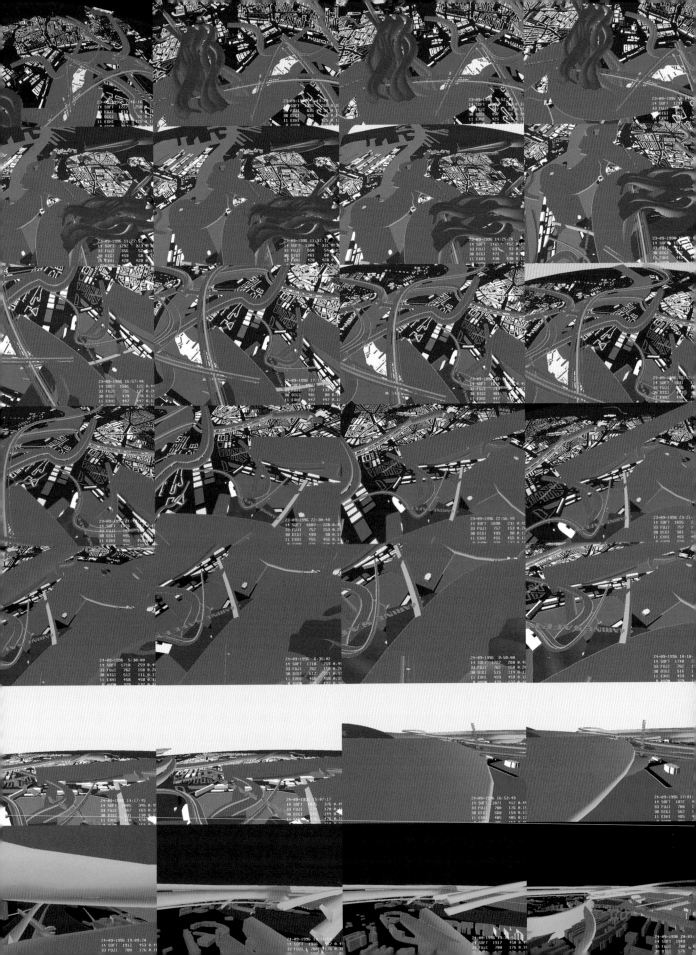

blowout

toilet block,
Neeltje Jans, the Netherlands, 1997

In **Rethinking the Work of Frederick Kiesler,** *Wouter van Stiphout states that people often focus on Kiesler's 'organic', a-tectonic forms as something sculptural, while for him this architecture clears the way to restoring the relationship of the human body to furniture, piles of papers, the table being set, the cat, and so on. An architecture that refrains from framing events through perspective and tectonics in order to have a direct, unfiltered and intimate connection with smells, bodies and images.*

The small outdoor toilet block has a progressive geometry that tries to split into two elements. At one end it is round, then inflected halfway by splitting into two parts before terminating at the other end. The spline-trajectories containing the different sections divide so that one dives into the earth and the other jumps into the air. The geometry is articulated by a steel structure that separates the men's toilets from those of the women, with one for a disabled person in between.

With some urgency one enters this small structure, but instead of being directly guided to B, the direction is multiplied, bent and twisted by other movements, such as the vector of the wind moving through the interior at high speed. The structure is open on both sides, with a grille on one side and an exhaust pipe on the other. With the vector of the wind and sound, one has to balance one's actions while going to the toilet: the building intensifies the dynamics between internal pressure and external forces of the wind and a distorted corridor in which one can hardly move when it is crowded. These 'external forces' are not just another 'natural element' in the architecture: they are media, furniture, motility — they connect one person to another, shape intimacy, build it up and release it. Finally, sitting on the toilet, orthogonal to the direction of the geometry, one can relax and let go.

A series of plasma-cut steel plates describes the precise
but vague geometry of the small building.

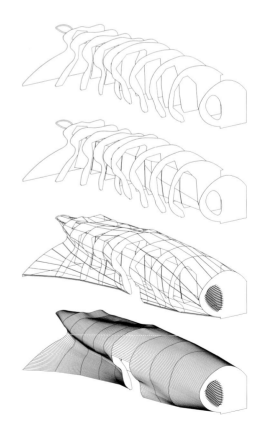

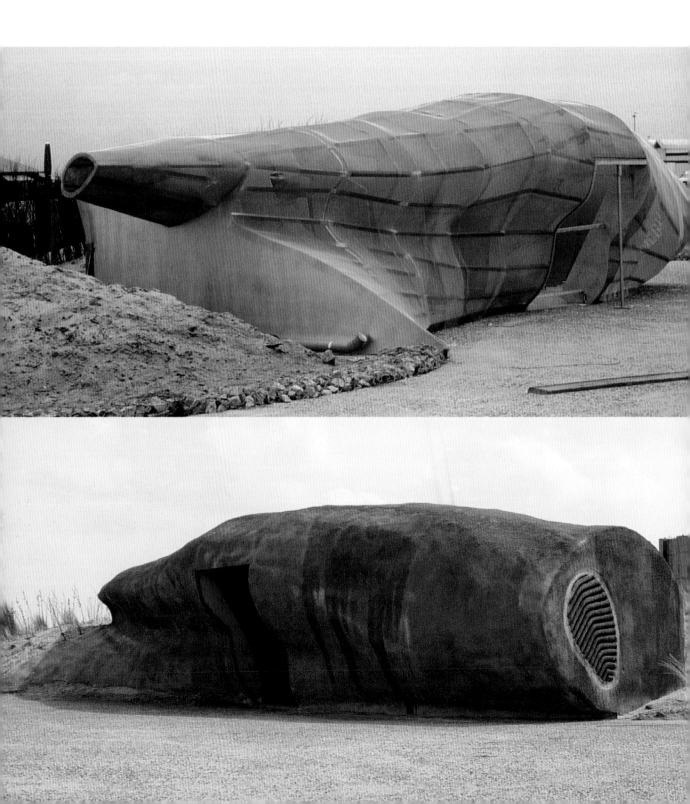

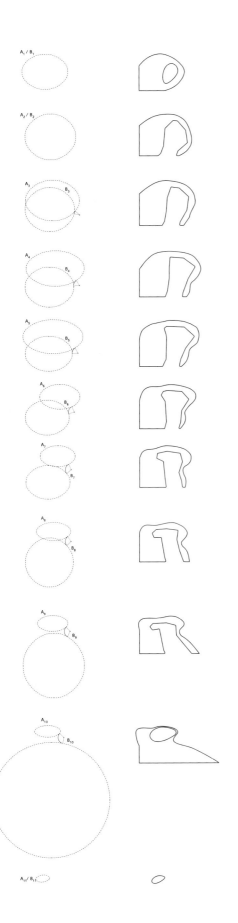

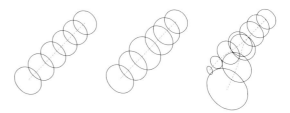

blowout is similar in shape to the nearby *H₂Oexpo*, the difference being that this also has concave geometry next to convex. The exterior form is created by spraying concrete on a wire mesh welded to the steel plates.

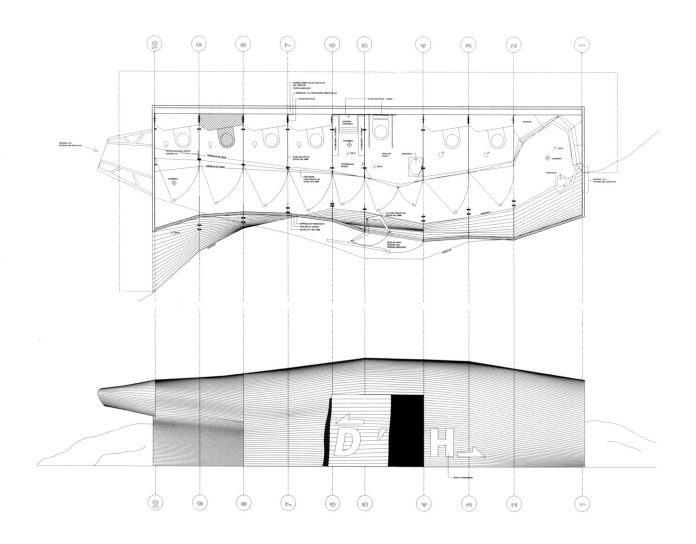

The structure is open at both ends to the wind for natural ventilation.

p 272

I always tell students that if they want to work with curves they must be as rigorous as Schinkel, Mies and Alberti put together. Curvature needs a very systematic approach. When a straight line has only two points (at both ends of the line) and a curve has multiple points (spaced out over the length of the line), it directly follows that mastering curvature means mastering a lot more information than before.

FOAM HOME

research project into the reconceptualization of the attic,
Nijmegen, the Netherlands, 1997

Why do attics or lofts seem so much more inhabitable than spaces that are simply empty? It is not so much the romantic shadows as the structural differentiation that offers so much potential. Miesian emptiness offers an openness that is too undirected, too generalized. This hyper-conceptual project – 'What if one were to add up all the attics in a city and reorganize them into a proto-housing scheme?' – was my first true exercise in branching and bifurcating structural systems.

In the phenomenology of Bachelard it is the technical spaces (basements) and constructive spaces (attics) that haunt the house's daylit living areas. There is no horror movie that does not celebrate these secondary spaces, where the tension of daily life returns as grisly flesh. A radical merging of the served and service spaces would heighten the intensity of habitation considerably. The structure would be continuously adjusted, not very different from the utopian projects of the 1960s: every act of living would also be one of building.

The project is a literal cohabitation of the generic and the specific, and the design procedure immediately equals the design result. The progressive differentiation of a bland Miesian structure into a complex three-dimensional one follows from an iterative technique that increasingly breaks the symmetry of the initial state. The formal deformation of a hall into an attic is guided by structural transformation that allows for a differentiation of inhabitation – it is not all attic, and some areas stay more generic than others.

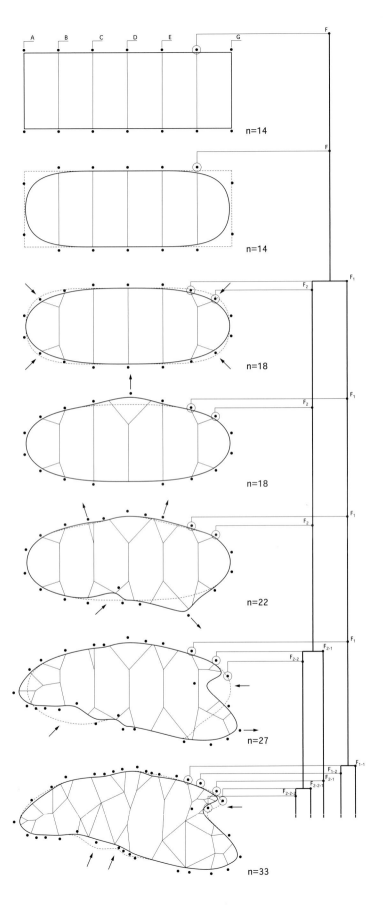

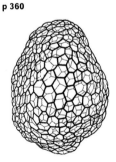

It was Francisco Varela who wrote information as 'in-formation', which has many implications. First, when we mention form, we imply information. Second, day-to-day references to information as something in the sky or in wires miss the point that it is actually bodies, goods and generally material forms that are informed. Third, the processing of information is a formative process that happens within, not outside of, time. So 'information' implies dynamics and complexity, not simplicity and reduction. Fourth, information is not something that just enters a form from the outside: it is the inner material structure of the form that allows for specific information. In that way information is a degree of difference that is contained by the form, where difference is built upon difference.

p 106
p 270
p 304
p 360

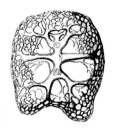

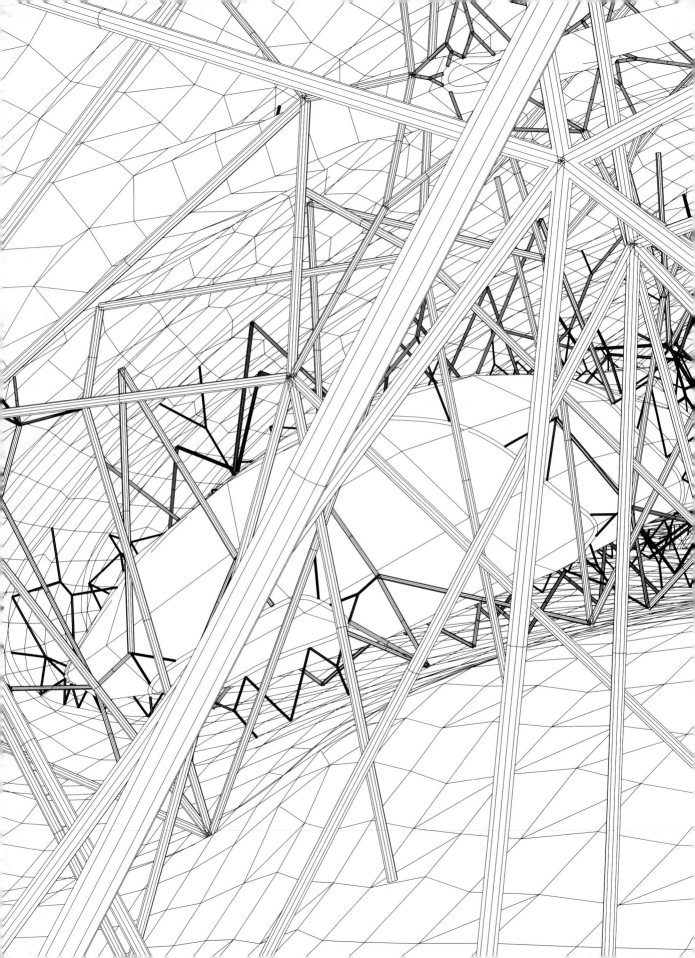

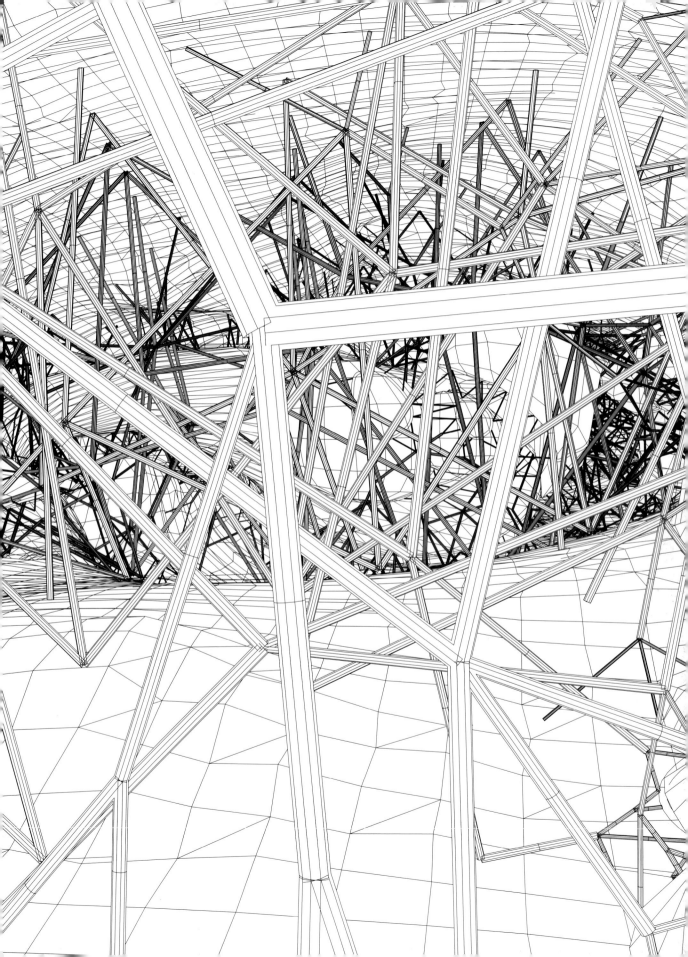

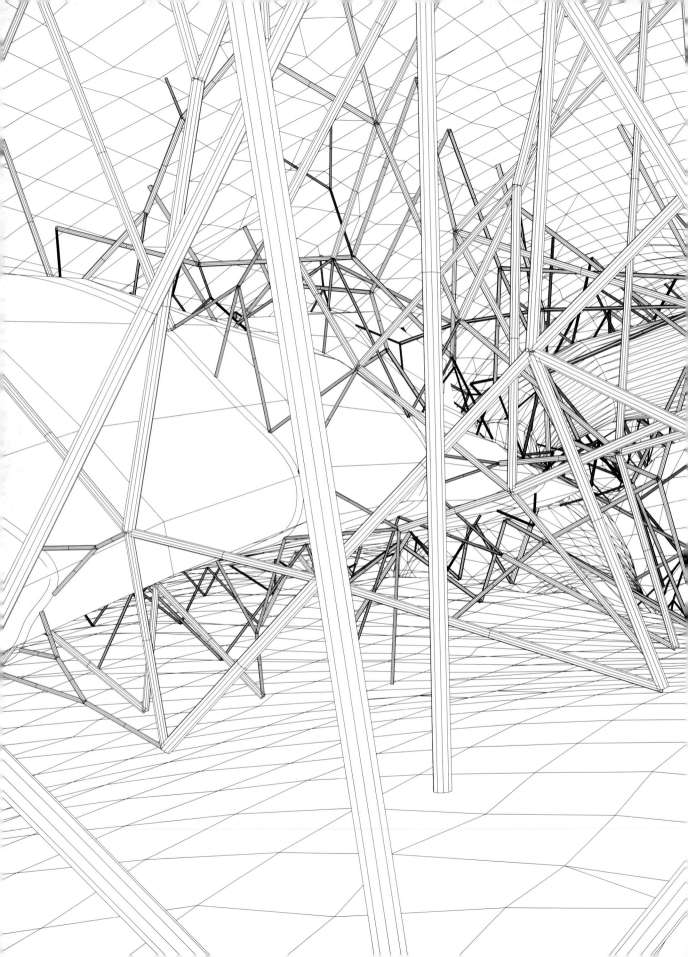

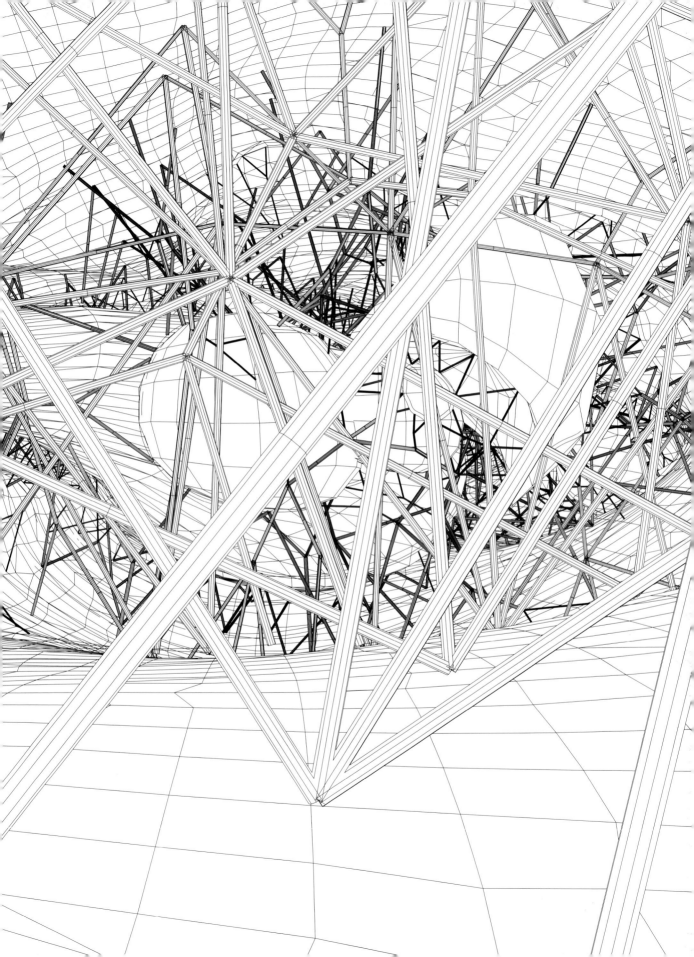

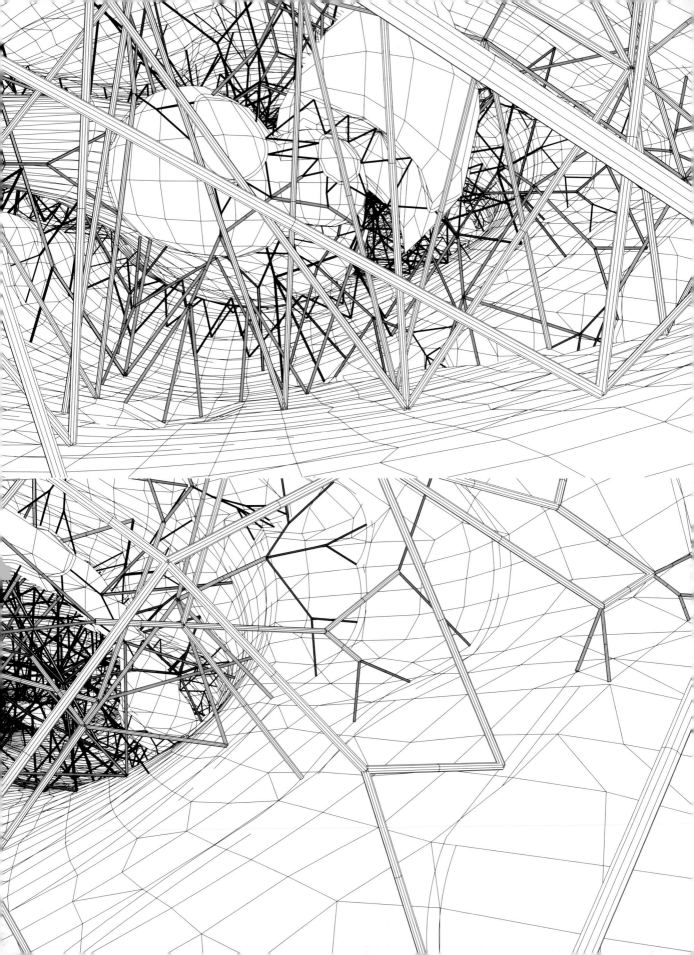

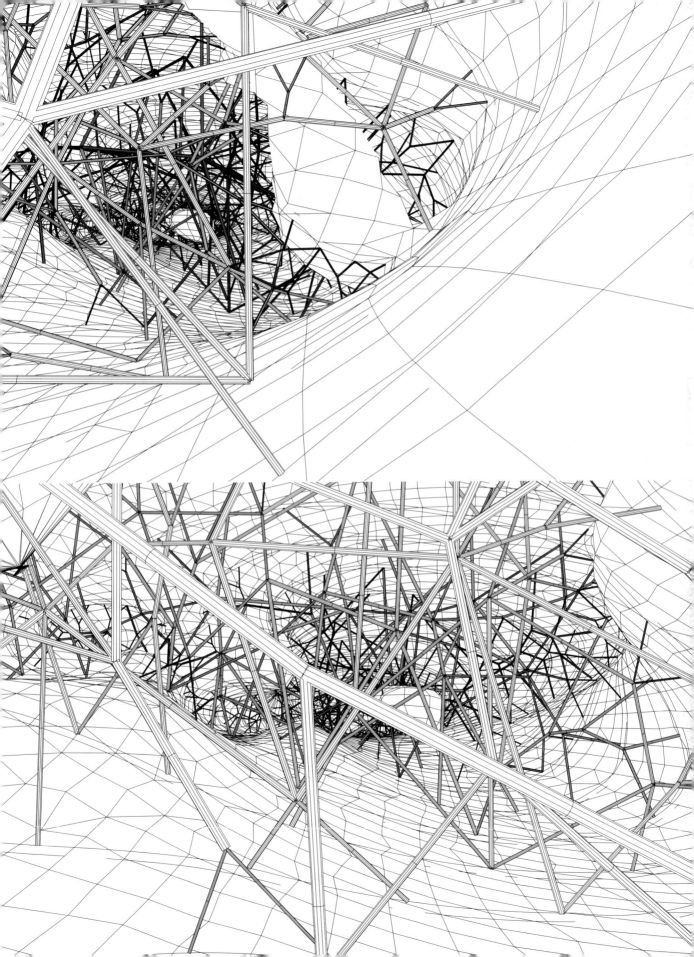

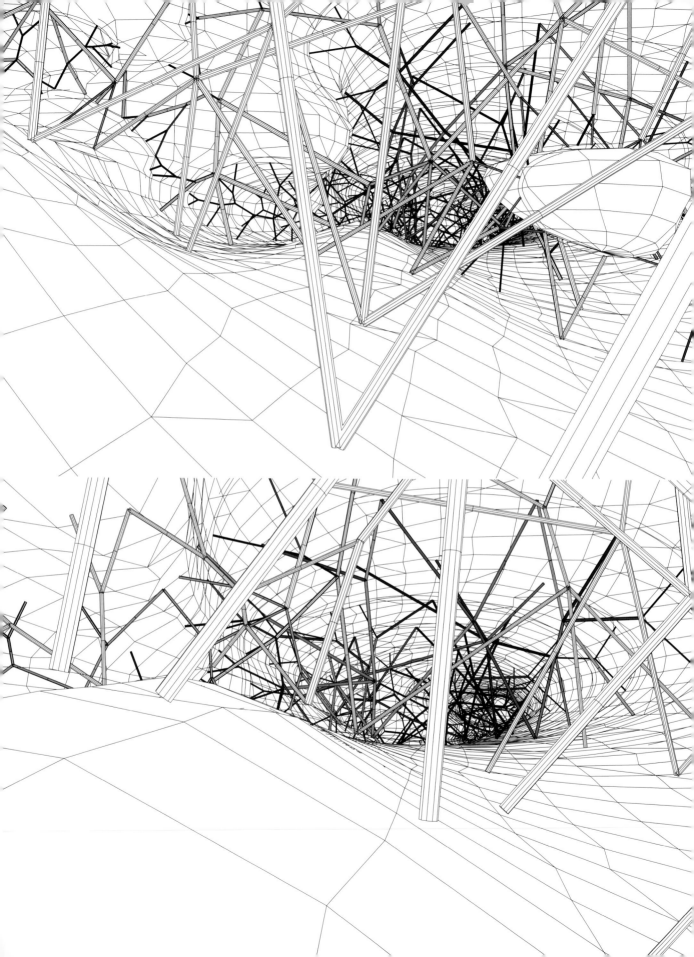

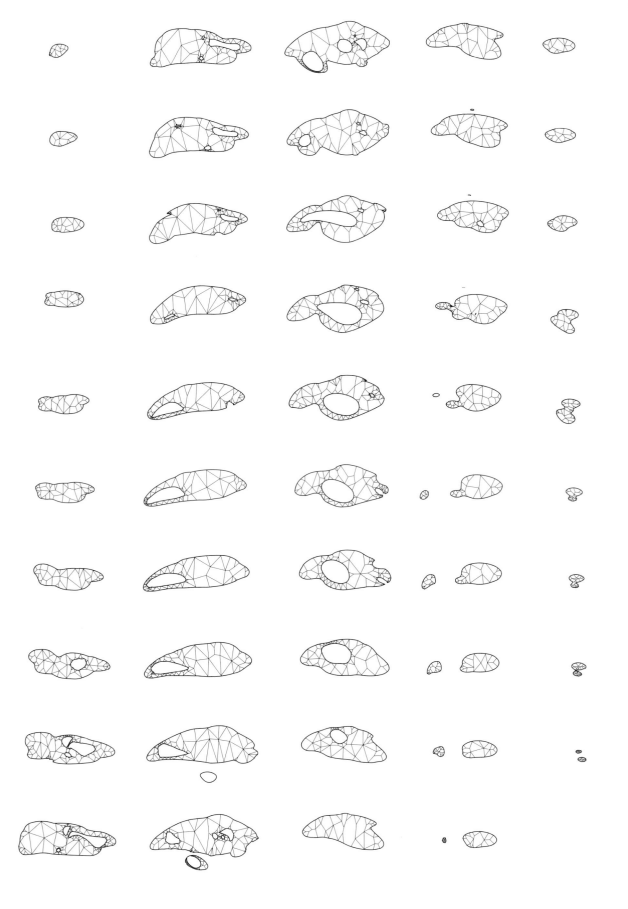

p 384

At the time of this project I had just edited the Comfort issue of Forum, a Virilio view on the hidden agenda of technology as a mass anaesthetic. We saw a clear reversal in the master-slave relationship between people and technology, an all-too-perfect service that could have only one outcome: a permanent floating in blissful safety. There are only two forms of technology: one that adds movement to the body and one that takes movement away — which is the technology of comfort.

"beachness"

research project for a beach hotel and boulevard, Noordwijk, the Netherlands, 1997

I define "beachness" as a certain state of mobility, with the beach conceived as a field of openness and indeterminacy, instead of as a place to dig yourself in. The loose architecture of such light materials as wood and fabric and sand (used as a street when wet and for a bed when dry), people and cars, sunlight and wind all are considered materials that combine into a plastic alloy of continuous transformation. Everything is mobile and moveable furniture.

The project — which was commissioned as a kind of science-fiction research into a future Dutch Coast — consists of two parts: a beach hotel and a boulevard that blends into the beach. When the beach is partly paved with asphalt, beach behaviour and road behaviour merge locally into an exciting hybrid form: cars will park as beach cabins, sometimes with their doors open, to be grouped together, then separate again; as cars and pedestrians mingle, cars will behave as pedestrians. In this dynamic mix of slowly moving and parked cars, pedestrians and cyclists, an active ground level develops on which we envision moving structures of steel and fabric that react to the wind.

The hotel is conceived as an integrated experience of 'radical wellness', not as a classic Hotel Bellevue. Rooms do not even need a view to the sea since all guests are there to reprogramme their lives and reset their biological clocks — a celebration of J. G. Ballard and Paul Virilio mixed into a psychedelic review of *The Prisoner* … The hotel is wrapped in translucent fabric around a vertical core of rooms that are themselves translucent. The 'belly' hosts a parking space that turns into a seafood restaurant above a salt-water swimming pool. The fabric enveloping the tower can be used for projections, like visualizations of the psychological states of the guests, or movies that can be watched from the beach.

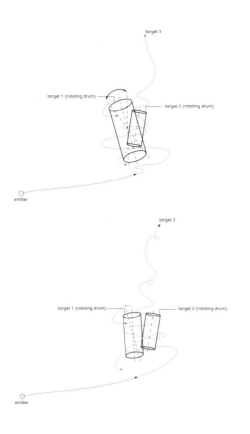

The tower's spiralling structure results from a complex choreography of rotating drums guiding a flow of monadic spheres. Tracing digital particles allows us to create movement that can never be drawn by hand. Since all spherical bodies are connected to each other by force fields, each movement has an effect on the other – an extreme version of the *three-body problem*. Movements happen within movements, making it completely different from any gestural way of working.

Iakov Chernikov
nr. 214, 1931

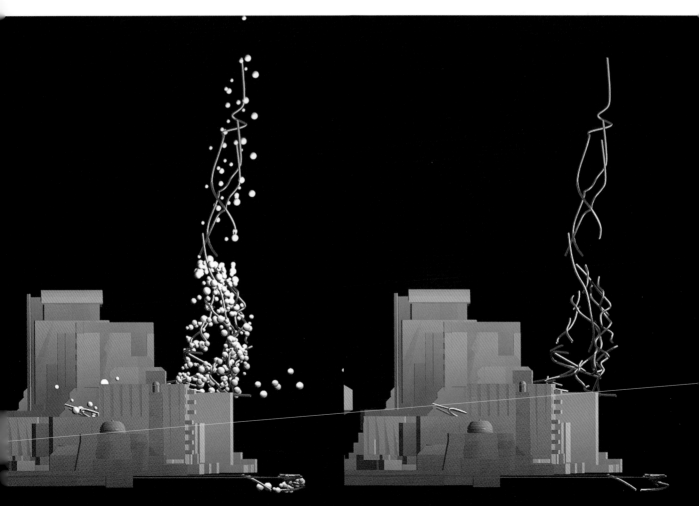

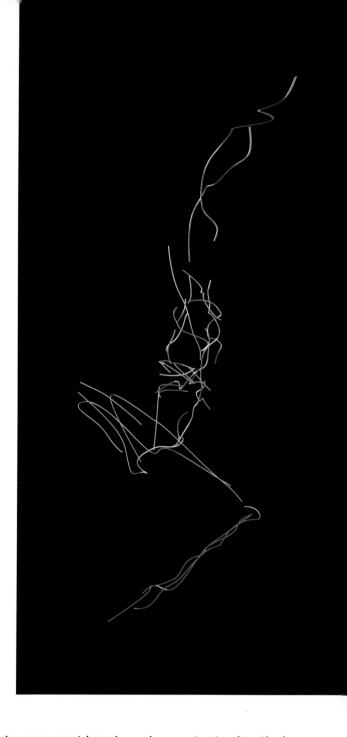

p 42
p 81
p 246

For me, tracing movement has always been a structural method, not a formal one. Although I have developed different techniques, earlier projects work with loose ends, loose figures of movement that are later reconnected in a structural configuration: a technique similar to Pollock's dripping method, where lines mesh together more like felt than weaving. We should remember, however, that Pollock's paintings are based on a complex choreography of feet, elbow and hand that make at least as complex arabesques outside of the canvas as onto it.

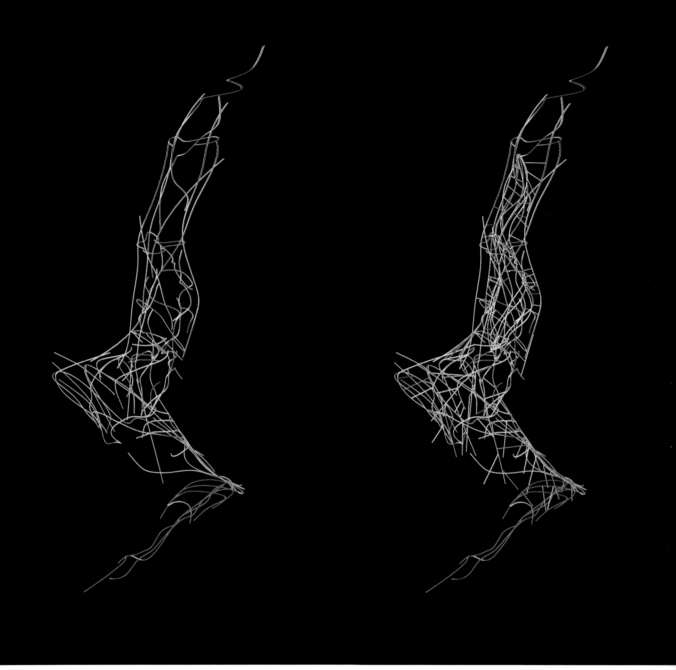

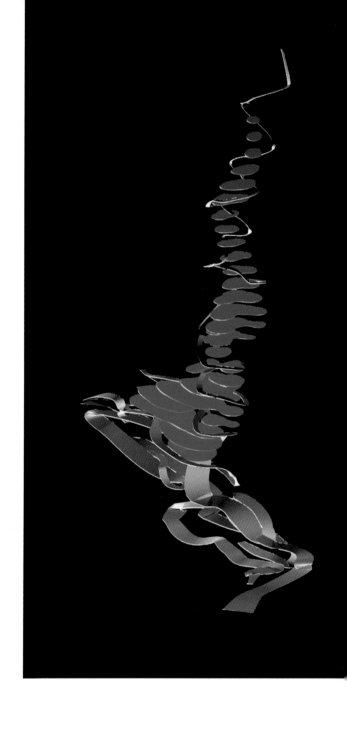

rooms

lobby

entrance

pool

conference rooms

fish-restaurant

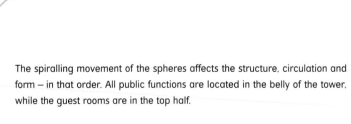

The spiralling movement of the spheres affects the structure, circulation and form – in that order. All public functions are located in the belly of the tower, while the guest rooms are in the top half.

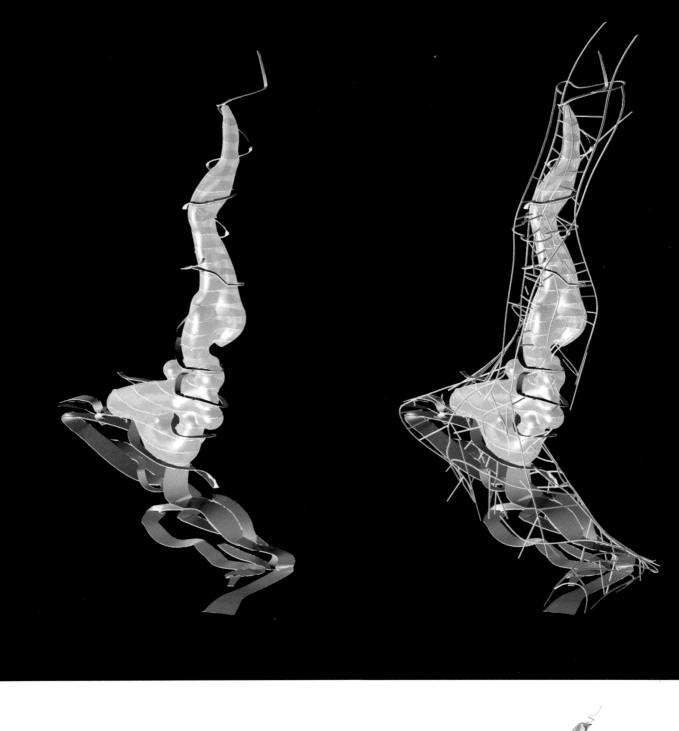

The translucent membrane wrapped around the tower permits a diffused daylight but at night becomes an enormous projection screen. When the sun has set, a projection of a new sunset starts, and after an hour another one, and again, each filmed in a successive time zone (westward) and streamed live over the Internet, until morning breaks again.

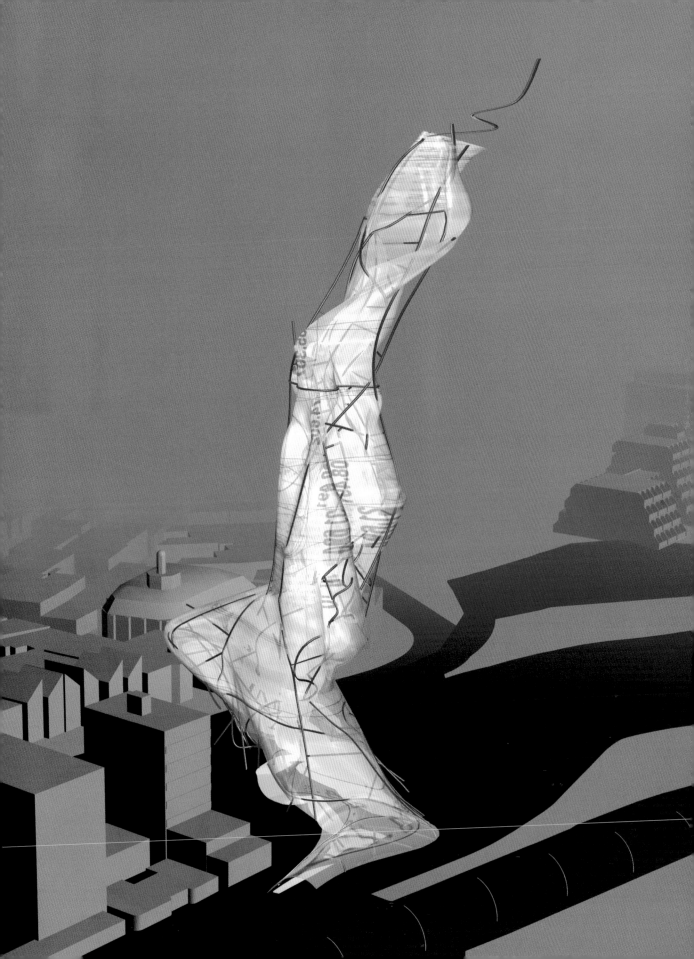

Tommy

a ceramic container for the Cor Unum company,
Den Bosch, the Netherlands, 1998

I wanted to make an object without any function, just to be held, without becoming an art object. Tommy loops back and forth between the optic and the haptic, the visual and the felt, as if made by a blind person. Tommy is conceived as a premature organism, born before it should have seen the light of day, and therefore slimy, ugly, even monstrous and unsightly — but just as moving as a baby. Tommy is a gesture created from the inside out and fully orientated upon itself. The path created in the computer traced a complex moving hand, a kinaesthetic sign. As it lies, Tommy desperately desires to be picked up and stroked, to be explored in the same way it was made.

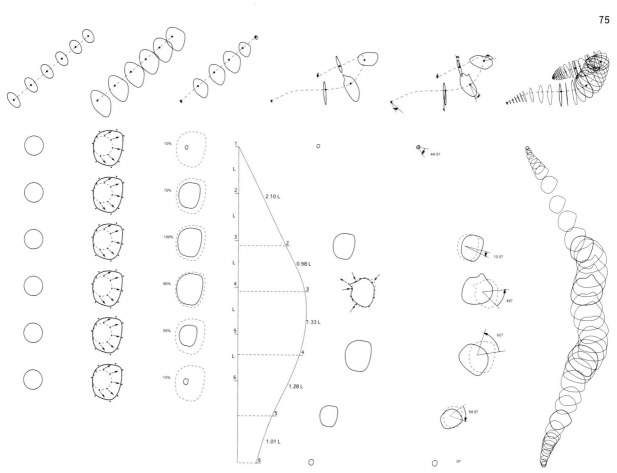

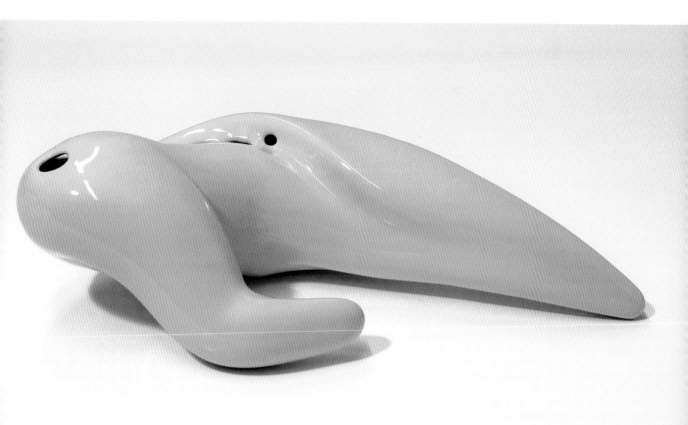

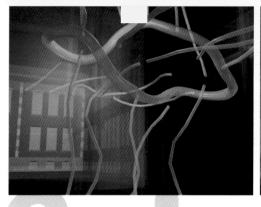
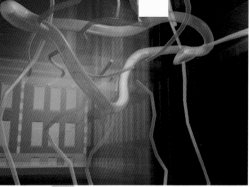

V2_Lab

offices and laboratory within the existing V2_ building,
Rotterdam, the Netherlands, 1998

Instead of regarding a renovation as something that simply completes an existing structure, I see architecture here assuming the role of furniture and textile as a means to introduce movement. We used complex digital choreographies to generate slight but distinct variations on an office typology. In this way we progress seamlessly from computer-generated processing of forces to human behaviour and work.

The *V2_Lab* is both a workspace and a place for receiving visitors to the V2_Organisation, an arts and technology institute that organizes the biennial Dutch Electronic Art Festival, DEAF. The *V2_Lab* specifically houses the work-spaces of artists in residence who collaborate with professionals from V2_ to produce elaborate interactive art works and prepare exhibitions.

      The space is designed to facilitate specific functions but also to stimulate new unknown situations. First, we looked carefully at the desired positioning of programmatic elements (lab space, audio room, video room, management spaces), which were to be elevated almost a full metre off the floor to allow views through the high window. This procedure operated through separation since tasks are generally separated. The second procedure stresses communication and continuity and uses flexible lines with the material properties of rubber, which are manipulated simultaneously with the lateral forces that connect programmatic elements. While the first operation works with the segmentation of dimensions, points, lines and surfaces, the second operation works mainly through 'springs', flexible digital points where forces can be passed on to make the line undulate. A continuous field vibrates within a crystallized space of functions and causes liquefactions and connections. The result is a space in which the determined states of objects are still readable and useable as functions but also where less determined states are materialized to stimulate new behaviours.

A

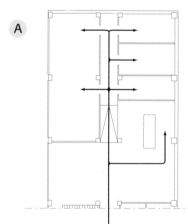

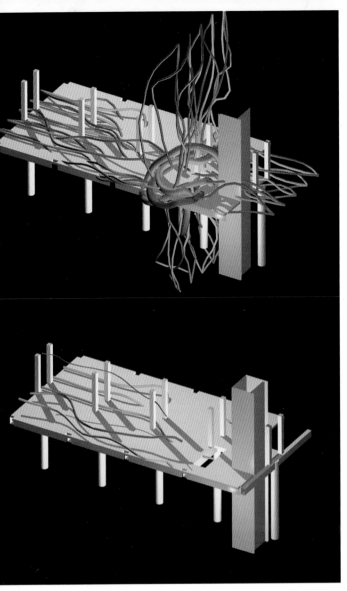

The line thicknesses correspond with the material properties of rubber. The software processes all the forces simultaneously, which makes the lines undulate in a complex manner. Five separate 'snares' are connected to a large central spring that responds directly to all effects, integrates them and sends information back into the lines.

Four stages of machining: A. programmatic mapping of separate functions (I – mobility), B. mapping of smaller movements in lateral directions (II – motility), C. locations where system II matches with system I, D. resulting floor geometry after connecting lines with ruled surfaces.

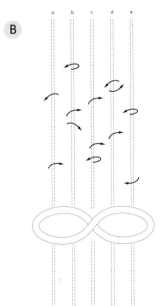

B

a   b   c   d   e

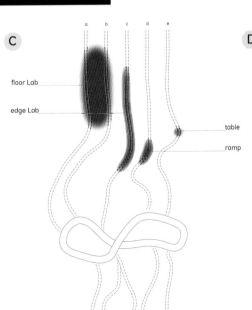

C

a   b   c   d   e

floor Lab

edge Lab

table

ramp

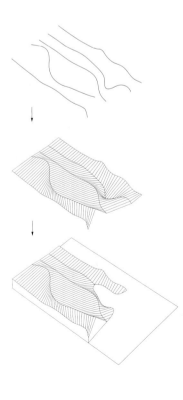

D

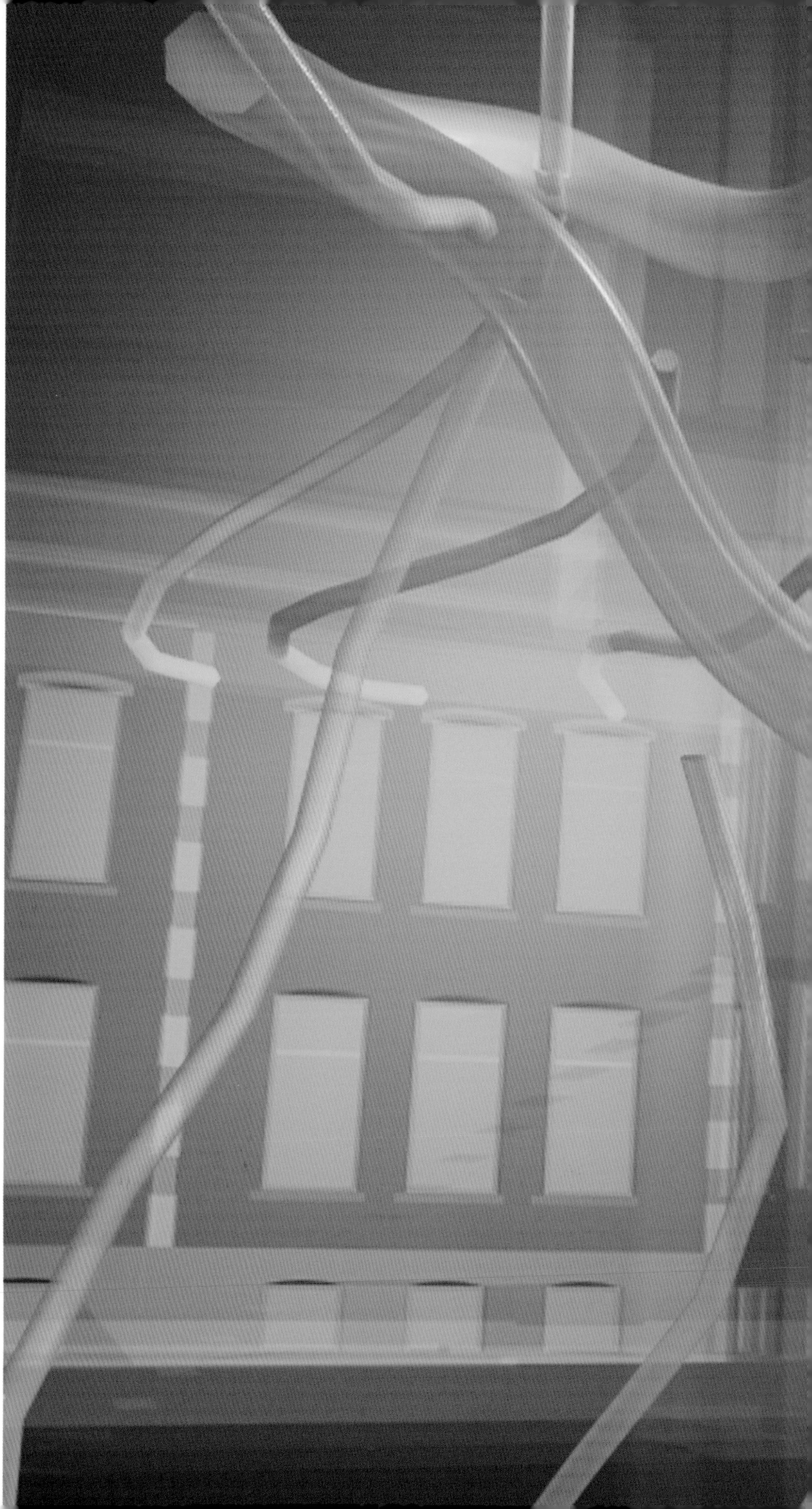

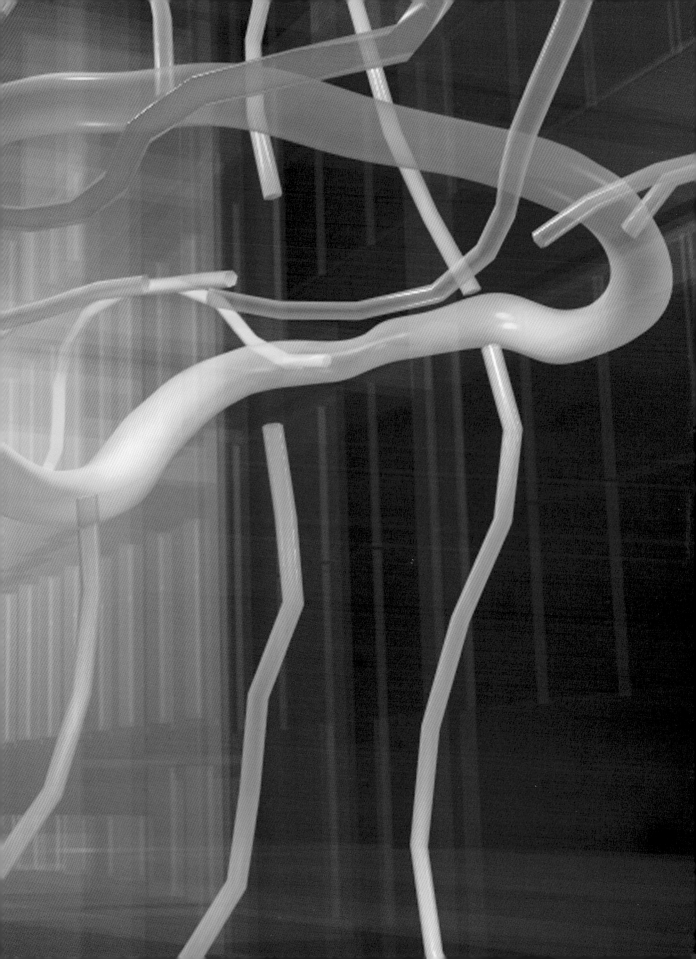

p 216

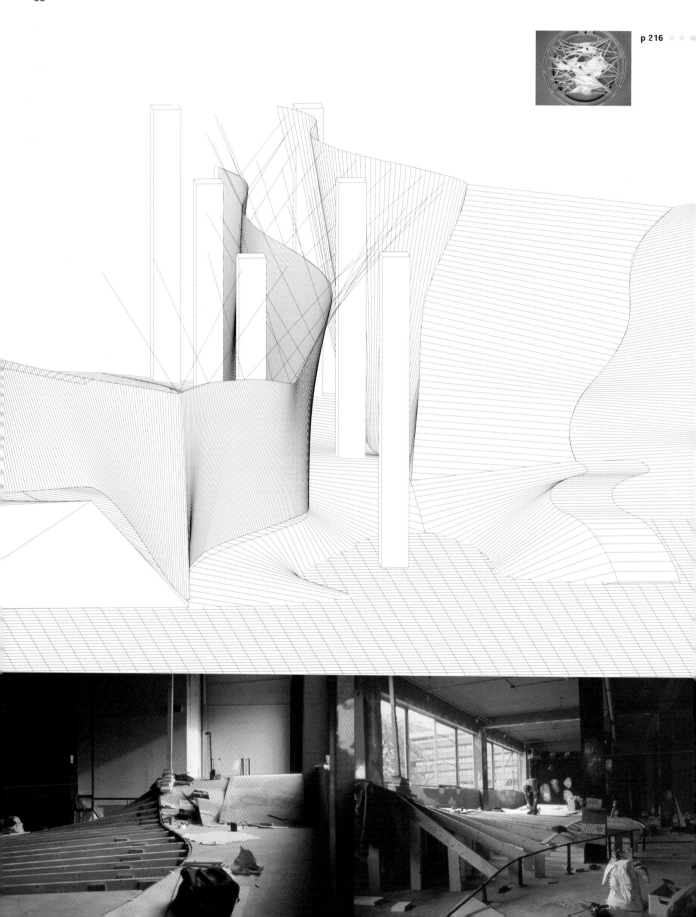

Two forms of rubber and two offices — Soft Office (p. 216) and the V2_Lab — use elasticity to create an architecture of flexibility and vagueness, but there are also differences between the projects. V2_Lab uses an indexical *technique in which movements are freeze-framed, while the* Soft Office *machine is a self-stopping, constructivist technique. V2_Lab, the earlier project, is all grey without a trace of horizontality, followed two years later by a more controlled* Soft Office, *in wood with floors accommodating standard office furniture.*

p 101
p 139

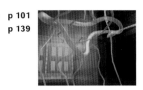

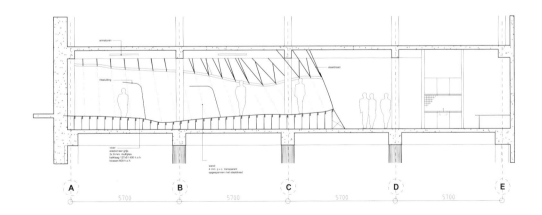

The design procedure focuses on the deep surface of the floor, where the extrusions of walls, rather than simply erected upwards, follow from the floor articulations.

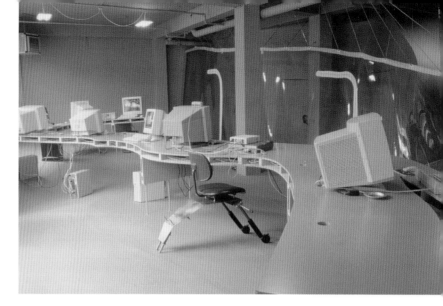

The thick plastic wall that snakes through the space acts as what Van Eyck called an 'internal horizon', an internal view. The wall divides management from artists, providing each with a distorted view of the other.

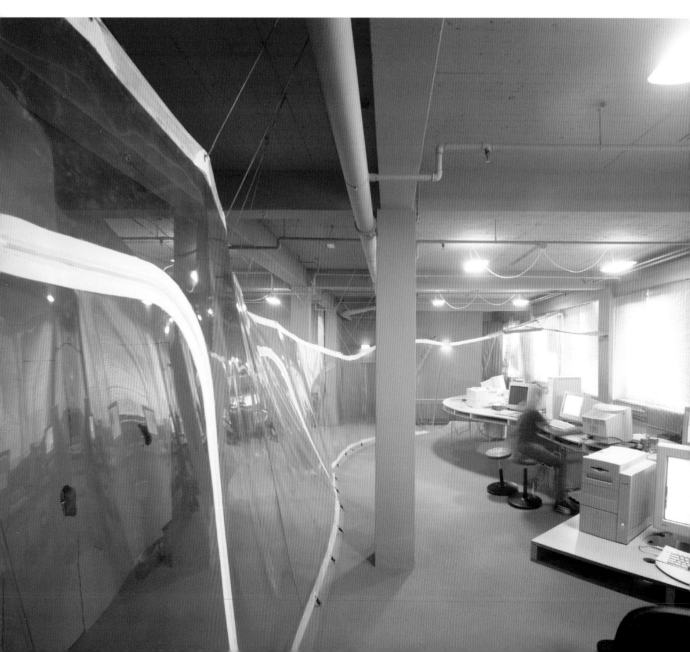

As in *H₂Oexpo* and other projects, one can study the effects of geometric vagueness on programmatic development *a posteriori*. Although most of the events (within the range of architectural definition) are predefined, some are new and emergent. The 'morphed' area between the table and the corridor proved especially full of potential. Sometimes small meetings emerge, either very actively, as when walking up the slope one is suddenly standing on the table of the general manager, or more relaxed, as when people are drinking tea lying down and conversing. These are not accidental 'freak' events, but intensifications of working relationships.

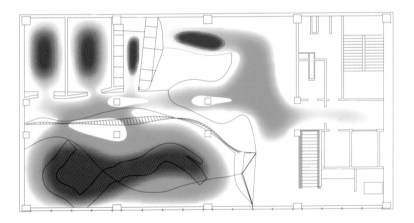

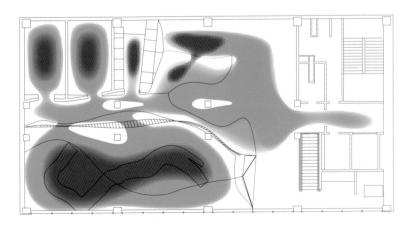

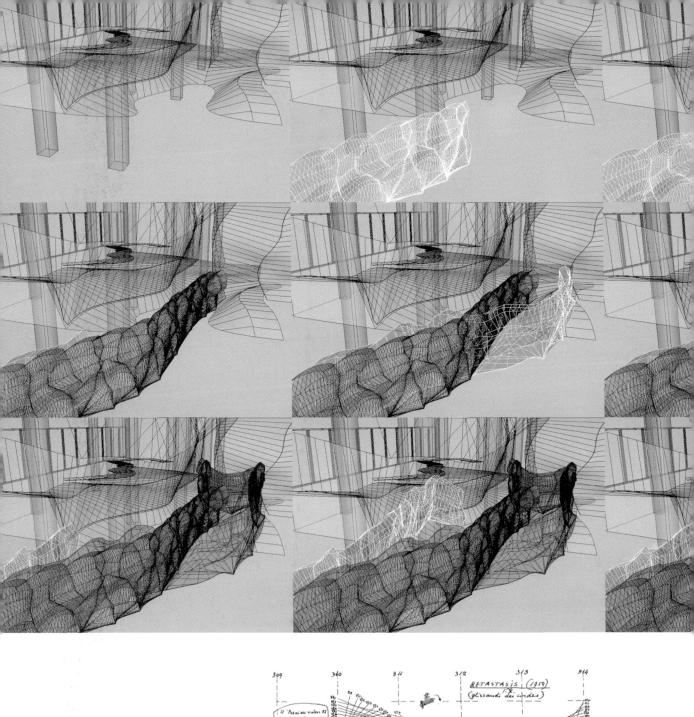
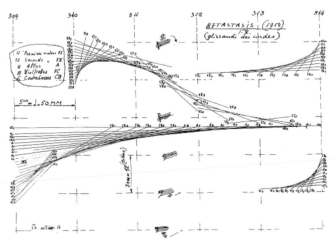

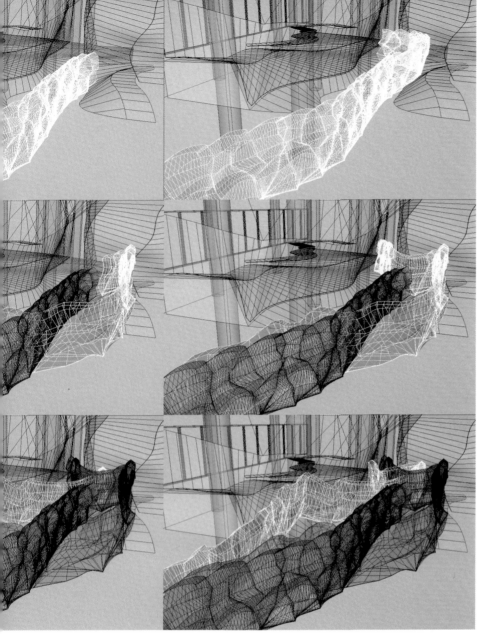

Three different types of entry to the V2_Lab graphed in space.
The joints of the human body are tracked in time and connected
afterwards to show the 'shape' of the movement.

The rubber lines with the springs that generated the design
return in the behavioural patterns in the office. Running lines
— which in architecture are always considered mechanical
and repeatable — develop variations that relate to people's
moods and habits. Habits are determined 'tracks' of behav-
iour, but feelings and moods make them variable. These can
only be mobilized if the architecture is flexible. If architec-
ture can respond only by reducing behaviour to predeter-
mined states, it will never work. This plastic interactivity of
vague geometry was studied carefully by Iannis Xenakis,
who used it for the design of the **Philips Pavilion** *and the*
score of **Metastasis** *with its multiple 'glissandi' that were*
never played in exactly the same way.

p 36
p 139
p 227

p 237

We were later asked to develop a new façade for the V2_ building. Again, we combined time-based design techniques with interactive electronic projections. Different street scenes from all over the world (here we see web images of taxi driver 'Mike at the wheel' from New York) alternate with interior views of people at work.

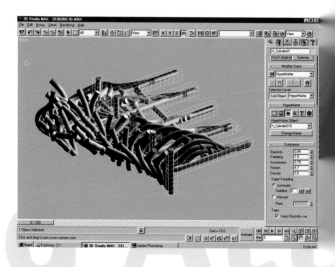

Flying Attic

installation for the UnderCover Foundation
travelling exhibition on the architectural rethinking of attic, the Netherlands, 1998

In **Flying Attic** *the constructive is conceived as flexible in every way. In each step in the design process, movement is absorbed by the structure and passed on to the next stage, from a skeletal structure in rubber to a flexible structure in wood to a human body. This self-supporting curtain was not only meant to show works but also to stimulate visitors to explore the structure itself.*

As with the *V2_Lab*, our main interest was the relationship between habit and emergent behaviour and how this can be made productive. For this we followed a stepwise machining procedure:

STEP 1 (diagram A, organization). Visitors are guided along the front wall (with an introduction to the theme of the exhibition), then guided back at the other side along four sections, each containing two exhibitors.

STEP 2 (diagram B, rubber). In the computer the organization diagram is constructed in 'rubber' (with the same elasticity and density as natural rubber) and distorted in time by exposing it to various forces. The tectonic model, with its cylinders, seams and interruptions, is replaced by a continuous topological model of springs.

STEP 3 (diagram C, materialization). In the design, the 'rubber' model becomes an assemblage of wood, foam rubber and a steel tube within a geometry of creases (hinges) and folds (bending). The tube and surfaces are soft and pliable but not weak or without resistance. This structure can be adapted to various galleries.

STEP 4 (diagram D, actualization). Apart from the fact that the structure conceals as much of the exhibition as it shows, deviating from the standard exhibition diagram, the materialization generates a complexity of behaviour that cannot be fully prescribed by a programme.

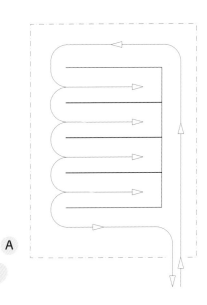

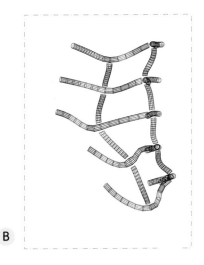

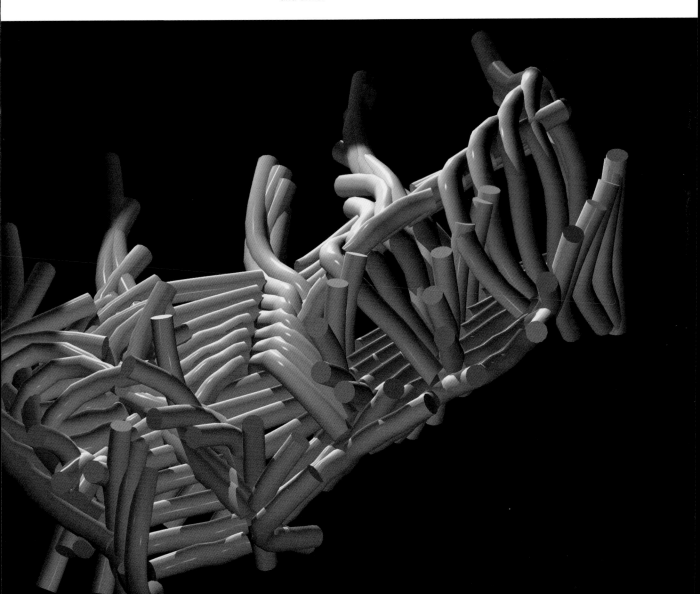

Organization diagram A contains the large-scale movement of visitors. Rubber diagram B has the same skeletal structure as A but inflected by the smaller movements of hands and arms.

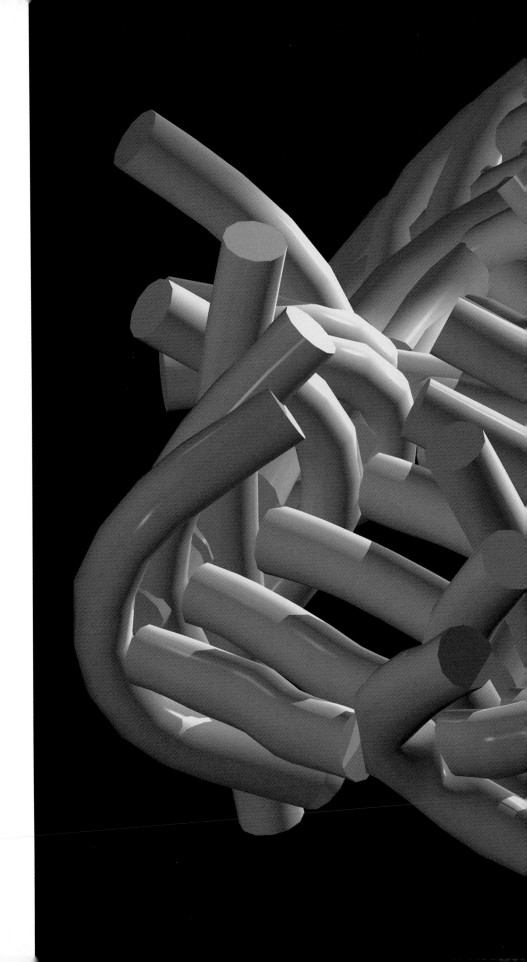

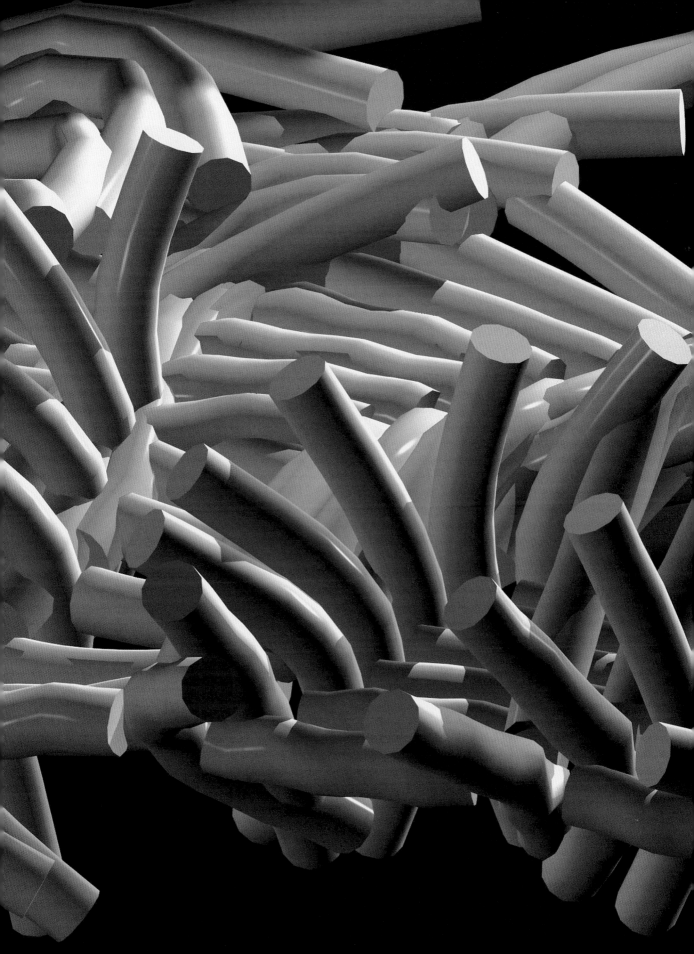

In the translation (or re-materialization) of the 'rubber' diagram (B) into wood and steel (C), the typology of diagram A is also considered. The *geometrical* information of B is read through the *formal* information of A. The walls of diagram A become flexible in the figural sense of geometry and in the literal sense of materials. Folds and creases materialized in an assembly of wood and foam rubber become a conceptual transformation of a *wall* into a *curtain* that is also structurally malleable.

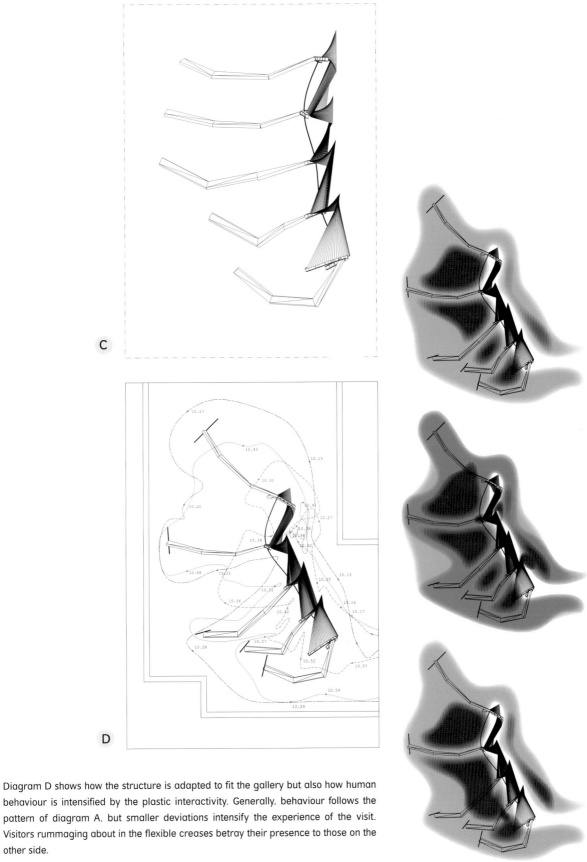

C

D

Diagram D shows how the structure is adapted to fit the gallery but also how human behaviour is intensified by the plastic interactivity. Generally, behaviour follows the pattern of diagram A, but smaller deviations intensify the experience of the visit. Visitors rummaging about in the flexible creases betray their presence to those on the other side.

Scientific visualization software is often occupied with showing the relationship between time and geometry. Generally, we think of shapes as discrete and time as continuous, but here discrete entities on different scales are understood as stages in a process of continuous variation, such that the geometry of a shape *at any moment* has the properties of time *as a flow*. In short, one can bridge time and form only by introducing the topological geometry of curvature.

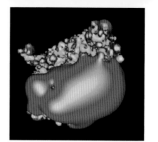

The Future Is Now

project for an exhibition on the 'future' related to the
Swiss pharmaceutical industry – in collaboration with
Harm Lux (curator) and Mike Tyler (artist),
Expo.02 Biel, Switzerland, 1998

There have been many futures. There have been prophecies, there have been utopias, there have been sci-fi extrapolations, there have been ideologies. No such thing exists any more. Although self-confidence has never been stronger, nowadays we acknowledge complexity, so we focus more on managing the near future than on planning and envisioning a general future.

The Future Expo was not conceived as a conventional exposition building featuring images of a so-called future. These are old futurisms; our future is now. We designed a structure where technology, human experience and environment exist in a single continuum. Instead of a museum that provides visitors with answers, we wanted to create a gap, an active 'reflectorium', an environment that raises questions.

From meteorology, morphogenesis in biological systems, catastrophe theory in events, fractal geometry in natural forms, we have learned that we should not stare at forms in space but understand how they develop in time, how they obtain their cohesion through time. The scientific visualization software we used to design this structure trains us to see shapes developing over time, to see pattern beyond form. Here, meteorological visualization generated a pattern of growth and expansion, as in cloud formation.

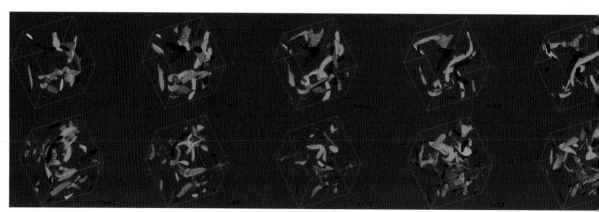

In visualization software often a cubical frame is introduced
to set the to-be-calculated data to a fixed amount.

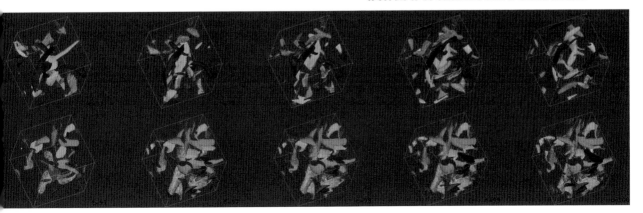

The built structure is densely filled with different kinds of sensors — light, temperature, pressure. These devices make the building sensitive to human presence; it knows who is there, what the person is looking at and where the person has already been. Simultaneously, visitors see images and hear sounds that are retrieved from a database of images of nanotechnology that move according to the visitors' interest and movement. Every visitor is equipped with semi-immersive virtual glasses, which enable him or her to see the actual built structure and images projected on the eyeglasses at the same time. Thus the visitor can move through the building, see other people, speak to them, walk around and at the same time see an image projected in front of his or her eyes. Because of the motion-tracking and eye-tracking system of the building's sensors, the computer knows where a visitor is and what he or she is looking at, then calculates an image and sends it back to the visitor and projects it on his or her glasses, as if he or she were seeing it on the wall.

section

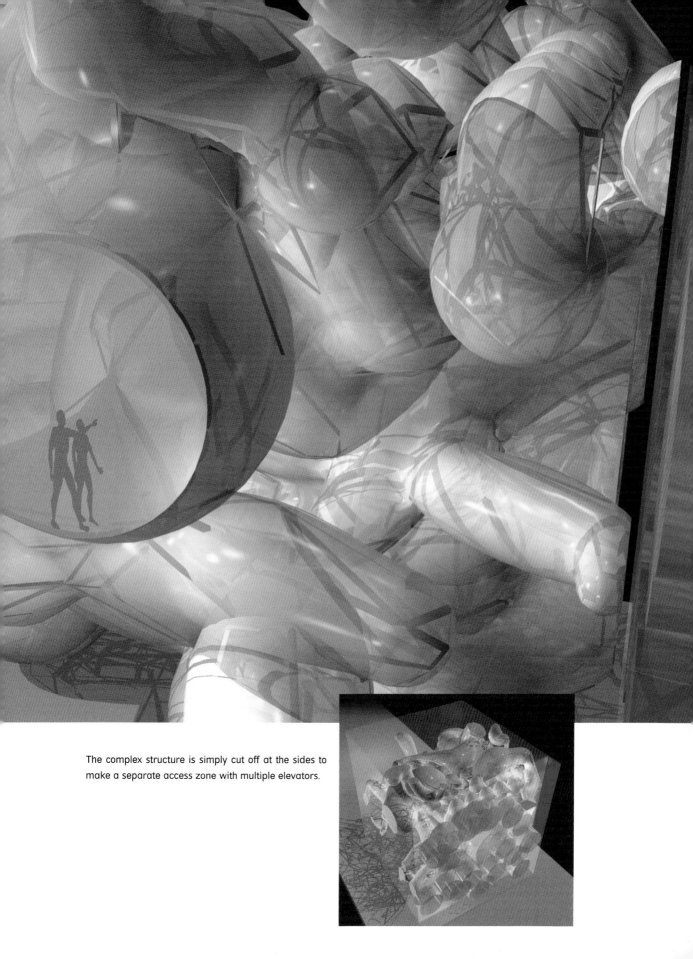

The complex structure is simply cut off at the sides to make a separate access zone with multiple elevators.

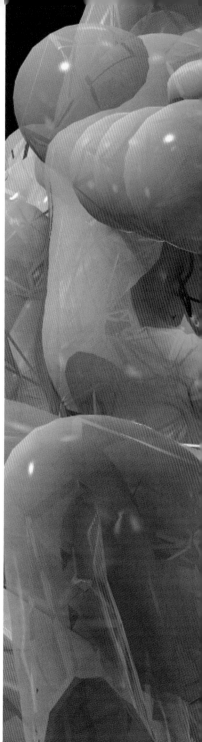

Three-dimensional nets have always been part of our research. Foam Home, Soft Office, obliqueWTC *and* The Future Is Now *are among the clearest examples. Frei Otto emphasizes that this type of structure relates to pneumatic systems, because an embryo starts out as liquid, then develops cartilage, which hardens fully after birth. In* The Future Is Now *the connection between 3D nets and pneumatics is direct, even though the spherical surfaces are not inflated membranes but rigid epoxy panels.*

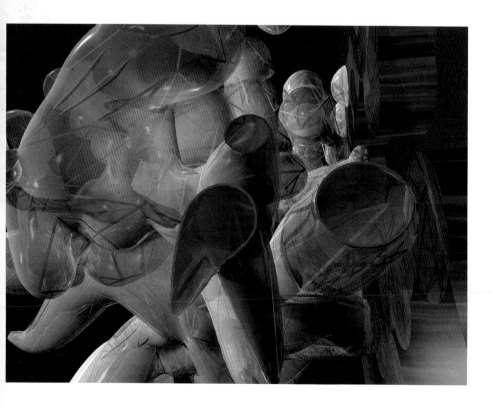

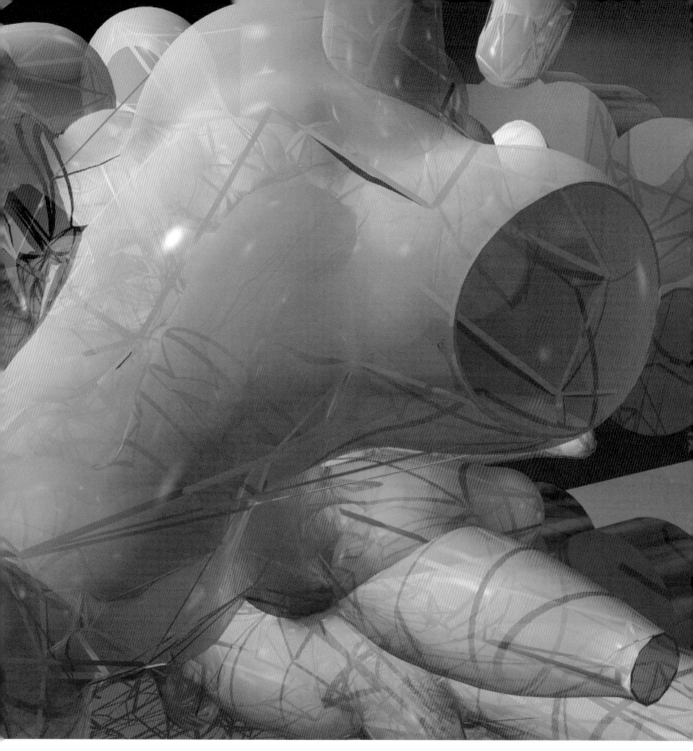

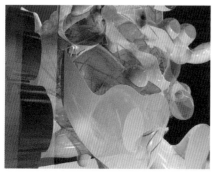

A structure like *D-tower* (p. 158), which is made of laminated epoxy in variable thicknesses, proves that this type of structure is not unbuildable. A tubular-steel structure in a polygonal network carrying epoxy panels connected through flanges would make it feasible. The translucent surface of the epoxy could be lit in different ways, both programmed and interactive.

Wearable computing devices make it possible for each visiting individual to have a unique exhibition experience. A tracking system would know exactly where each visitor is in the building, and in which direction that person is looking. A wearable computer would then send the right image to a semi-transparent LCD screen in the glasses. The visitor would not just see the space where he or she is, but also the image and text fitting in the perspective view. Someone without glasses would see only translucent walls and coloured light.

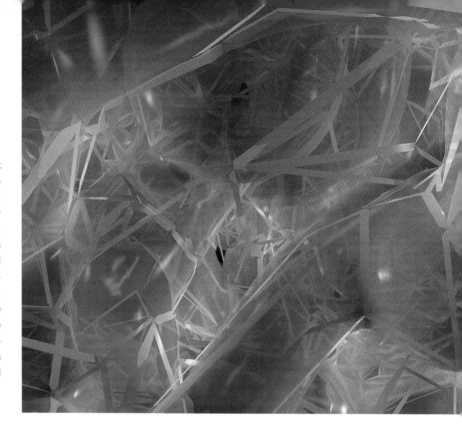

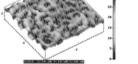

actual image (seen without glasses)

virtual images (with glasses)

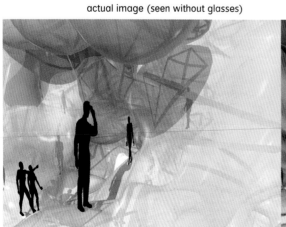

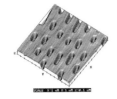

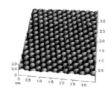

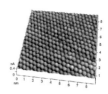

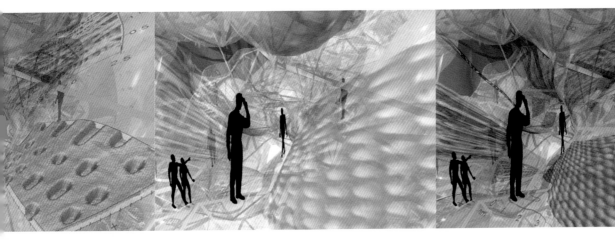

myTwinn©

OffTheRoad_5speed

research into non-standard prefab housing along highway A58,
for housing corporation TRUDO, Eindhoven, the Netherlands, 1999–2000

Mass customization is a hugely important issue in our culture and therefore in architecture. Can we have products that are as individual as ourselves and yet remain affordably priced? Is it possible for inhabitants of a new neighbourhood development all to have different houses? This raises the question of variation. One answer is metadesign, that is, to create a specific house one must first design a generic house template. This generic house is a virtual matrix of relationships that can be specified for each inhabitant and then built.

OffTheRoad_5speed is an integrated approach to the design of large urban structures and the small scale of the house and its interior within one continuum of five interrelated machines or machine-states, as in a gearbox. All speeds, from the scale of the highway to the smallest, most intimate behaviour in a house, are absorbed by interactive, variable, responsive systems, which all have their own characteristic limitations and thresholds. Not one of the five systems, however, reaches a state of equilibrium, because all movement at the moment of freezing is passed to the next stage (the changing of gear), while at every level the movement is shared with a specific sphere of action, dependent on the speed of the body:

1st gear: interfering (urbanism). Perpendicular to the highway A58 with four lanes of traffic, a set of 100 lines was stretched out over 2,500 metres. All lines were divided over 20 points ('control vertices') and connected by springs with 'rubbery' properties, making the whole system into a continuum of moveable points and bendable lines. Two large spheres of action were attached to the system and respectively read in two directions, back and forth. This resulted in an interference pattern, where the sets of lines were a variation of one system, a complex pattern emerging out of a simple initial state.

2nd gear: bending (typology). Because in first gear every line was doubled or split as a result of bending it in two directions, all the points on the lines also doubled up, in as many different ways as the lines themselves. Thus, whenever

1st gear

Each line consists of two lines on top of each other, each containing a certain number of houses. When the system is not transformed, it simply forms a grid with semi-detached houses. The double lines are moved out of position with forces running over the highway, resulting in a complex moiré pattern.

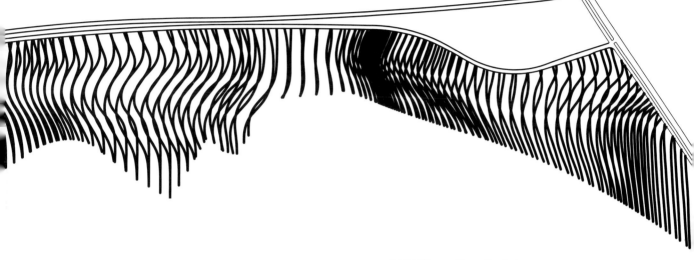

moiré pattern used to position the houses

moiré pattern transformed to a landscaped ground surface

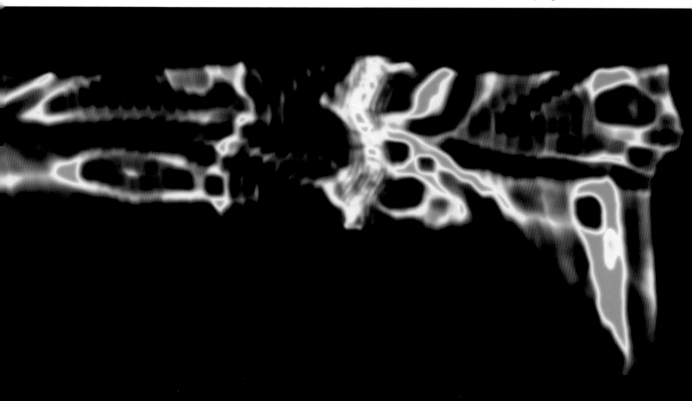

The software we used in the design of the *V2_Lab* and *Flying Attic* was somewhat different from that used here, where lines obtain their material properties from 'springs' that are like elastic bands *between* the lines instead of *in* the lines themselves. The points in the lines are used to *position* the houses, while the springs inform the orientation of each house.

a house is attached to the points on the lines, the typology of connection is varied. In this case, the 'double' type, the duplex, is varied towards the detached house and the row house. At each point, we attached a plot of 23 by 6 metres, which was rotated in the same direction as the accompanying spring. At first, almost all these rectangles overlap, but according to a 'bending principle' they gently bend away from each other, increasing the curvature on a local level.

3rd gear: tunnelling (programme). Because of the rather aggressive outdoor conditions (highway noise), lots are initially completely covered by structure (no front or back garden). The central, 23-metre curve that forms each house's spine is then split into three lines, each functioning as a 'motion path' for three types of radial forces corresponding to three scales of activity. The three types of radial force are:

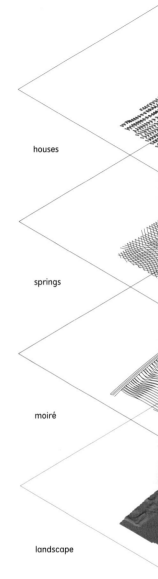

houses

springs

moiré

landscape

    a. large (1): for example, parking your car, making music, sitting together, having a party, playing in the garden
    b. middle-sized (3): such as cooking, making love, barbecuing, washing
    c. small (5): things like reading a book, going to the toilet, sewing, working on the computer

8

All forces have their own rhythm up and down their motion path, from slow to speedy. All the lines making up the outer surface are interconnected by springs. The result is 3,600 different houses, of which the middle 1,050 were used for this scheme.

4th gear: panelling (manufacturing). All houses are prefabricated. As all houses are completely different, flexibility in the manufacturing process is essential. The houses' topology is made up of 24 complex curves structured lengthwise, which allows the mathematical information of the curvature to be numerically available to another system. This system consists of a high number of pistons on flexible ribs connected to a synthetic mouldable sheath. After being placed into the correct position, the sheath is injected with high-density polyurethane, which expands in contact with open air, fills up the volume and almost immediately dries into a rigid foam that is processed in a spraying device to make it watertight and ready to use on site.

5th gear: lifestyling (living). A client is supposed to buy the house as an empty shell that can be adjusted to his or her needs. The shell can stay completely empty or be filled with walls, or a combination. All walls are removable and offer the client the option to alter the house or change functions. The requirements of a single person, a couple, a couple who work at home, a large family, an elderly couple are all different and change with time. The house can adapt and grow as an individual changes from being single into a couple, into a large family, into an elderly couple.

Sears Roebuck House #109, 1909

Industrially produced houses began by mail-order. One could order a house for any possible site, including slight modifications (and without meeting an architect). This developed into fully prefabricated systems, generally in wood, since steel and aluminium never proved successful on the housing market. The dream embodied in the kit house was threefold: retain as much of the assembly as possible at the factory, minimize and keep lightweight the number of parts and make every component modular to optimize variability.

transport by truck

online assembly

component diagram

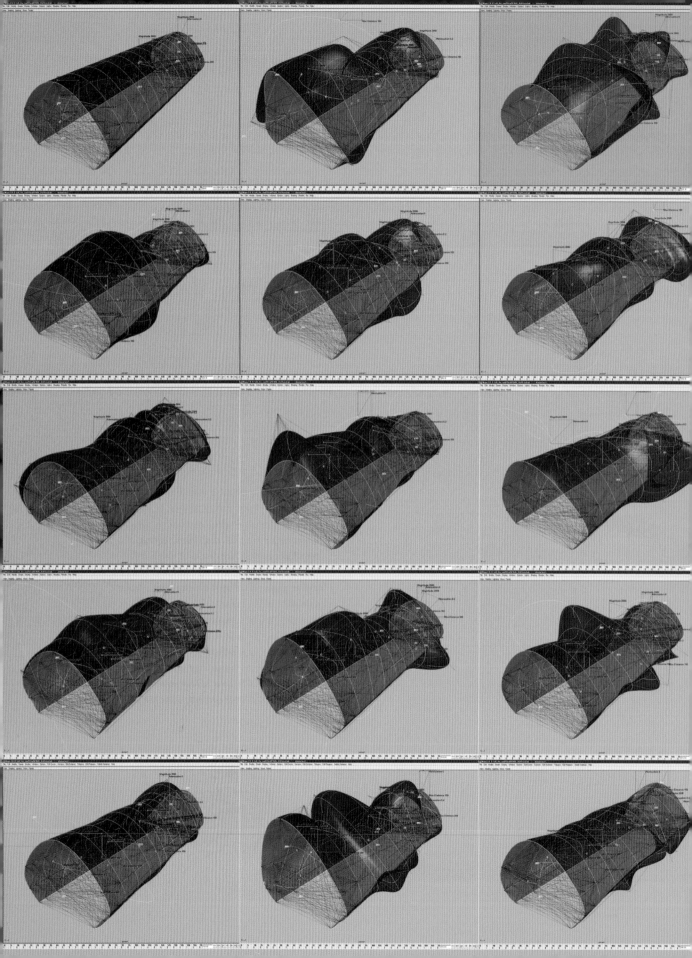

3rd gear

myHouse© is based on three scales of human activity (group, couple or individual) that are simultaneously graphed and imprinted on the outer surface of the house. The procedure begins with a virtual, generic type (frame zero, top left) derived from a shed typology. The radial forces are then fed into the system and create a concaved and convexed geometry that contains programmatic elements. Unlike the kit-of-parts house, myHouse© is based not on a modularity but on continuous variability. This is why the house can be sold only over the Internet (and not through a catalogue) since the house's shape and price must be generated and visualized in real time.

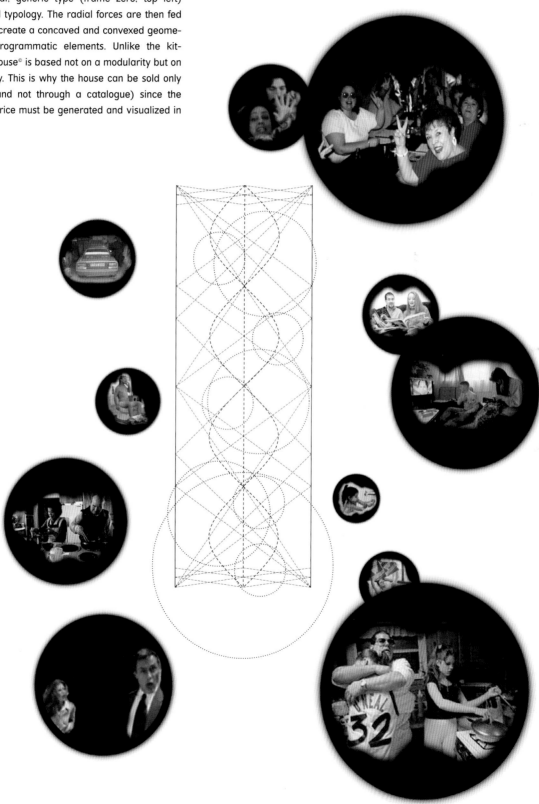

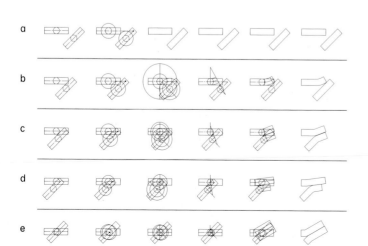

2nd gear

Rectangular houses are bent to the site generated by the flexible grid of the 1st gear. We developed an algorithm that recalculates the relation between the two houses, preventing them from intersecting. As the connections are reconfigured, the street orientation changes considerably: street views might be closed with row houses, half open with semi-detached houses or open diagonals with fully detached houses. Roads are of a typical serpentine suburban low-speed nature, since the main road is only a few minutes away.

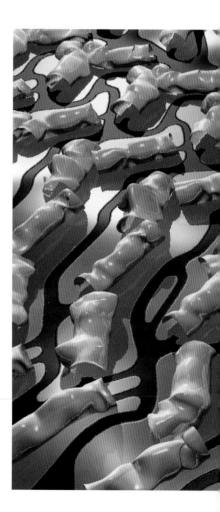

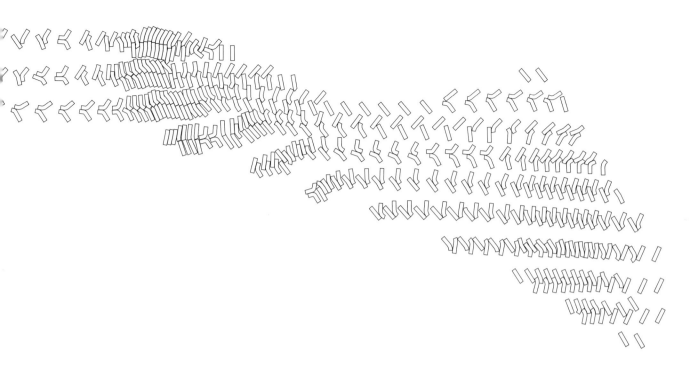

perspective view (after applying 3rd gear)

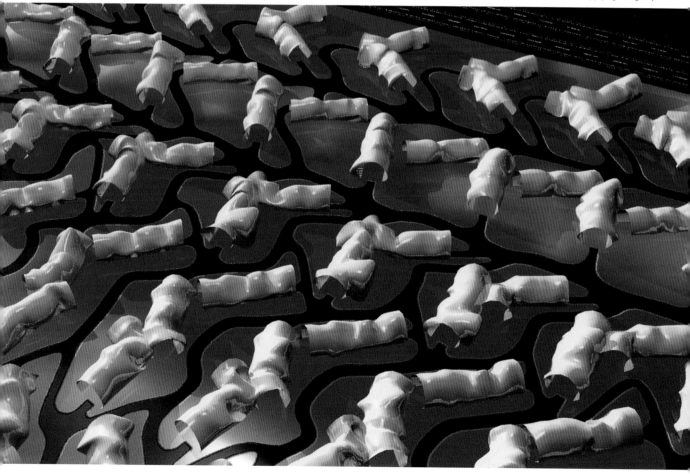

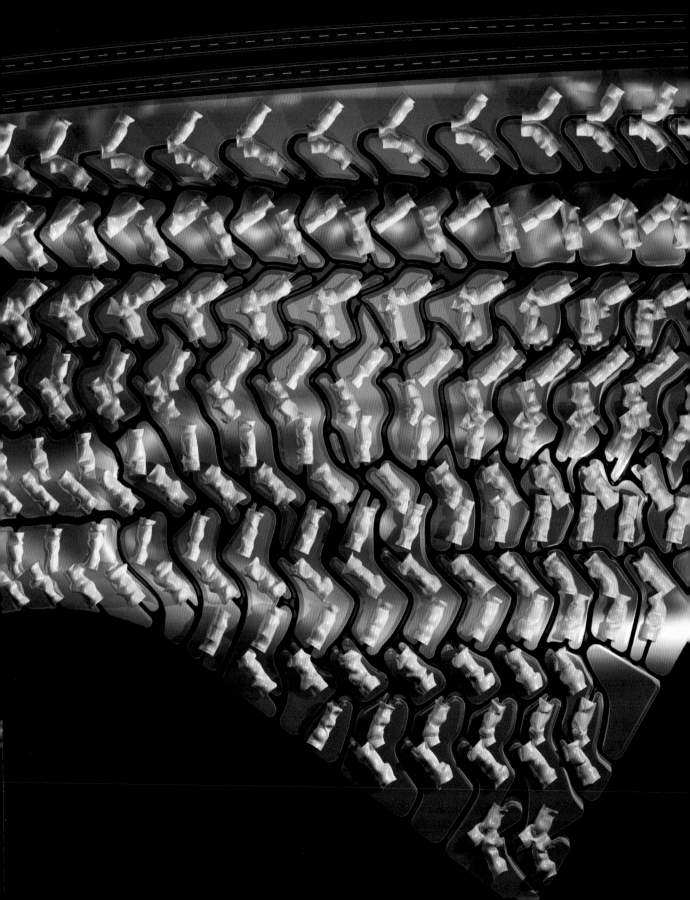

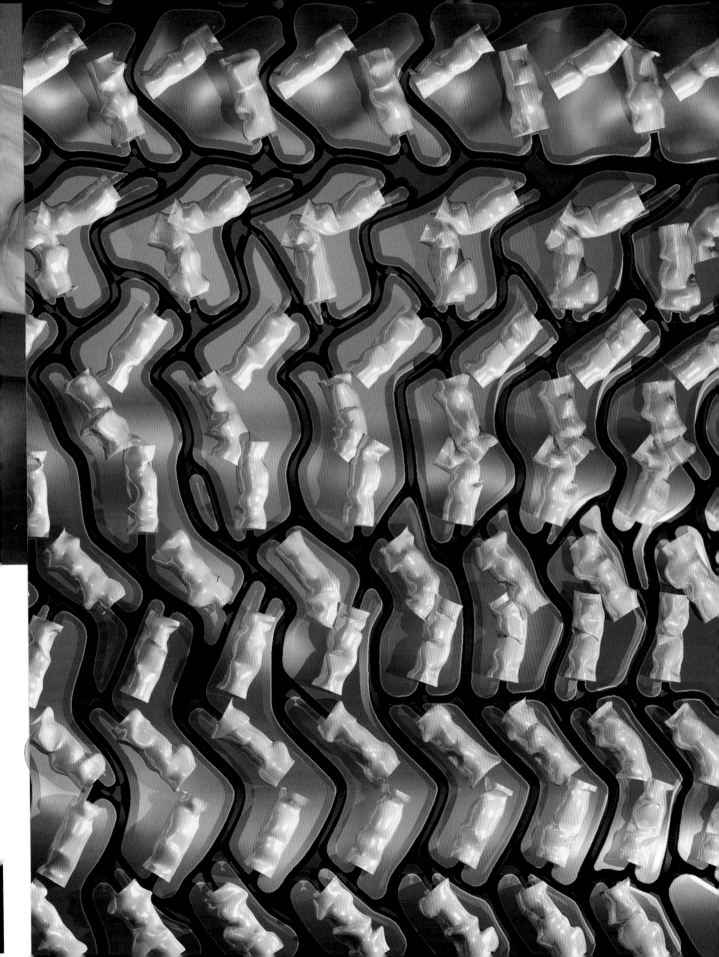

myHouse©

Lewis Blackwell and Scott and Laurie Makela,
Whereishere (1998)

FACES

FACES

installation of *Whereishere* in the 'Taste' exhibition,
Bonnefanten Museum Maastricht, the Netherlands, 1999–2000

Just once, I wanted to do a project without form, pure objects, pure colours. Objects are like faces, and faces are like objects — I tried to link them as directly as I could imagine.

In Edgar Allan Poe's short essay 'The Philosophy of Furniture', the eye of the writer travels from one object in a house's interior to another, judging them, approving and enjoying them, while the proprietor sleeps on his sofa. Through Poe's writing, we immediately understand that the objects are looking at the owner, travelling through his body's interior and mapping out his personality. The interior of a house is also the interior of the body.

In the 'FACES' installation we do not localize a clear interior either. In fact, the installation comprises four rooms, in three of which we can look at the objects and in the fourth the objects look back at us. The rooms follow the categories of Lewis Blackwell's book *Whereishere*: in the first three — **Obsession** (yellow), **Means** (orange) and **Materials** (green) — every object is positioned as part of a furnished interior but without the background of chairs, cabinets, sideboards or tables. Only the scheme of their relations remains in the form of large steel tubes. Visitors looking at exhibited works are tracked by sensors, activating small cameras that film their faces, their excitement and their experience, and project the emotions one by one on the walls of the fourth room, **Audience** (white). Each visitor to the exhibition becomes visible not only to others but also to him- or herself as objects of desire. Advertising usually shows only the blissful faces of people enjoying their belongings; here the objects advertise themselves.

Means

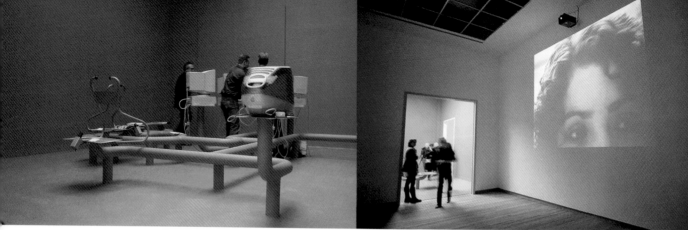

Audience

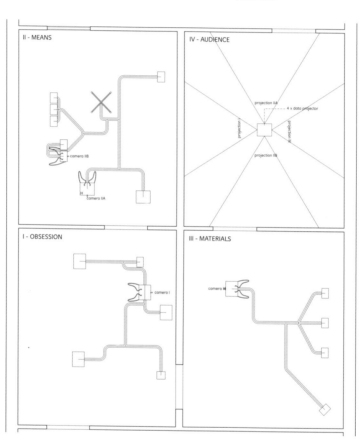

Obsession

Materials

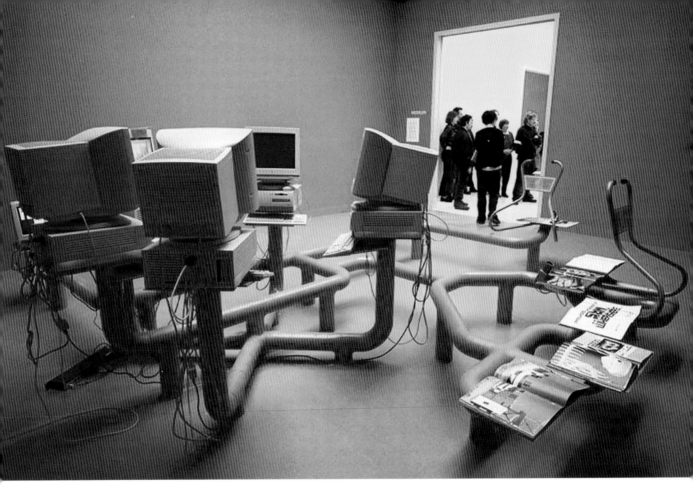

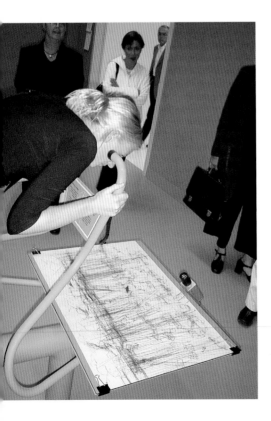

Visitors usually entered the fourth room last and realized they had been filmed, which made them return to the first rooms. After a few months of the exhibition, an archive of thousands of faces has been built up.

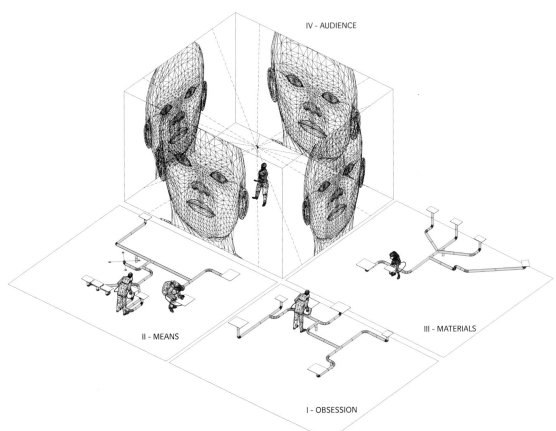

IV - AUDIENCE

II - MEANS

III - MATERIALS

I - OBSESSION

The positions of the camera-projectors containing different angles are mapped on the continuous surface of the screen, making it distort.

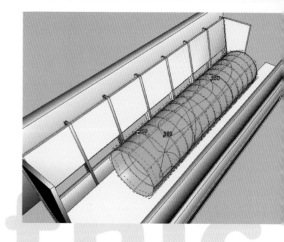

De Gothic Stijl

exhibition design for *The Virtual House of De Stijl*, in collaboration with curator Jean Paul Baeten and photographer Hans Werlemann, Netherlands Architecture Institute, Rotterdam, the Netherlands,1999–2000

How does one exhibit the work of Theo van Doesburg? A historical approach is one option, but in his case not appropriate. Van Doesburg experimented often with time and image relations or image and architecture relations, speculating avidly on the future. To avoid art-historical clichés we opted for an atmospheric presentation in which image, screen and architecture merge into a complex whole.

Theo van Doesburg
Arithmetic Composition,
1930

The research carried out by Theo van Doesburg into the relationship between time and image ran strangely counter to architectural Cartesianism. Cubes and planes in motion created sequences of cubes, which, when rendered simultaneously, broke away from each other, whereas similar tracking methods of such contemporaneous sculptors as Antoine Pevsner or Naum Gabo resulted in a *constructivism* of dynamic form based on continuity instead of fractures. Van Doesburg occasionally came close to that sense of wholeness, mainly when working with diagonals, as in the *Aubette* interior, where the oblique grid of colours (almost) transcends the separation of wall and floor.

We have worked with a similar approach, in which the diagonals first emerge as a result of rotations before merging into a system of connections. Selected works were photographed by Hans Werlemann in a non-orthographic manner, zooming in and out, and taking diagonal views. These movements were then plotted on a virtual screen that distorted heavily with the different perspectives. This screen was then strengthened by a wooden structure that not only tried to re-create the form but also read the vectors as structural information. All beams split in two directions, vertically to follow the section of the screen, horizontally to connect to adjacent beams, so that the structure becomes a three-dimensional network of diagonals.

Hans Werlemann
2000

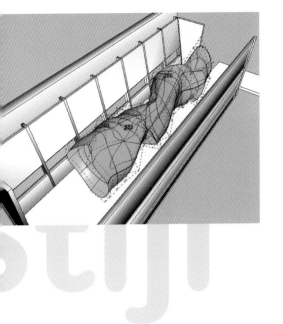

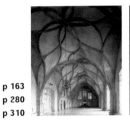

p 163
p 280
p 310

Naum Gabo
Linear Construction #4.
1959

In architecture there are opposing views on the relationship between time and form. One states that motion deconstructs form (deforms), the other that motion actually constructs form (informs). The first view posits a form that is a priori a whole (generally a cube or a sphere) before being deformed, the second — also mine — assumes that form is an a posteriori result of interacting elements that configure through movement, be it bending, torquing, twisting or similar operations.

four views from different angles

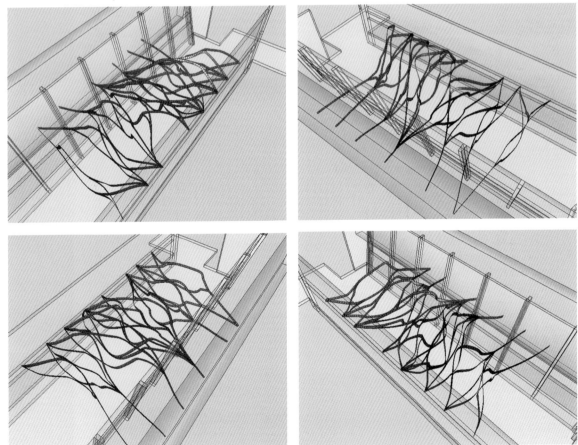

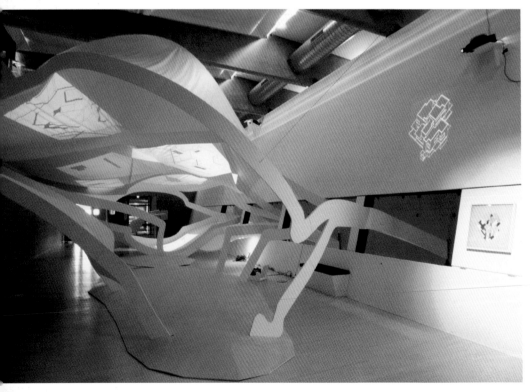

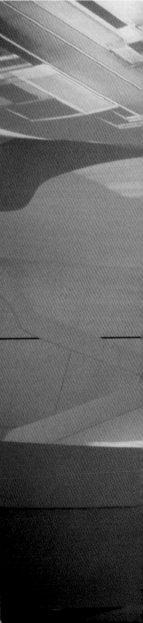

In the exhibition, curator Arielle Pélenc conceives four groups – (A) 'Vision Machine', (B) 'Emergent Worlds', (C) 'Connected Worlds' and (D) 'Invisible Worlds' – with works of very different sizes, from large Surrealist paintings by Yves Tanguy to tiny 'photographs of thoughts' by late-nineteenth-century Spiritualists. These image-body relations are broken down into spatial categories: helmet (D), capsule (A and C) and dome (B) – each with specific viewing distance to the work. The different scales were used to choreograph the 'vortex forces' (rotating forces with a spherical radius) on a skeleton with four arms, each of which has its own range. For example, if we need a large space for a small number of Surrealist paintings, the vortex force is large but its reach quite short; likewise, for a large number of small works the vortex force is relatively small but the reach of the skeletal arm long.

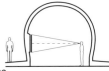

dome

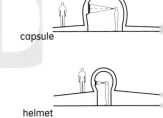

capsule

helmet

wetGRID

exhibition design for 'Vision Machine',
Musée des Beaux Arts, Nantes, France, 1999–2000

How can we involve action in perception? This is one of the critical questions in designing an exhibition space. Architecturally it means that there is no a priori segmentation of floor (the surface of action) and wall (the surface of perception). In this case, the question was central to the content of the exhibition itself, since 'Vision Machine' was suspended between passive recording and active hallucination.

The exhibition 'Vision Machine' is an arrangement of 250 paintings, drawings and installations by a diverse group of artists, including Pollock, Kupka, Ernst, Tanguy, Polke, Barry, Mikami and Atelier van Lieshout, and architects, such as Parent/Virilio, Kurokawa, Hauserman, Schein, Archigram and others. The exhibition explores the area between the emerging view and the projected view, between subjective and objective vision. The design methodology consisted of steps, machining stages, in which each piece of new information is passed on to a new level.

In the first stage, the four rotating forces interact with a linear structure derived from the museum. These four vortices connect conceptually to four types of vertigo and hallucination, according to the grouping of curator Arielle Pélenc: 'Invisible Worlds' shows visualizations of invisible forces; 'Emergent Worlds' displays images that relate to self-organizing visual patterns; 'Vision Machine' focuses on images that become spatial in their arrangement, as in installation art; and in 'Connected Worlds' architecture becomes a construction of vision, as in the capsules and domes of the 1960s. Each of these worlds is represented by works of varying size and media, and thus the forces generating the form in the first stage of the procedure relate to these scales. In the second stage the rotating lines transform into a paper model, which is digitized into a set of complex, blister-like volumes that emerge from an undulating surface. The volumes were sliced in the computer to generate a set of lines that form a diagrid of curved ribs to be cut out of plywood using precise CNC laser-cutting techniques.

Atelier van Lieshout
Super Orgone helmet, 1998

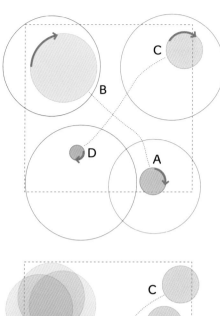

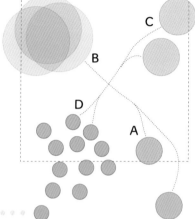

Since translating Baudrillard in the early 1980s I have been fascinated by vertigo, considering it as a constituent force of reality rather than a loss of reality. Many of my earlier projects were heavily influenced by this idea, especially H₂Oexpo, with its oversized well, and "beachness", with its spiralling geometry. All of these projects use the concept of proprioception, of a body relying on its own internal balancing system instead of being kept upright by an architecture of vertical cues — posture as an emergent property produced by an interaction of architecture and body.

p 36
p 65
p 97

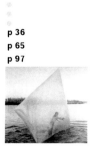

four subsequent stages of vortex interaction

The works were hung directly on the complex surface and orient them-selves according to the surface's manifold directions. Some works hang exactly vertical, others tilt only a few degrees, others much more and some turn the full 90 degrees, hanging upside-down on the ceiling, so that the visitor's body is actively involved in seeing and must position itself according to the initial forces of vertigo, a remnant of the original forces that created the works.

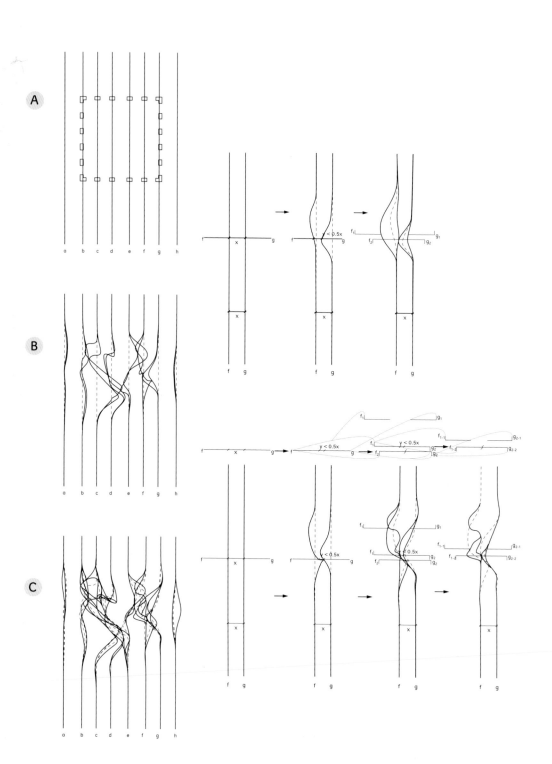

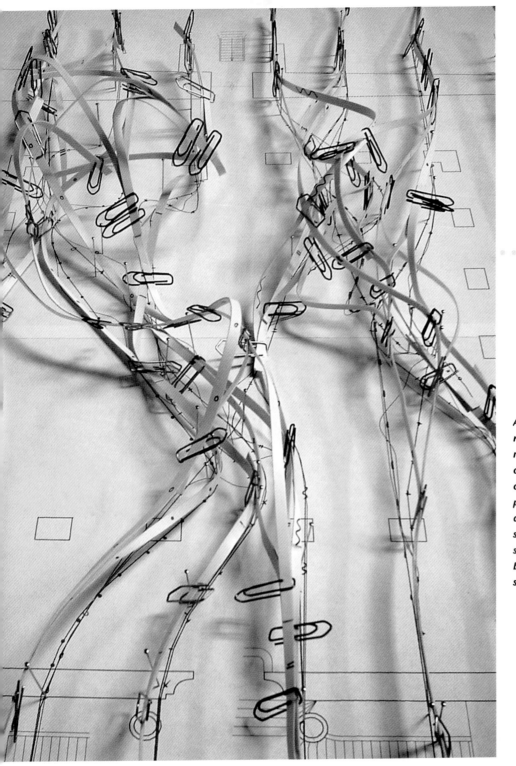

p 177

After meeting Frei Otto in 1998 I realized that the indexical techniques of animation software could give us only a simulation of complexity, not a real complexity. Complexity is not the deformation of primitives but a structural transformation from simple to complex (without being reducible to the original state).

p 216
p 246
p 260

We used complex digital choreographies to start the procedure but not to end it, and opted for a combination of digital and analogue techniques. The regularly spaced lines reflecting the structure of the existing museum (A) are moved away from their formal symmetry (B), then returned to equilibrium through an analogue technique with paper (C). The final *Formfindung* was determined through a simple added algorithm: if the lines in the digital animation move closer by more than 50% of their original distance, the analogue paper line is split in two and connected to its neighbour by a paper clip. This function ensures that the procedure stops by itself instead of having to be freeze-framed. Ultimately, this is a Gothic principle: producing surfaces by bifurcating lines.

We digitized the lines of the paper model (in green) and closed them into a surface. This is called 'lofting' and has a striking effect: if one closes two lines it results in a 'ruled surface', a (single) curved surface that is made up of straight rules. If one forms a closure between three or more lines it also curves in the other direction, a double curved surface. In this case the structure is one of blisters: double-curved volumes emerging from a single-curved surface.

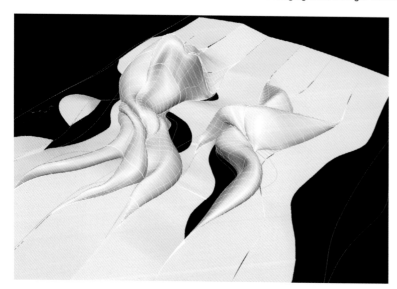

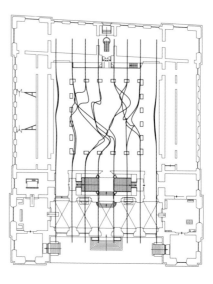

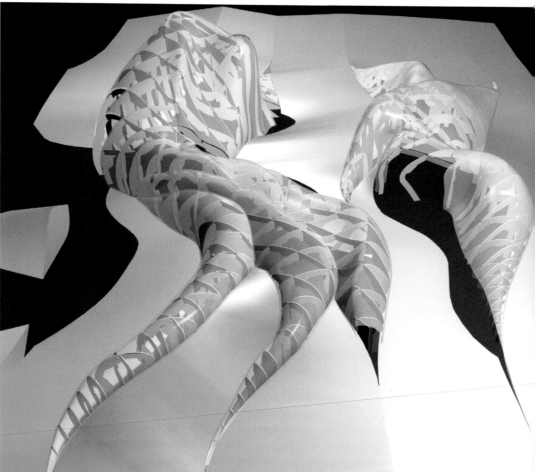

The complex structure of volumes that is articulated by smooth curvature and sharp internal edges is sliced in two directions, making up a diagrid.

143

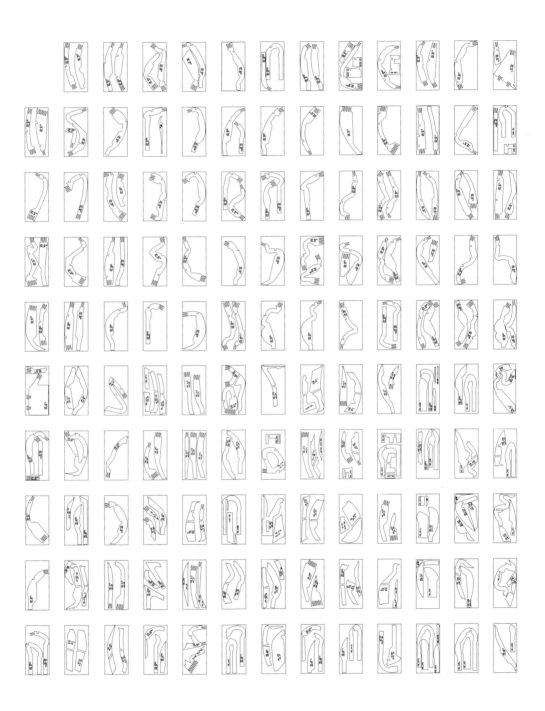

In the past this kind of curvature would have been inconceivable in architecture because each curve would have had to be reduced into circle segments, drawn onto large sheets of paper (including the radius and the angle of each arc), then cut by hand from plywood sheets. Today we don't even need to know the formulae of cubic curves because the mathematical information of the complex geometry can be passed directly from the computer to the CNC machine, which cuts each of the lines out of the plywood by laser.

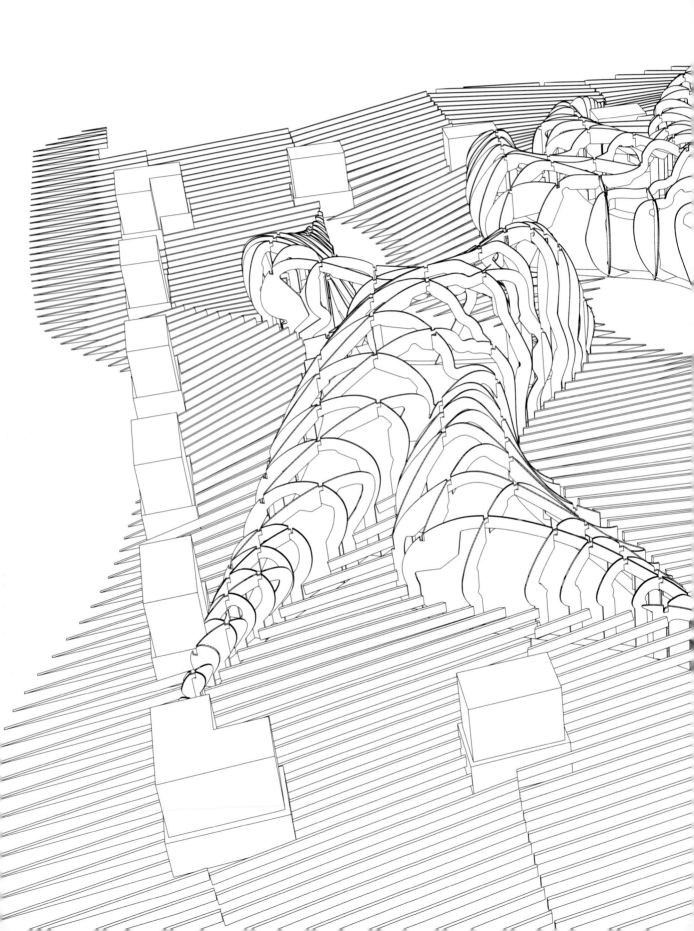

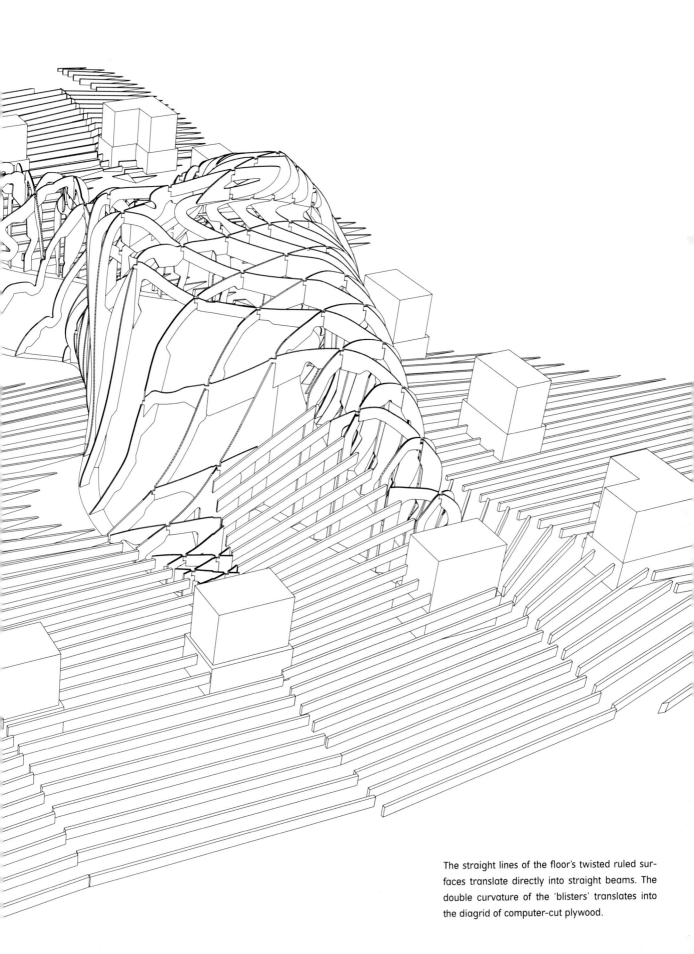

The straight lines of the floor's twisted ruled surfaces translate directly into straight beams. The double curvature of the 'blisters' translates into the diagrid of computer-cut plywood.

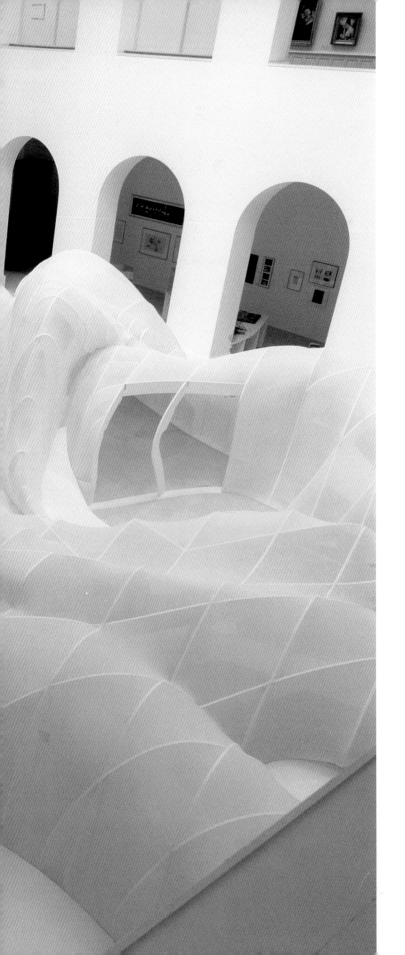

The daylit white arches and plaster walls merge with the white ribs and cotton of the installation.

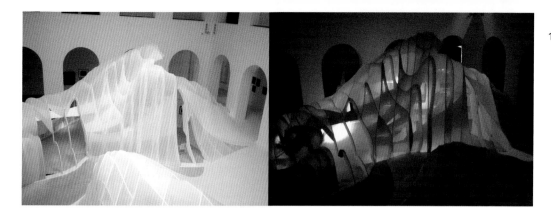

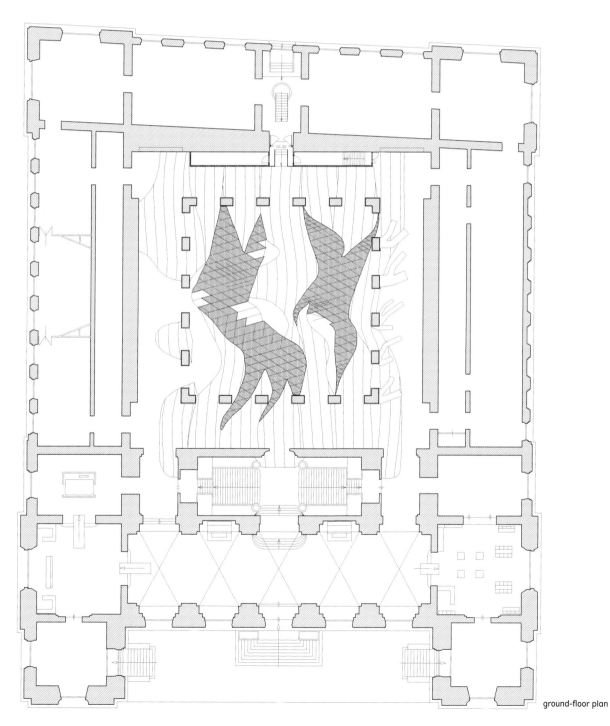

ground-floor plan

The works have specific groupings; sometimes an artist is clearly organized in a row, sometimes that row breaks up to connect the works conceptually to those of another artist.

view of the 'Invisible Worlds' area

Frederick Kiesler
Vision Machine, 1938–42

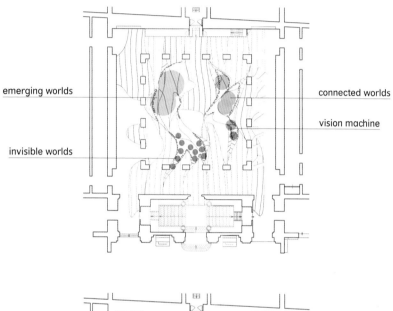

emerging worlds

connected worlds

vision machine

invisible worlds

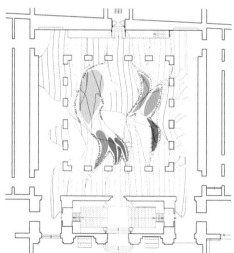

Forces corresponding to the perception spaces 'helmet', 'capsule' and 'dome' were mapped onto a continuous surface, which expressed them more as groupings than as separate elements.

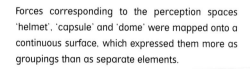

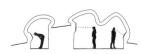

The choreography of vortex forces that produced the structure affects the position of visitors' bodies and limbs. To see, one has to act: a tilting of the neck, an arching of the back, a bending of the knees, and even more extreme positions, such as looking straight up and losing the sense of top or bottom of the works.

Henri Michaux
mescaline drawing,
1969

Strangely enough, the design procedure of the tower (a 'tower' having been requested by the client) starts with a pulsating sphere. The symmetry of the sphere is 'broken' by a choreography of alternating contracting and expanding forces – it inflates as much as it collapses.

D-tower

public artwork: interactive tower, questionnaire and website for the city of Doetinchem, in collaboration with artist Q. S. Serafijn, Doetinchem, the Netherlands, 1998–2004

We conceived a tower that would change colour according to the emotions of a town's inhabitants, questioned in a daily survey. An urban object that shows the hidden feelings of a whole city ... what could be more intriguing? What if art ceased being metaphorical to become real and operational, the inverse of the route to abstraction – though the object can hardly be called realist. The tower doesn't just stand in public space, it orients itself in a public sphere that includes the electronic realm of the Internet.

D-tower is a complex alloy of different media, where architecture is part of a larger system of interactive relationships. It is a project in which the intensive (feelings, qualia) and the extensive (space, quantities) change places, where human action, colour, money, value and feelings all become networked entities. The project consists of a physical building (the tower), a questionnaire, written by the Rotterdam-based artist Q. S. Serafijn, and a website, all of which are interrelated. The tower – designed by NOX – is a 12-metre-high structure where standard and non-standard geometries combine in a complex surface made of epoxy formed by a computer-generated mould (CNC-milled styrofoam). The structure is similar to a Gothic vault, where column-line and shell-surface share the same continuum.

The building is directly connected to the website in two ways. First, the website shows a visualization of the responses of a number of selected inhabitants to the questionnaire. The selection repeats every six months and reflects the topography and ethnography of Doetinchem's 50,000 inhabitants. The survey deals with everyday emotions, such as hatred, love, happiness and fear. Every month the questions become more detailed, and answers are graphed in landscapes made visible on the website. Second, the four emotions are represented by green, red, blue and yellow, the colours of the LEDs illuminating the building, and are directly related to the website, where the responses are compared and weighed. In addition to the website, which displays which emotion is

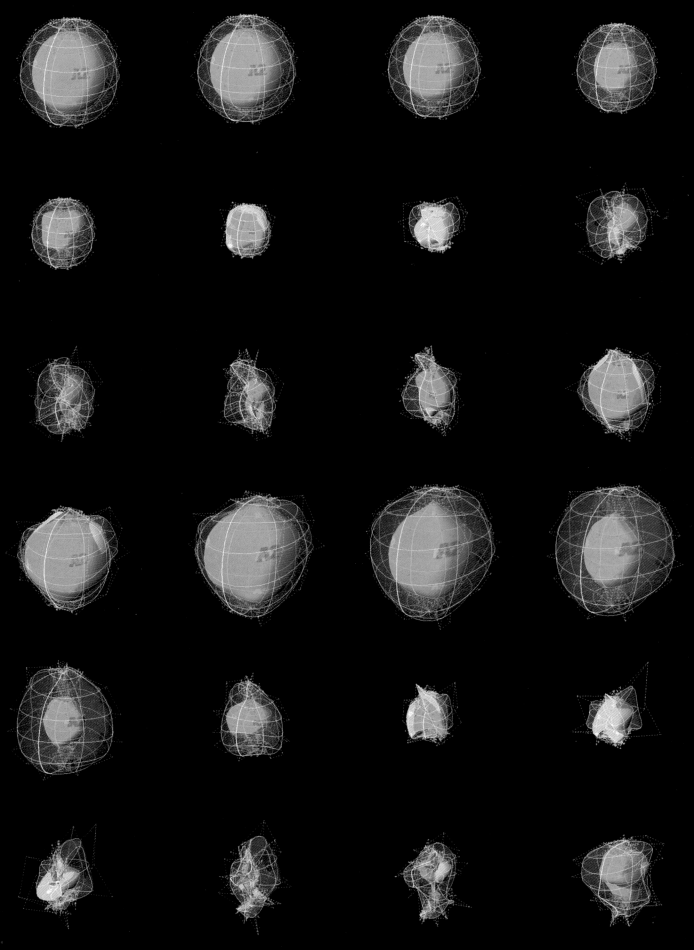

stronger in what street or neighbourhood, the tower displays the overriding emotion at that moment. Each evening the tower thus takes on the colour of the number one emotion that day...

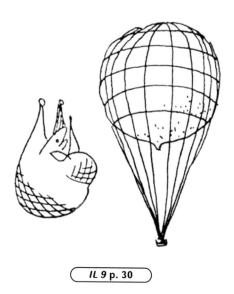

balloon

IL 9 p. 30

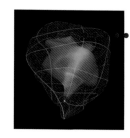

At the point where the sphere, which starts out convex only, seems to have as much concave geometry as convex, we suspend the animation.

shopping bag

We again turned to Frei Otto's books for help. In *IL 9* (*Pneus in Nature and Technics*, 1977) two possibilities for turning a sphere into a vertical structure are placed next to each other, a balloon and a shopping bag. The shopping-bag diagram made me realize I already had the content of the shopping bag, so to speak, but was missing the handles. Tracing the complex geometry of the concaved sphere with lines, we constructed the handles upwards with bands. Then, as with Gaudí's inversion technique, it was turned upside-down: what hangs through tension, stands through compression.

When the tower is digitized, we can also make it stand up by turning it upside-down. Though it does not stand up straight, the geometry allows the four legs to stand as a twisted tripod. The contracting and expanding forces on the sphere, together with the exact vertical direction of gravity, result in complex diagonal legs that make the object appear to rotate upwards as much as downwards.

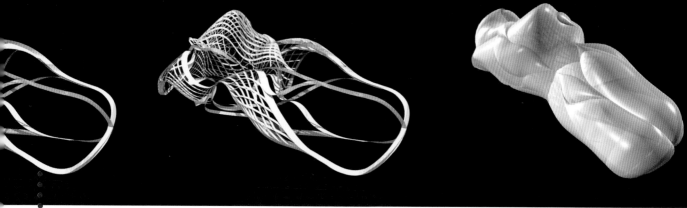

A-life, an earlier version of *Son-O-House*

The use of iterative techniques returned in the design of *Son-O-House* (p. 174). The project consisted of a geometry, both continuous and creased. The idea was to have large linear constrictions bifurcate into smaller mesh elements that were smooth, a powerful tool for directly relating the geometry of zero or single curvature with double curvature. The first incisions act as primary structure, which is closed with straight rules or simple arcs, while the lattice that follows after bifurcation is double-curved, like a shell that does not rely on the hierarchy of primary and secondary elements. The methodological relationship between single and double curved was fully developed in the *Pompidou Two* project (see p. 304).

One option to transform the deformed sphere into a tower was the 'balloon option'. Here we tried to 'recalculate' the shape through iterative inflation. One inflates a balloon partly, tapes certain areas, inflates it further, tapes it again, and so on. The symmetry of the pneumatic sphere is broken by taped incisions or constrictions; its scaled stepwise deformation is similar to certain growth processes (see p. 370, Manuel DeLanda, 'Materiality: Anexact and Intense').

p 304

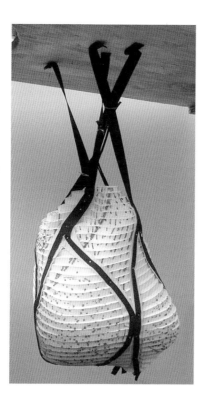

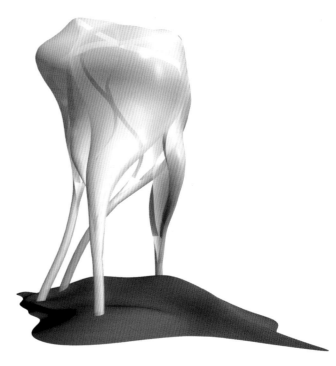

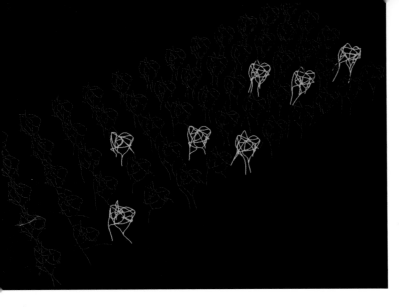

In the *finite element analysis* the tower shows complex dynamic behaviour. The columns *transform* gradually into surfaces, there is no substructure and all forces are simultaneously transferred through the epoxy surface. Because the epoxy is hand-laid on the styrofoam moulds, the thickness of the material can be easily varied according to the loads: at the bottom the epoxy is 18 millimetres thick, at the top only 4.5.

After digitizing the hanging model and turning it upside-down, we created numerous variations on the positions of the legs. What is interesting is that in all the variations the top stays the same while only the legs change position.

The 'original' sphere is an object with a fully rotational symmetry, but this is not completely lost when 'broken'; broken symmetry is not the same as asymmetry. During the process of breaking, some areas are left untransformed and remain within symmetrical configurations while others develop into local asymmetries. In this case, some parts repeat two, three or four times, while others are unique. The result is an object with a surface area of 200 square metres, but made with less than half the amount of mould surface.

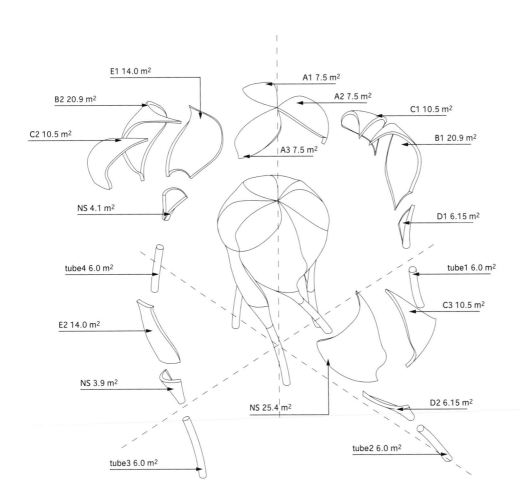

E1 14.0 m²
B2 20.9 m²
C2 10.5 m²
A1 7.5 m²
A2 7.5 m²
C1 10.5 m²
B1 20.9 m²
A3 7.5 m²
NS 4.1 m²
D1 6.15 m²
tube4 6.0 m²
tube1 6.0 m²
C3 10.5 m²
E2 14.0 m²
NS 3.9 m²
NS 25.4 m²
D2 6.15 m²
tube2 6.0 m²
tube3 6.0 m²

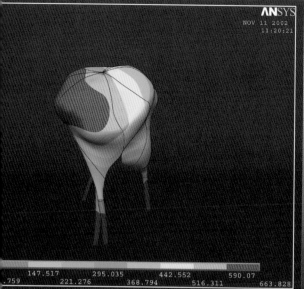

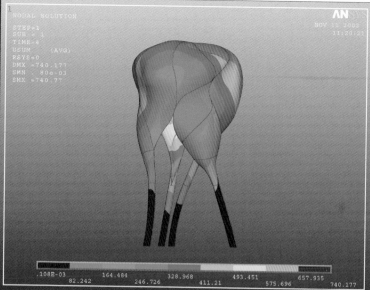

Surface to line. When Gaudí was confronted with the problem of tiling the double-curved surfaces of the benches in Parc Güell, he had a brilliant solution: to use the waste pieces of standard square tiles that had fallen onto the factory floor and been broken into multiple polygonized fragments. Similar cracking occurs in craquelure and so-called Voronoi Diagrams. For me this marks a shift from thinking in joints to thinking in cracks (or cuts, shifts, tear-ings or constrictions). Instead of segmenting the surface beforehand, one can segment it during the geometrical for-mation itself, organizing both smoothness and sharp creases. In our machining procedures we must develop geo-metrical articulation, structural formation and panellization simultaneously, not in sequence.

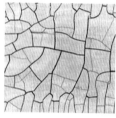

p 192
p 231

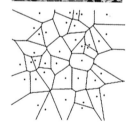

Line to surface. Rather than breaking a surface into lines we can follow the reverse procedure, a Gothic logic: lines bifur-cating and weaving into surfaces. For anyone interested in continuity, Gothic line-surface configurations are mind-boggling. Simple curved figures are interlaced into a mani-fold of larger configurations, not only for aesthetic reasons but also for structural ones. In no architectural style has the figure of the arabesque been developed beyond the orna-mental except by the Gothic builders.

p 135
p 140
p 272
p 304

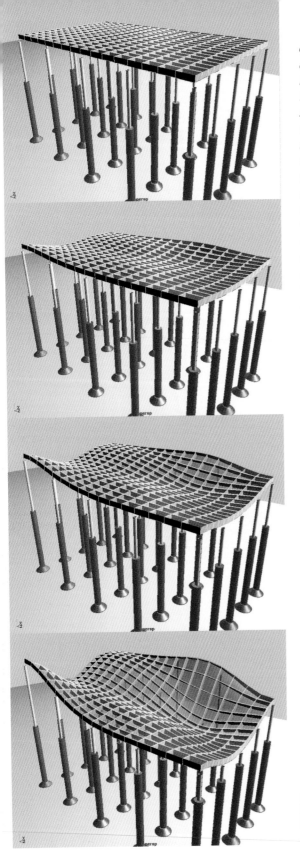

Our task today is to translate the use of flexi-curves and French curves into surfaces. The flexi-curve is a wooden slat used in ship-building since the seventeenth century and bent into curvature by leaden weights, an early form of analogue computing. The digital splines we now use are generally cubic functions. If we built a table that could be adjusted numerically into a double-curved shape made up of splines in two directions, we would have a flexi-mould: a mould to make moulds. This would change building technology considerably, since it would mark a shift from standardized pre-made elements to variable non-standard elements. We could also consider translating French curves into 'French surfaces'. We could analyze any double-curved surface during the design phase into zones of curvature similarity. When these zones are digitally reassembled into a surface, it will be much smaller than the initial one. Imagine summarizing a face to the size of a cup: the cup would be a mould to create a face. Such a matrix-mould would act as a 'mother' to a complex series of differentiated panels.

p 124
p 270
p 356

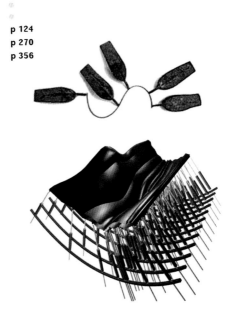

The continuous variation of the mould can occur only within a certain range of stretchability. A flexible material is generally weak and would not be able to withstand the weight of such materials as concrete. However, when sufficiently layered with air pockets that allow for flexibility and can be vacu-formed into a rigid state, it can carry considerable loads.

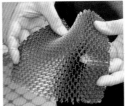

165

flexi curve

There have always been two methods for drawing irregular curves, the flexi-curve and the French curve — though transposing mathematical information to a building site is another story. The first is based on the classic spline (see opposite); the second is a kind of 'curve-mould', where any complex curve drawn in pencil by hand could be retraced in ink along a continuous assembly of curves. Each profession had its own sets of French curves: the lines used in wallpaper design, boat building or highway construction are all different families of curves. Each kind of curvature varies in degrees that are contained in the template.

French curve

For the tower, we opted for a combination of CNC-milled styrofoam for the mould and hand-laid epoxy with glass-fibre laminate. The 3D-milling machine simply follows all the numerical data of the double curvature. The epoxy panels all have flanges that are glued to each other, strengthening the surface so no substructure for the tower is needed.

CNC-milling machine

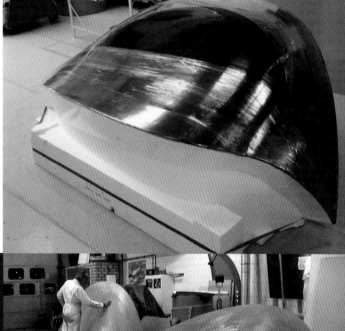

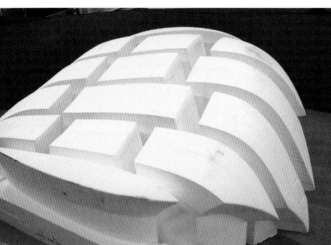

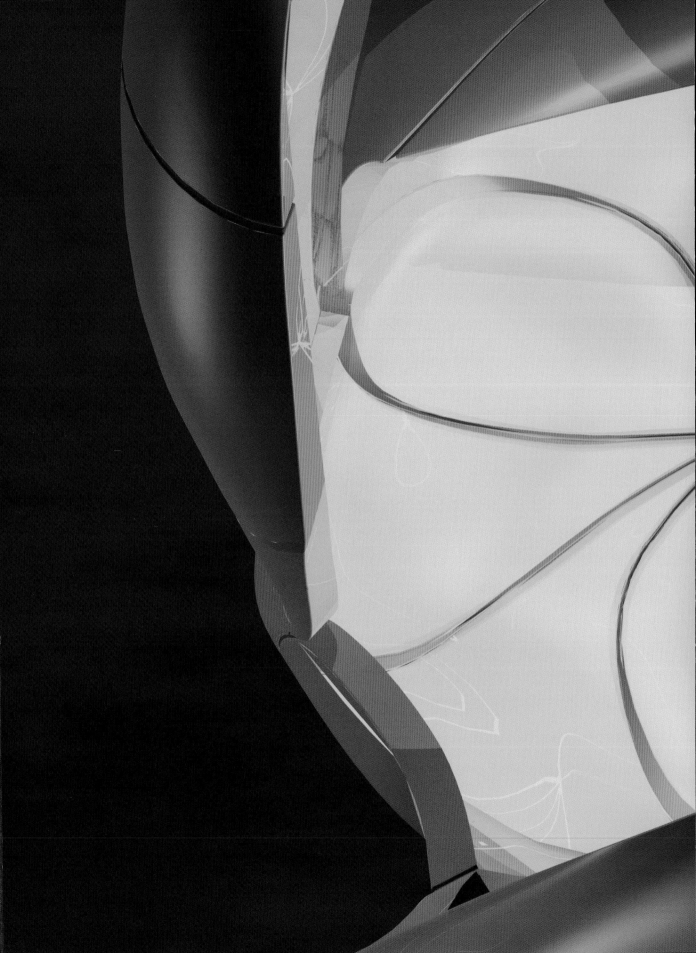

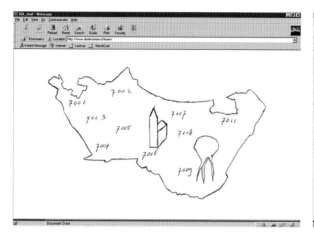

Doetinchem's 50,000 inhabitants are distributed over ten zip-code areas (left). On the website each area is represented as a line.

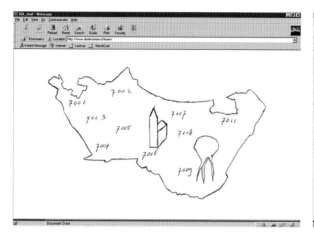
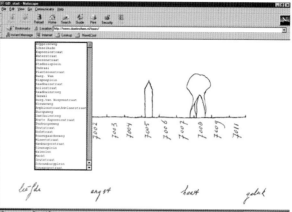

Q. S. Serafijn's website operates on two levels: one globally accessible and the other accessible locally and only with a password. The local informs the global. Every year 80 inhabitants are selected to become the Chosen Ones, representing the city and its neighbourhoods. They participate in an electronic survey on their emotional lives. About 300 questions on four emotions – love, hatred, happiness and fear – are posed so that they can be answered from 'not at all' to 'very much so'. The nature of the questions evolve over the year, starting out fairly general but growing very inquisitive and detailed by December.

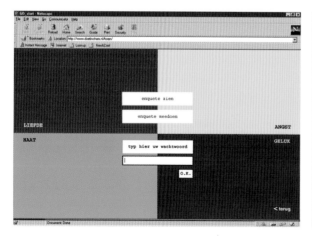
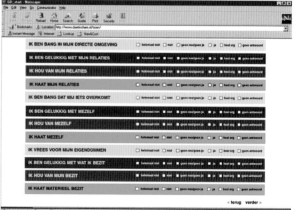

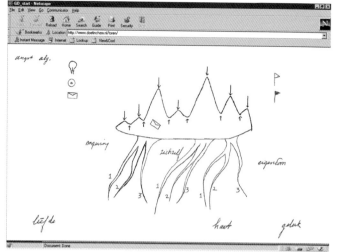
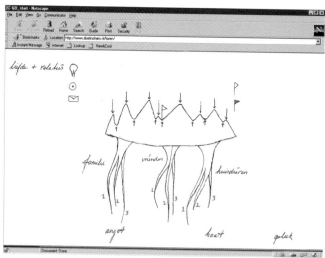

Answers are continuously mapped on a graph based on the linear representation of Doetinchem. Each visitor to the site can check the city's emotional state because the site shows not only the state of the day but a huge archive that builds up over years. Next to the landscape visualization, the 80 Chosen Ones are allowed to leave personal messages and pictures as clickable little flags and letters.

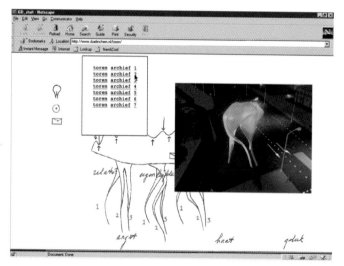
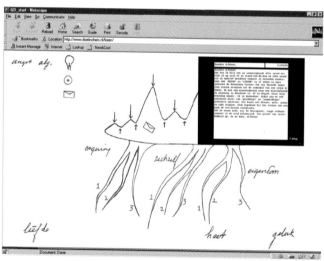
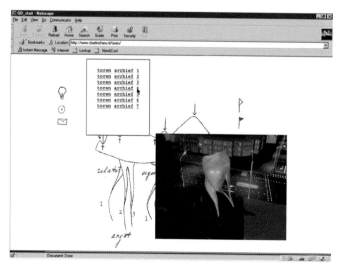
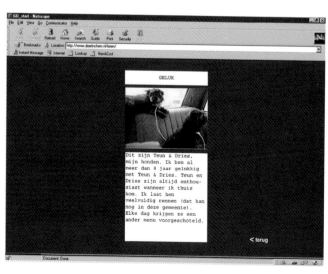

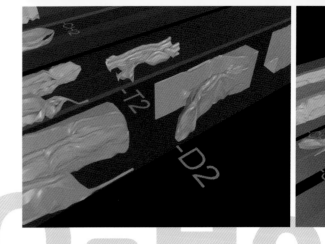

Son-O-House, a house where sounds live

public artwork for Industrieschap Ekkersrijt,
in collaboration with composer Edwin van der Heide,
Son en Breugel, the Netherlands, 2000–04

Son-O-House *is one of our art projects that allows us to proceed carefully over a period of three to four years to accumulate knowledge that can be applied to larger and speedier projects. Not a 'house' in the real sense, Son-O-House *is what we call 'a house where sounds live', a structure that refers to living and the body movements of habit and habitation. In *Son-O-House *a sound work generates sound patterns activated by sensors picking up visitor movements.*

Along the highway between Son en Breugel and Eindhoven is a large industrial park with a special quarter reserved for IT and new-media companies. The artwork is meant to strengthen the identity of the area, not only as a technological statement but as a social space where people can organize informal meetings, relax during lunch-hours or simply enjoy its beauty. The structure allows people to hear sound in a musical structure and to participate in the sound's composition. It is instrument, score and studio at the same time.

The structure is derived from a house's typical action-landscapes: a fabric of larger body movements through a corridor or room, together with smaller movements around a sink or a drawer. This carefully choreographed set of movements of bodies, limbs and hands is inscribed on paper bands as cuts (an uncut area corresponds to the motion of a body, a first cut through the middle corresponds to limbs, and finer cuts to the hands and feet). We staple the pre-informed paper bands together at the point where they have the most connective potential, from which the curvature emerges empirically. The outcome is an arabesque of intertwining lines (white paper model) that is a reading of movements on various scales and a material structure, since the paper curves stand upright in concert with each other. We have only to sweep these lines sideways to marry the open structure of lines with the closed surface of the ground. This results again in a porous three-dimensional structure (purple paper model), which is similar to the structure obtained by the combing, curling and

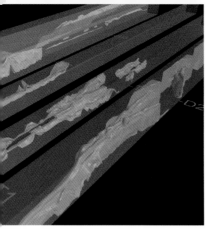

This 'kinetogram' shows greater intensity of movement than any standard motion diagram with running lines.

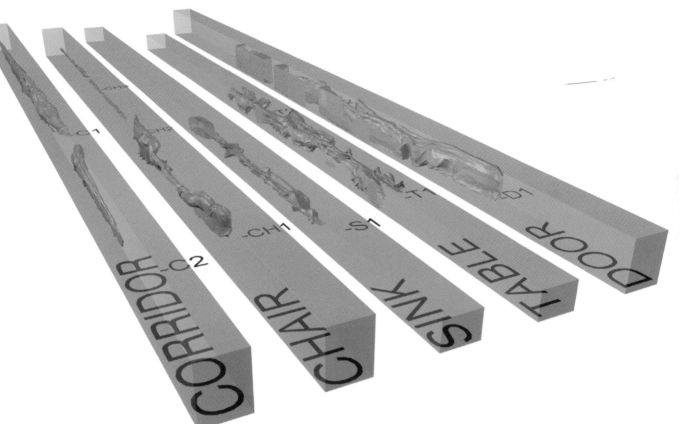

First, we set up a camera to record body movements in home situations. The computer then analyzed the movement by comparing film frames through software that draws contours around each package of changing pixels. If we place cameras at different positions in a house, we can see that movements are actually complex structures of three cooperating scales: body, limbs and extremities. When we put the frame-contours one after another, the different scales of movement become apparent.

parting of hair. We digitize this paper analogue-computing model and remodel it into the final structure of interlacing vaults that both lean on each other and cut into each other.

In the house-that-is-not-a-house we position 23 sensors at strategic spots to influence the music indirectly. This system of sounds, composed and programmed by sound artist Edwin van der Heide, is based on the moiré effects of closely related frequencies. Unlike most interactive art, visitors do not influence the sound directly but through the real-time composition that generates the sounds. The score is an evolutionary memoryscape that develops with the traced behaviour of bodies in space.

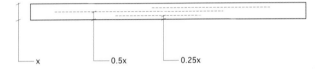

x   0.5x   0.25x

Normally kinetograms would be mapped onto a plan and then extruded vertically into a structure. Here, however, we chose to map the movements onto more abstract paper elements that still have the potential of becoming a floor-element, a wall-element or both. The paper was either uncut (body), cut in half (limbs) or cut in half again (hands or feet) to indicate the body's coordination of movements.

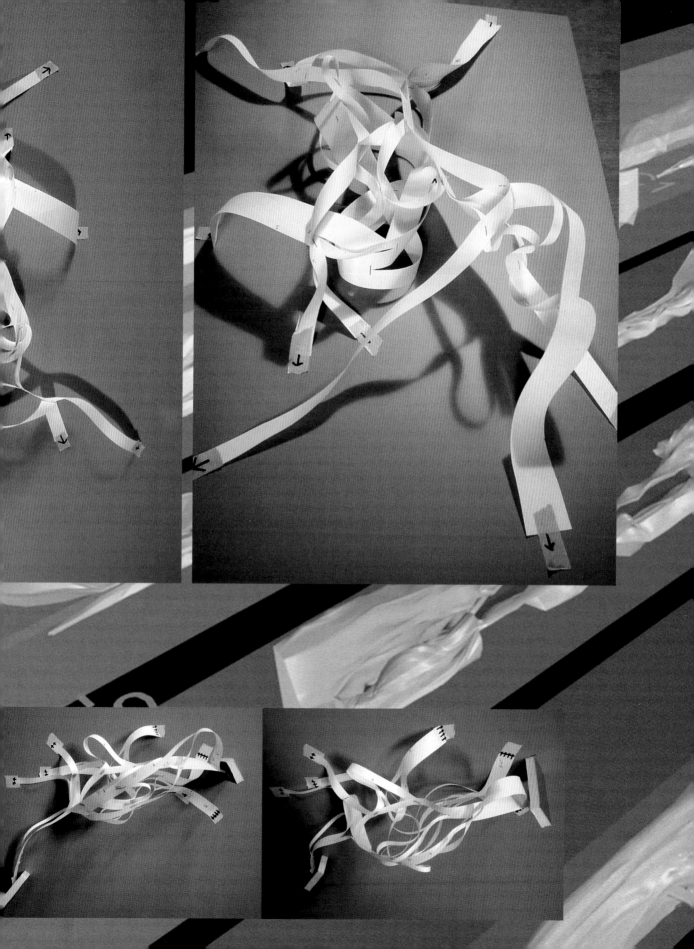

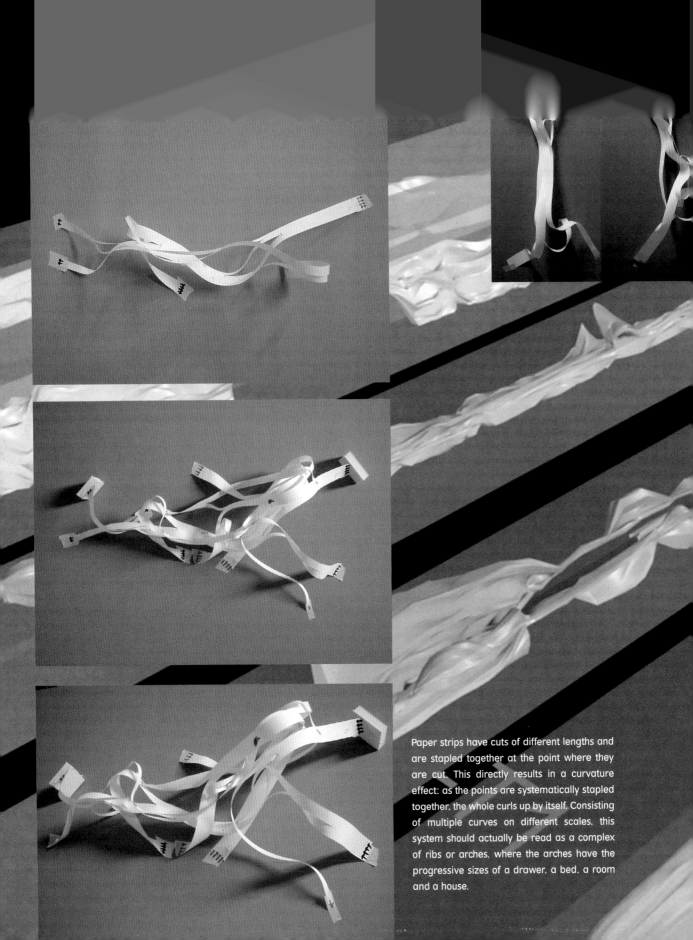

Paper strips have cuts of different lengths and are stapled together at the point where they are cut. This directly results in a curvature effect: as the points are systematically stapled together, the whole curls up by itself. Consisting of multiple curves on different scales, this system should actually be read as a complex of ribs or arches, where the arches have the progressive sizes of a drawer, a bed, a room and a house.

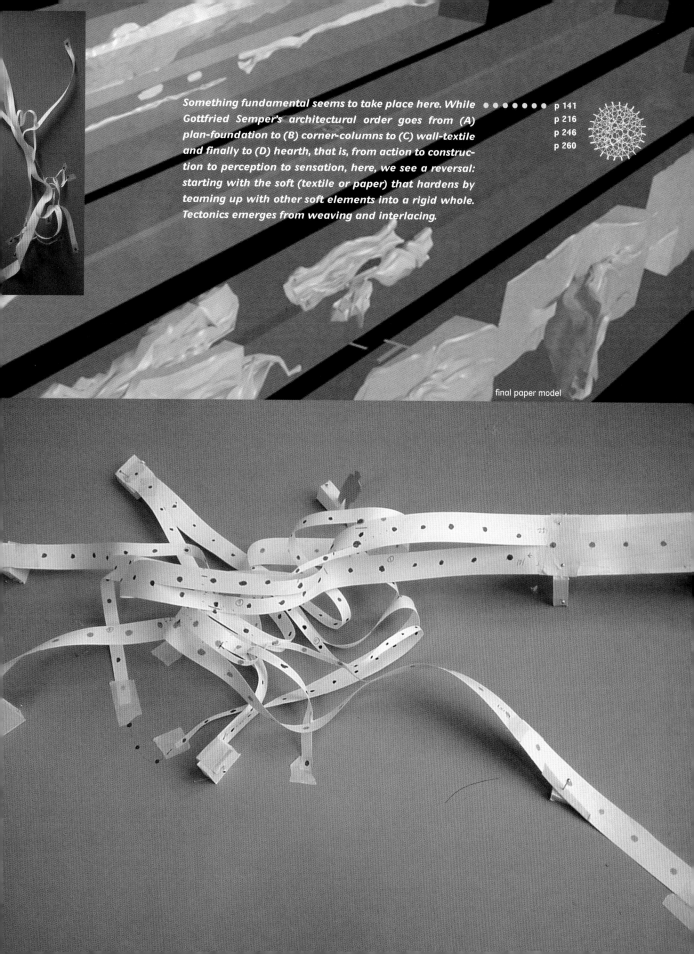

Something fundamental seems to take place here. While Gottfried Semper's architectural order goes from (A) plan-foundation to (B) corner-columns to (C) wall-textile and finally to (D) hearth, that is, from action to construction to perception to sensation, here, we see a reversal: starting with the soft (textile or paper) that hardens by teaming up with other soft elements into a rigid whole. Tectonics emerges from weaving and interlacing.

p 141
p 216
p 246
p 260

final paper model

The final analogue-computing model. The white paper arabesque is extended sideways by purple paper bands according to a tiny algorithm: the lines sweep out sideways following the initial direction of the white paper while trying to connect as quickly as possible to another surface. This means that sometimes lines that start out quite vertical need some length to reach the ground, while at other times they find another surface immediately and stop. The result is a structure that both closes and tears open, similar to the combing of hair with curls. The final digital version differs from the analogue one especially at the ends, where recombing the curls produces four duck's tails.

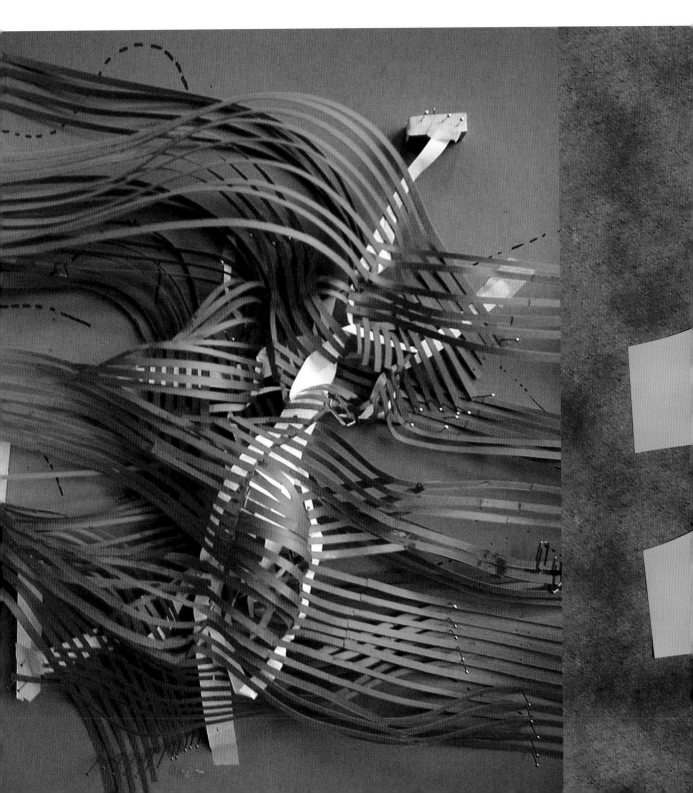

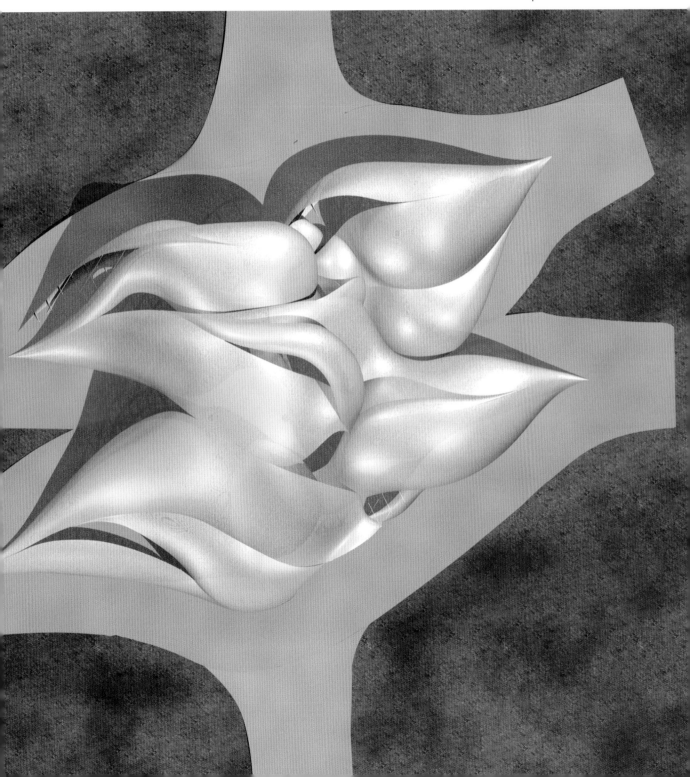

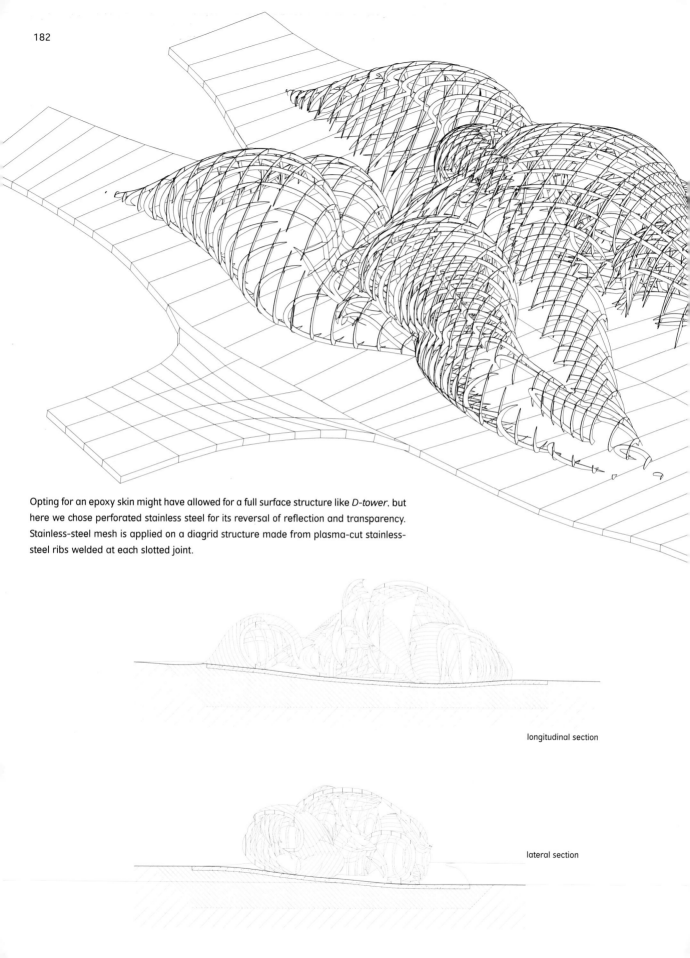

Opting for an epoxy skin might have allowed for a full surface structure like *D-tower*, but here we chose perforated stainless steel for its reversal of reflection and transparency. Stainless-steel mesh is applied on a diagrid structure made from plasma-cut stainless-steel ribs welded at each slotted joint.

longitudinal section

lateral section

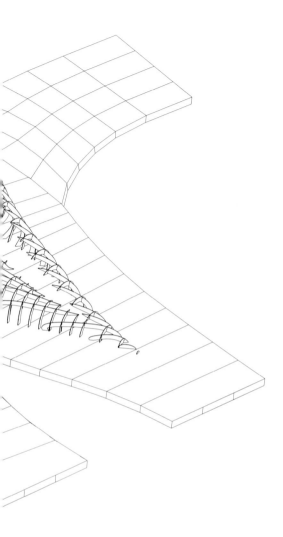

Structurally, *Son-O-House* is not just a complex set of intersecting vaults. The surfaces of the shells on top of the structure actually have a different curvature from the more linear elements towards the tips close to the ground. The tearing allows not only access but structural integrity. The curvature increases towards the ends, transforming the shell into a beam and a surface into a line.

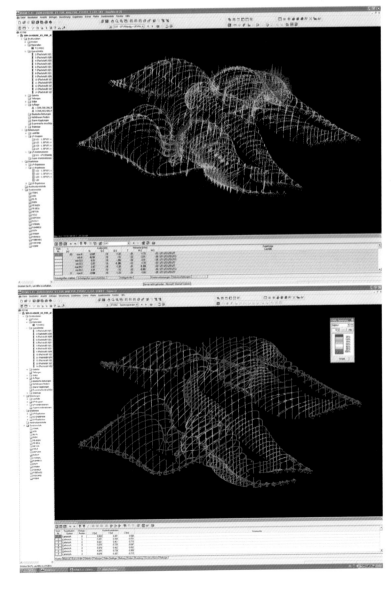

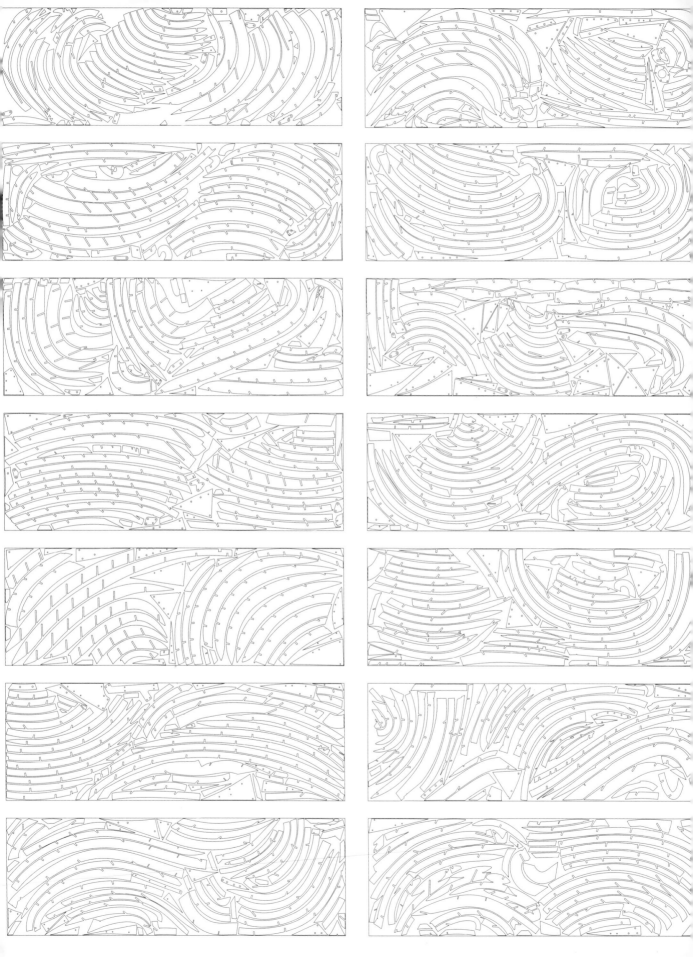

185

All parts of *Son-O-House* are flat: the outer surface is made of flat strips of expanded stainless steel, and the substructure is made of intersecting ribs of flat stainless steel. Moreover, we made all rib curves fit in 21 rectangular plates of 6 by 2 metres of stainless-steel plates with a 1-centimetre thickness.

double curvature with similar curves

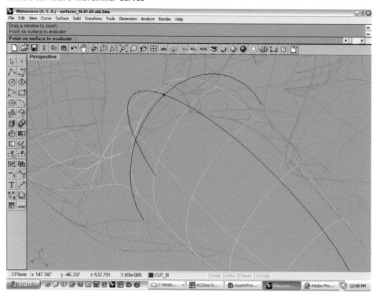

joint

Though the double-curved structure of *Son-O-House* is of a non-standard geometry, the surface is covered with standardized, pre-cut strips laid in an algorithmic manner that 'reads' the geometry. When the double curvature of a certain area consists of similar curves in both directions (quasi-spherical), nine strips close into a hexagon. When the curves are too dissimilar, the seventh strip 'breaks' away from the hexagon.

closed hexagon

For the steel contractor we made a model and a brochure with rules and tips, but no drawing. The surface has an 'emergent pattern' and no predetermined layout, since everything depends on the position of the first strip, where the other strips follow either a closed-hexagon or open-hexagon rule. There are 1,000 strips cut to 2 metres in length and 17 centimetres in width. The first 50% of the surface is covered with an unmodified strip, the next 45% of the surface is covered with strips hand-cut on the short end to fit (yellow dots) and the last 5% is covered with strips cut on two or more sides (red dots). There is no waste.

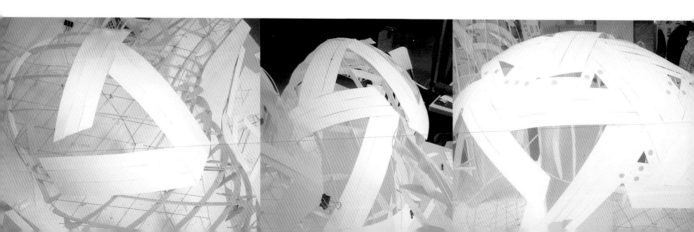

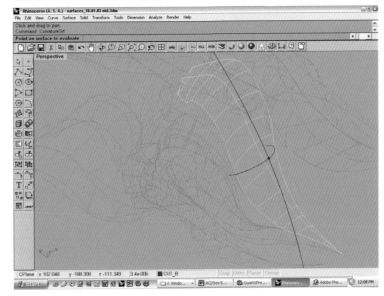

crack

open hexagon

The panellization of complex double curved surfaces is a hugely important issue, aesthetically and methodologically. Tessellation is generally viewed as the subdivision into or addition of tile modules. The least interesting method is triangulation, the subdivision of a surface into triangular facets, where three points always form a flat plane. The most interesting techniques are based on variability, which is a 'textile' way of thinking, where flexible bands precede the hardened ceramic tile.

It would not be possible for us to use this labour-intensive technique to cover the surface on larger buildings. We could use only fully pre-cut panels. In that case, the surface of a digital 3D model would need to be covered with a self-organizing pattern following the same rules as the hand labourers did with *Son-O-House*.

p 163
p 202
p 231

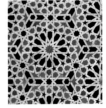

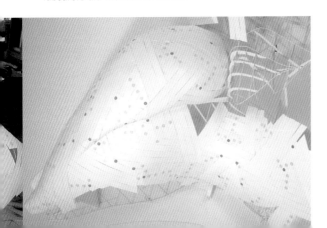

The three scales of movement indexed on the paper strips return clearly in the final structure. Some areas are accessible to the whole body, others only to hands. As in H_2Oexpo or *wetGRID*, the visitor actively engages the architecture through a wide range of postures. This is intensified by a real-time calculated sound structure that interacts with body positions and body movement.

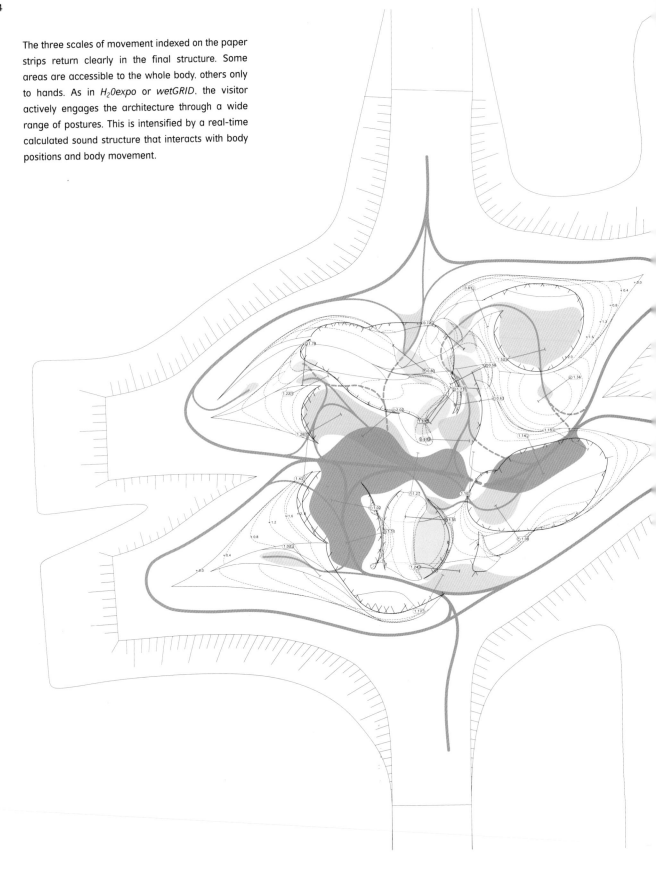

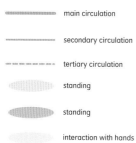

- infra-red sensor
- main circulation
- secondary circulation
- tertiary circulation
- standing
- standing
- interaction with hands

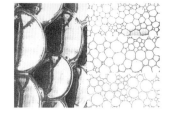

IL 9 p. 92–94

Galerie der Forschung

expo centre for the Österreichische Akademie der
Wissenschaften in a fourteenth-century monastery,
Vienna, Austria, 2000

The Umbau *(conversion) in Vienna is an art in itself ... the whole city is scattered with hidden jewels. Here we deployed our interest in Gottfried Semper, particularly his ideas on textile and adornment. What if architecture were to occupy the space between rigid tectonics and soft furnishing?*

For the project, two typical Viennese phenomena played important roles. The first is the notion of the urban interior, where the narrow street or square has such an intimate quality that it feels like the interior of someone's house. The other is the phenomenon of the *Umbau*, where occasionally interior conversions seem to act as catalysts in the urban tissue and function equally as urbanistic hinges and as architectural statements. The project plays with this inversion of roles in which the exterior is treated like interior decoration and the large interior of an old Jesuit monastery becomes like an urban site.

In a literal shift from tectonics to textile we took the vault structure of the monastery and treated it as textile adornment: the vault spheres are moved through the space, along with the activities, and leave traces of use, which are then hardened in wood structures. Following this method, the Semperian space between the carpet and the wall – between cladding and structure – becomes so large that it gives rise to an 'urban circulation' between programmatic elements. A few clubs, an info centre, bookstore, café and lecture room with a small exhibition space are all actors on an urban platform of continuous exchanges and interaction – daily activities drenched in the incessant smell of waxed wood.

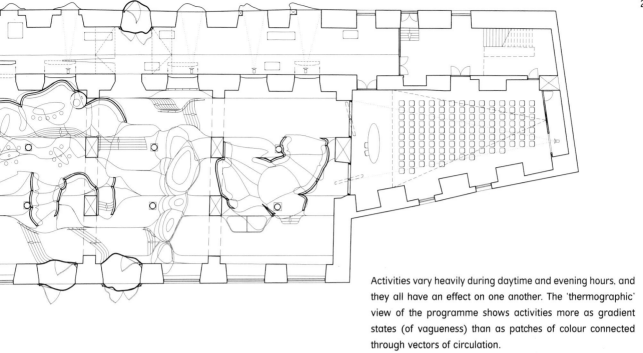

Activities vary heavily during daytime and evening hours, and they all have an effect on one another. The 'thermographic' view of the programme shows activities more as gradient states (of vagueness) than as patches of colour connected through vectors of circulation.

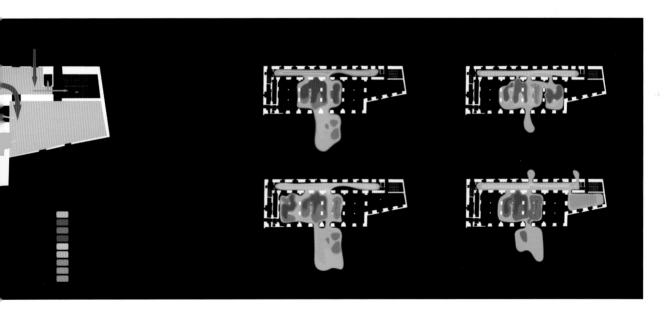

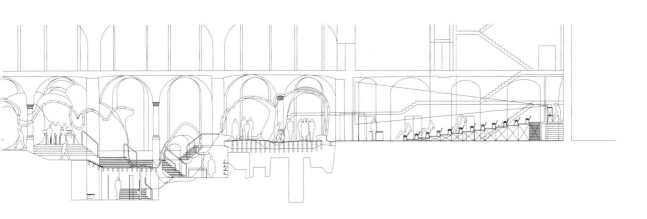

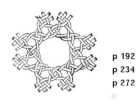

p 192
p 234
p 272

The Semperian notion of cladding (Bekleidung) comes from his strong interest in textile, not just as one of the four elements in architecture but as its main element. The architect as Wandbereiter (wall fitter) is not just a Nietzschean obsession with masking and surfaces; it means a structural interest in weaving, interlacing, crochet and the like. For Semper the knot was etymologically related to the Naht, the seam, which is based more on the continuity of bands and threads than on the architectural segmentation of tiles and parts (see also p. 342, Andrew Benjamin, 'Notes on the Surfacing of Walls').

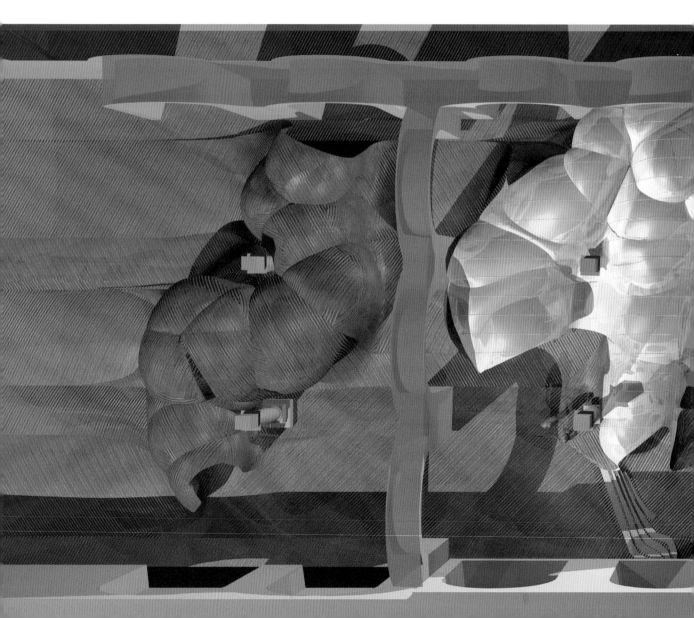

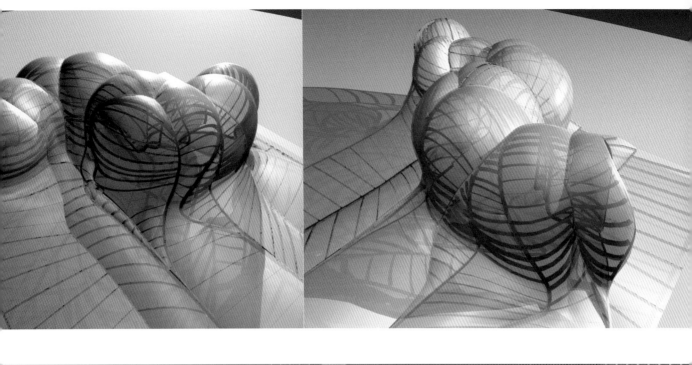

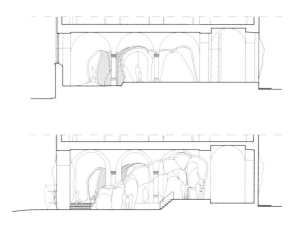

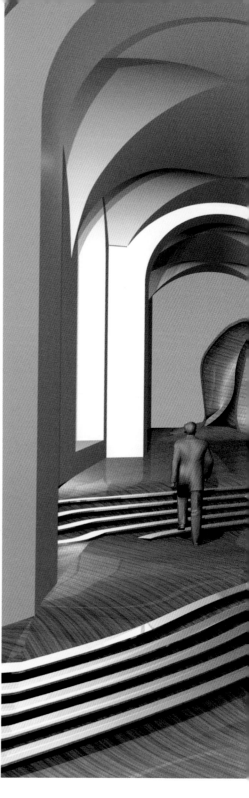

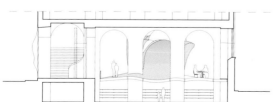
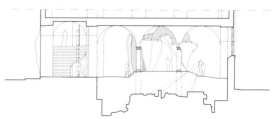

Exterior spaces are adorned with interior references:
curtains, lamps and wallpaper.

The small square in front of the gallery is lit by a huge suspended lamp.

Lars Spuybroek

NOX FLURBS ©

NOX exhibition,
Venice Biennale, Aedes Berlin, Vivid Rotterdam, TAMA Tel Aviv, 2000–01

How does one exhibit architecture? If through panels and models, the whole spatial experience is lacking. We have always tried to make installations out of images, i.e., create a certain thickness around the image, a zone that the visitor can enter, either through interactivity or through spatialization of the panel itself, as in this case. For the most part, flurbs© are flexible panels that have a relation to both ground and wall, switching back and forth between diagram and image, explanation and experience.

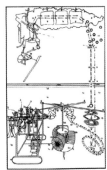

p 7 ● ● ● ● ● ● ● ● ● ● ● ● ●

How does one diagram what is already diagrammatic? In this diagram of an artwork that is itself already a screen or a diagram, Duchamp's Large Glass *schematized by Jean Suquet, it seemed to me no accident that the* Large Glass *looked like a computer screen and not like a canvas, since it is a cybernetic work describing a process of flows and exchanges. Duchamp was the first artist to use arrows in his art, and essentially the* Large Glass *is more an interface than a surface, which marks an important cultural shift from visual to operational surfaces.*

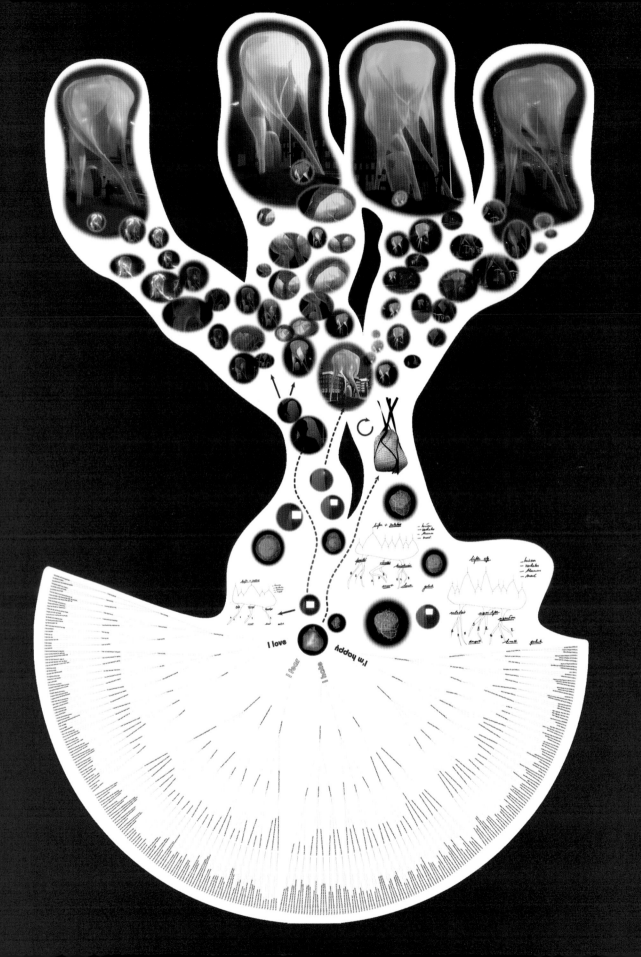

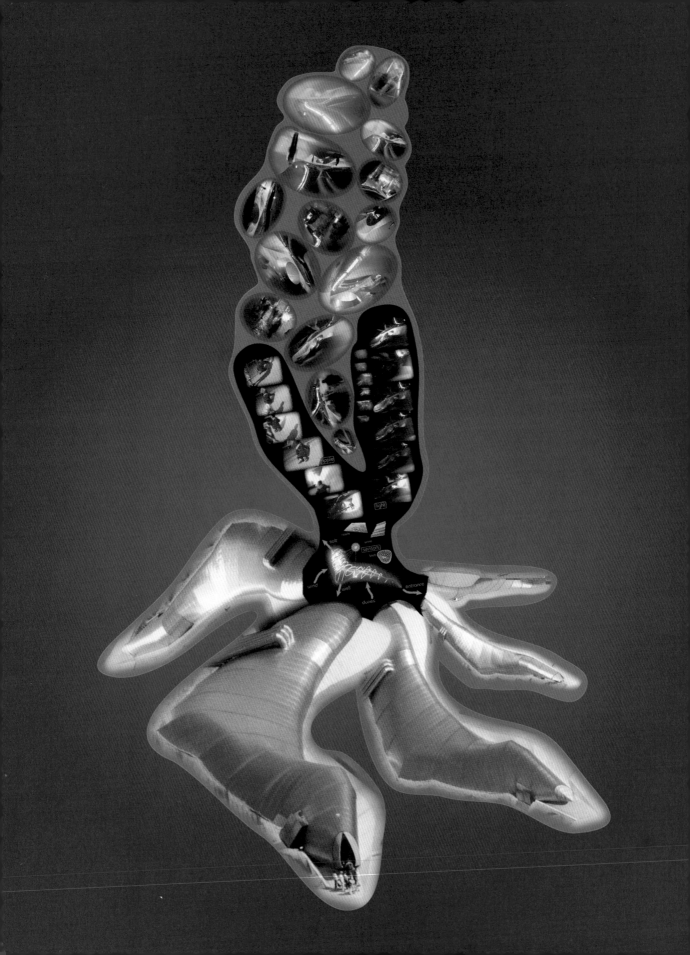

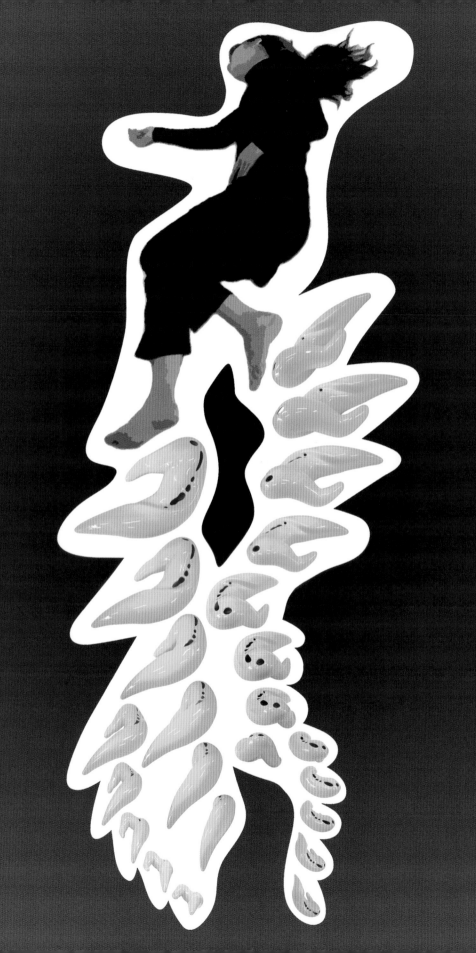

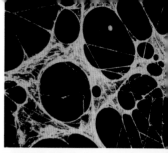

In the books of Frei Otto there are two categories of research. One applies to specific projects, the other is more fundamental research into *form finding*: forces working on balloons, lacquer, wool threads and so on. The second one is the main source of interest to us, and here he basically developed two techniques: line-to-surface and surface-to-line generation. Sometimes lines mesh together into surfaces, sometimes surfaces are torn and stretched into linear elements. Both methods create porous systems ('nets') where the holes are not positioned accidentally nor subtracted afterwards. Holes co-evolve with the geometry. In this project we used the analogue techniques to study surfaces that can both contain expansive open spaces for communication and contractive closed spaces for concentration.

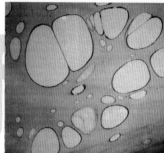

Soft Office

headquarters, office, interactive playground and shop for Anne Wood/Ragdoll television productions, Stratford-upon-Avon, United Kingdom, 2001

Soft Office *is a building in which work and play are closely interwoven. Half of the building is reserved for young children to play with interactive environments (that are also present on the web); the other half is for adults to work in a 'flexi-office' where no-one has a specified workplace and where the environment is intended for functional, formal conduct and informal, creative conduct, such as writing, discussing and presenting.*

'Muscular movements in general are originated by feelings in general.' Herbert Spencer, *Dancer & Musician*, 1895

We are all aware that our emotions, moods and feelings influence the way we move in space, that our intensive movement is related to our extensive movement. The scheme of this external movement always seems skeletal, a mechanical framework of goals and tasks, not just in our lives but in our work. To control events we often resort to routines and habituation, but if behaviour and scripting were nothing other than the blind repetition of former actions, nothing would ever happen (except maybe on the level of chance), and yet, uncontrolled events make organizing and managing the work process impossible. And though modern management theory recognizes that rigidity is a necessity in organizing tasks around set goals, a certain relaxation of their implementation has become vital. Flexibility is, first and foremost, of the mind. The object of our research in this project was to gauge how much flexibility of mind could be stimulated by a flexibility of architecture. To realize this we had to move away from the either-or choice of closed rooms and open landscapes, while bringing both together in a connection that could be directly experienced.

   In analyzing existing flexible offices, it became clear to us that there is a positive, daily tension between the intended, traditional, static planning philosophies and the viable, dynamic structure that is actually the productive force, not the one or the other. In calculating the desired surface area of an office for

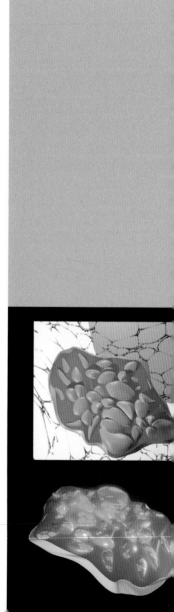

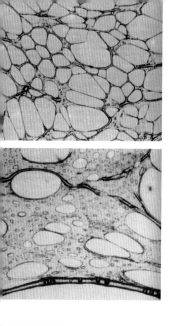

IL 35 p. 238

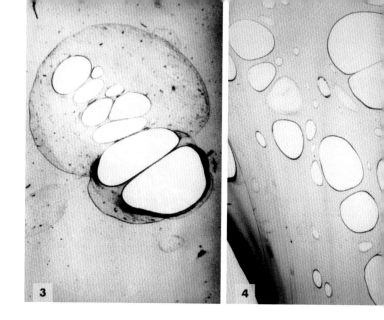

3

4

Since the machining methodology can be abstract in its initial stages, we did some quick first runs from diagram to design, to clarify our way of working to the client and to give an indication of a possible visual result. We took two of Frei Otto's diagrams of two-dimensional porous systems and extruded them upwards into architectural systems. On the left was a 'Turkish-bath office' option that contained only cells; on the right a second option with an open landscape scattered with dispersed rooms based on the wool-thread modelling technique (see p. 352, 'The Structure of Vagueness').

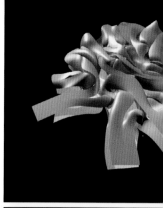

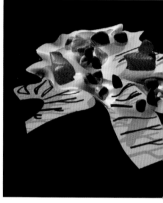

60 people performing different functions (marketing, administration, online production, offline production, management, origination), one would normally require at least 900 square metres. If one studies the occupancy rate of spaces that incorporate time-space relationships, however, one begins to see a largely differentiated usage over time in the dynamics of an office culture. This dynamic structure allowed us to make the office area with 625 square metres. But it is not only the quantifiable office space that has to change – leaving the structure the same while reducing it by a third would not do any good. The spaces and furniture of the office need not be designated to a particular person, nor strictly designed for a type of work, but destined in essence for a state of mind. We established standard office spaces of general connectivity next to informal meeting spaces and small individual capsules for work demanding concentration. The *active* programme is a continuum of *expansion* (communicative behavioural types) and *contraction* (the necessity to shut off, to discuss, meet or write, either in small groups or alone). The *passive* programme, more a subprogramme, is one of bathrooms (which can play an active role in office cultures), cleaning rooms, editing suites and the like.

In contrast to the office space, the children's space – the 'Scape' – is a field or landscape of objects where a substantial part of the movement is propelled by mock-ups from children's television programmes. Where the adults in the office find a lateral freedom in a longitudinally oriented system, the young children's movement in the Scape is gravitational and spiralling. They move 'around 'n' around' the mediated objects. For other areas a different approach is needed, a place where the building comes alive and interacts with the children, which we call 'Glob'. Glob is a world designed by globally networked children and is present in the building and on a website. Glob is a 'living organism' (some of its responses are calculated with genetic algorithms) that has the special ability to interact with children and will grow, love and play. Glob creates an experiential environment for the children and touches their senses and humour. Together they will create drawings, music and stories.

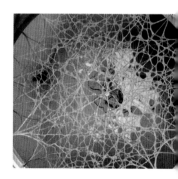

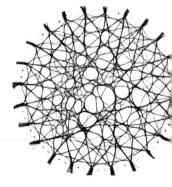

To understand how porous systems operate on the slack of wool threads we remade Otto's experiments in the office. For our purposes, however, we needed a three-dimensional system, working with thin rubber tubes and wet lacquer.

The diagrams of Frei Otto were constrained to two dimensions only and could not provide us with enough information to render them spatial, therefore we mixed the porosity on the plan level with the vertical elevation.

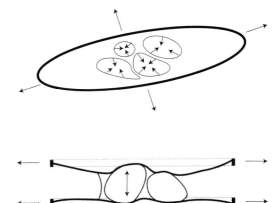

We needed a machine that produced open spaces for communication and closed spaces for concentration.

Initially, the rubber and lacquer behave exactly like wool and water in a similar arrangement, since the lacquer is still very fluid. Then, after one or two hours, we vertically separate the two rings. Since the lacquer is drying, it behaves more like the rubber of the tubes; the lacquer surfaces stretch and interact with the curves in the rubber tubes. A porous three-dimensional structure that is not straight plan-elevation but networked in different directions emerges.

p 141
p 179
p 261

Our stance on the research of Frei Otto should be clarified. Where he was forced into the position of engineer, always coming second to the architect, we try to integrate the two roles. That makes the operation 'impure' to both professions, however, and it might suggest why some people object to the techniques. In our methodology it is deliberately unclear what is floor (action), column (construction) and wall (perception).

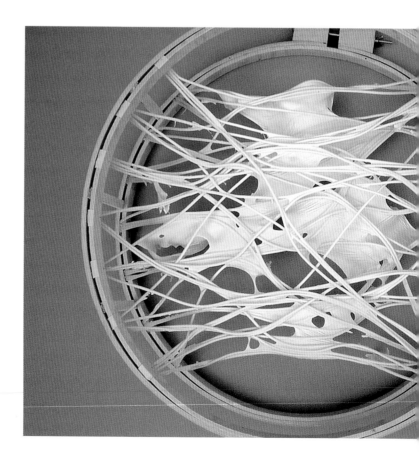

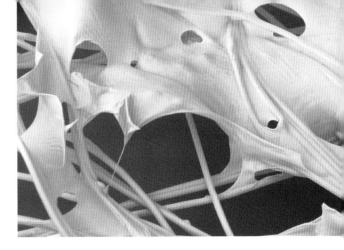

The structure's porosity is now fully three-dimensional, though within the typological range of a one- to two-storey building. It is interesting to note the difference between typology and topology: the typological limits of the framework are set beforehand (where the tubes meet the boundary of the wooden ring, they have absolutely no room to manoeuvre), and topological flexibility is generated later, but only in the middle area.

 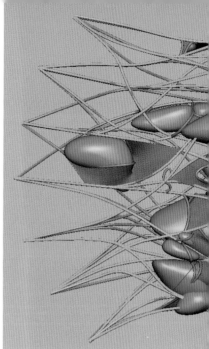

As with our other analogue machining techniques, the method is by no means intended to produce a 'final' design right away. It is much more a structural and formal expression of a 'meta-programme', which has the necessary ratio of open spaces and spongy spaces, even a scale, but which does not contain the exact position of all the rooms. Diagrams always need to have *potential*, room for development within a clear sense of direction. After digitization (left) the programme is carefully filled with deformable volumes (middle) that finalize the nesting process: the addition of extra surface is no longer interactive with the overall geometry. At the end (right), the model's extremities are rearranged to fit typologies that are more generic.

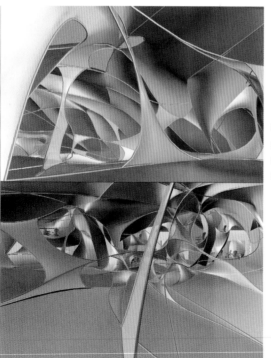

Reworking from diagram towards design is never direct. Even the digitized model has abstract qualities that contain redundancies. In our topological view of programme and behaviour it is vital that this vagueness is never eradicated.

In the final plan, which is more of an X-ray, the spatial continuity of generic spaces at both ends of the design is visible. On the left is the large hall for the children's spaces, on the right four more formalized office bays, and in the middle a specific area for informal interaction.

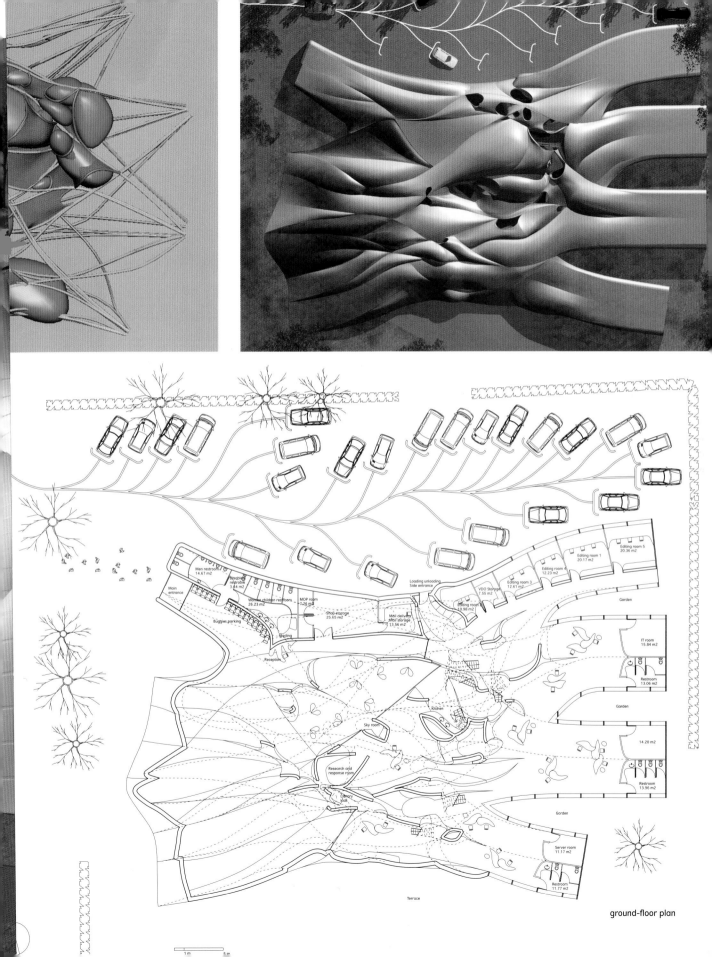

ground-floor plan

1 m   5 m

interactive scape

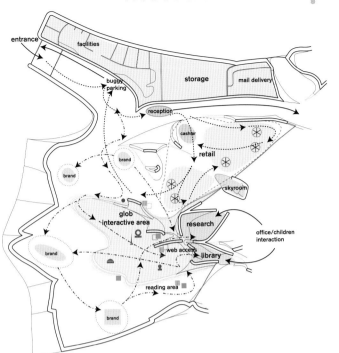

SCAPE
Children will explore in and out of the light as the nearby house is situated under the bright 'sun' and in the distance is a magical glow of Glob.

Spot lights on the brands creates a magical theatre scape for the children. Lights are incorprated in a flexible system to work around the changing environments of the brands. Towards the back of the Scape is Glob, the magical interactive organism that communicates with the children. Glob with its sensitive skin interacts with the children and displays a special colored glow according to its mood.

SHOP
Shop & Play Split
Parents and grandparents explore the shop, kids explore the Scape. View and buy the merchandise in one area. Storage is separated from the shop next to the mail delivery room.

LIGHTING
Spot Lights with colored gel, Flood lights
Digitally programmable lights [mix colors]

EQUIPMENT
Projectors, Monitors, Cameras, Speakers, Headphones, Microphones, Netphone, Internet

SENSORS
Button on/off sensors, motion sensors, light detecting sensors, touch sensors, pressure sensors, electromagnetic field sensor [theremin-change pitch of sound], velocity sensor, digital panels.

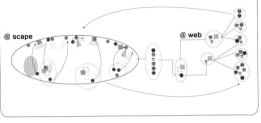

BUTTON SENSORS	EQUIPMENT	MOVEMENT	BRAND
pull rings	sensors / lights	······· parents	✳ toys
bending arms / push buttons / rotating knobs	camera / projector / monitor / speaker / microphone	··—·· children / —— both	brand / brand

Playing children on one side, working adults on the other. A glass wall separates the two landscapes to carefully avoid the neutrality of an open hall and the determinism of room division. The children's space, Glob, has areas for varying installations based on children's television programmes and a more defined area filled with electronic devices and sensors. Glob is meant for children to interact with the building: they can make it laugh or change its mood. Children in other countries can upload their portraits and have them projected in the Glob-zone through web interfaces.

flexi-office

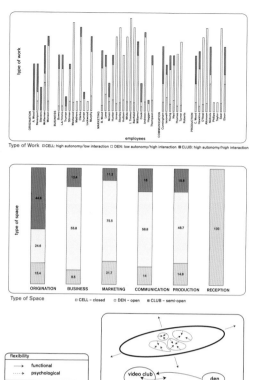

Type of Work ☐ CELL: high autonomy/low interaction ☐ DEN: low autonomy/high interaction ■ CLUB: high autonomy/high interaction

Type of Space ☐ CELL – closed ☐ DEN – open ■ CLUB – semi-open

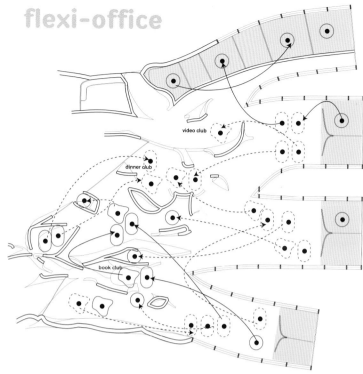

Topology offers something completely new in architecture. Between determined states (space X–behaviour X, space Y–behaviour Y) we can now have less determined states that are more open to other actions. Very different from Mies's undetermined open Cartesianism or Tschumi's 'space of accidents', it is more active because, though already formed, it is not yet defined. No-one ever believed that in architecture the informal could take form without becoming determined – how can something have a shape without having a name? This redundancy engenders variation of behaviour that is not 'wild' but that has a flexible relation with more defined states of behaviour, such as tasks and routines (see p. 322, Brian Massumi, 'Building Experience', and p. 352, 'The Structure of Vagueness').

p 36
p 97
p 139

After studying Francis Duffy's research on flexible office typologies we designed spaces for states of mind and types of work rather than for specific activities. Nobody has his or her own workplace. An office can thus be two-thirds of the size of a 'normal' office, since it is designed for an average number of personnel present at any one time. This is especially productive in communications and creative businesses.

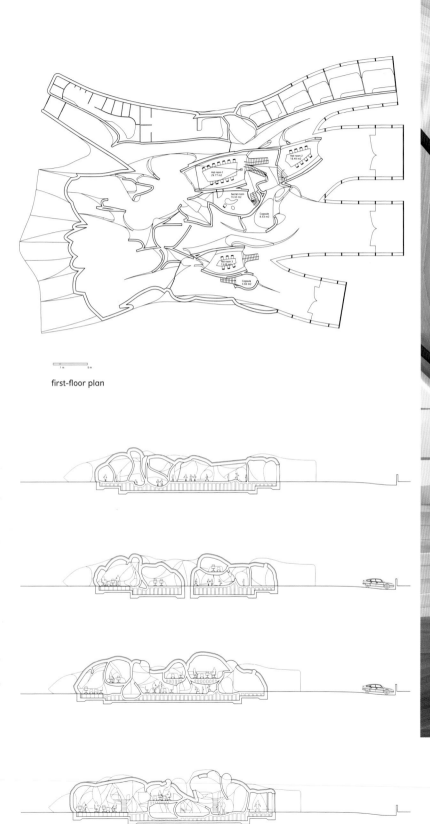

first-floor plan

lateral sections

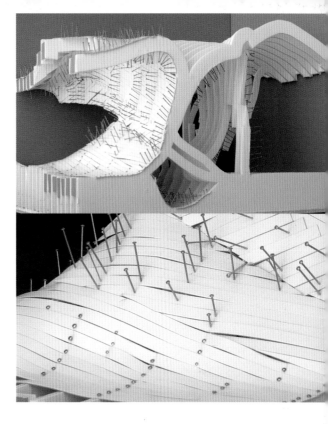

Strips of wood follow the ribs' double curvature by twisting and bending, respectively a rotation orthogonal and in parallel to the centreline. Since the amount of torsion and inflection is limited, the number of planks that can be placed side by side is also limited. One must shift direction to continue to fill another limited amount of surface, an action that is repeated until the whole surface is covered. As in *Son-O-House*, the surface is filled with joints (between the planks) and cracks (between the groups of planks).

The wooden panelling is perforated because the space behind the surface needs to be accessible for cables, lights and air ducts. Most of the technical infrastructure, however, would be in the floor.

On first sight, this project seems to reflect a classic Semperian separation between tectonics and textile, but it is slightly more complex: all variation is a sweeping or spreading of the corners over the façade's length. All modulation is serial and follows the vertical rhythm of the adjacent factory.

Maison Folie

multipurpose hall, studios and exhibition spaces, media library, daycare, artists' communal space, offices and a soup restaurant for Lille, Cultural Capital of Europe 2004, invited competition, first prize, Lille, France, 2001–04

A complex of buildings result from the renovation of an old textile factory into a conglomerate of art-related functions plus a new multipurpose hall used for concerts, theatre productions, fashion shows and performances. As in Rotterdam, Hamburg or Glasgow, art moves into abandoned industrial buildings to transform and revive the identity of a city.

In Lille, a city made of cities, the idea of the network prevails. It is necessary to survive and is a basis for vitality. Fundamentally, this notion of a network is scaleless: networks contain networks. Lille flourishes within a global network of high speeds, but it is itself a network, a multinodal city. Maison Folie is again a smaller and even finer network within one of these municipal nodes, Wazemmes. The design is based on three different levels of the network:

    a. Programme: recognizing that the programme's heterogeneity is already an explicit expression of this social dimension and fits perfectly within the differentiated composition of the old factory, as well as recognizing the dilapidated quality of the existing buildings.

    b. Landscape: using an older but related concept of the network, the landscape, to modulate potential exchanges implied in the programme, to stimulate (but not to provoke) unexpected encounters.

    c. Image: producing an indelible image that will form part of local dreams and memories, local psychogeography, and connect to the global levels of art and media.

Programme

In its social context the programme stimulates a lively and vital criss-crossing within the district of Wazemmes, especially in its fitting within the old factory and its differentiation of scales, which is more like a small city. Austerity is therefore the keyword for this aspect of the design: the more economical we are, the more programme we will be able to provide for. Quantitatively, it requires a

respectful and modest treatment of existing buildings, and qualitatively, the programme's internal dynamics of differences (age, culture) demands a precise treatment of the ground.

Landscape

Social exchanges, the interaction between programmatic elements, are stimulated by an architecture of continuity, an uninterrupted connective surface linking hammam to playground, to a brasserie, to the art school, to an exposition, to the party room, to the artists' residence, to the *salle de spectacle*, to the neighbourhood's inhabitants. It is not difficult to imagine the programme's fluctuations at different times of the day or days of the week. To stimulate unexpected encounters, we incorporated these functions in an undulating landscape, a *mineral garden*, that includes patches of smaller green gardens, private or public. The landscape allows everything to interact more easily, and promotes movement from activity to activity.

Image

The section of the programme that requires a new building (*salle de spectacle* with its studios) is a technical but introverted programme. It is best served by an assemblage of boxes that shut themselves off from the city (except for the foyer) but fit exactly within the urban scheme of the neighbourhood. Since Wazemmes is such a damaged district, we decided to finish the street with a façade. We made the black box glow with a luminous skin that transforms with movement in and around the *Maison Folie*, a shimmering, almost holographic dress that incorporates the pulsations of art and life. The articulation of the façade was generated through continuous variation and modulation of the vertical tectonics of the old factory's façade: vertical lines bent in a complex pattern, which, animated by the sun's position, produces a spectrum of effects as one walks or drives by.

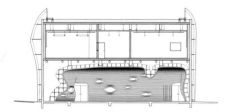

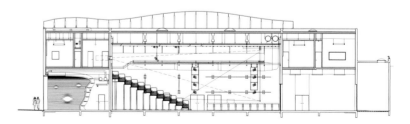

We decided on a cautious approach when renovating the existing building. No building could be fully restored to its 1880 original state, since subsequent alterations had also left their mark.

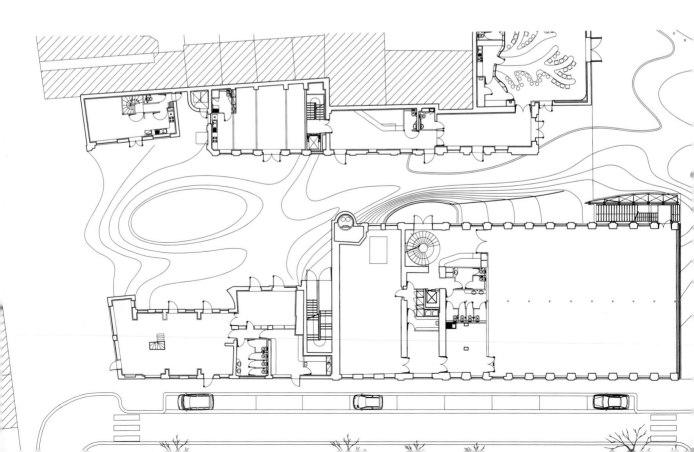

The new building was meant to match typologically the urban fabric, without variability of massing or structure, only of texture.

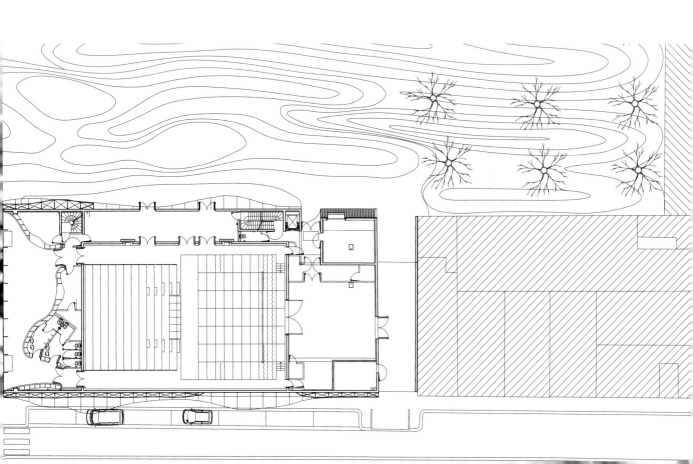

African Village

Rem Koolhaas
Lagos, Nigeria, 2000

ParisBRAIN

a transurban scheme for the area west of La Défense, Paris, France,
research project for the exhibition *Expériences d'urbanisme* in the
Institut Néerlandais, Paris, 2001

The exhibition on urban visions included such notorious Dutch works as Constant's **New Babylon**, *Aldo van Eyck's* **orphanage**, *Piet Blom's* **Kasbah**, *Theo van Doesburg's* **Aubette** *and OMA/Rem Koolhaas's* **Yokohama Project**. *We investigated these historical options and their relation to early Situationism and contemporary phenomena, such as globalization, migration and transnationalism.*

We considered the relationship between *action painting* and psychogeographical mapping as a means of developing intensive design techniques. What directly relates the two methods is that they are tracing methods. Although the gestural move of a Situationist's 'step out of the system', creating 'moving accidents', is different from Jackson Pollock's gestural dripping technique, both actions leave traces. Pollock made traces into a system of paths, while Guy Debord tried to get off the path and create a trace. For both Pollock and Debord the idea of landscape is crucial, be it lines meshing into a complex network or a psychogeographical space where the grid is short-circuited by momentary *dérives*.

In our machining procedure, we used Frei Otto's wool-thread technique for optimized path systems, but in a slightly different manner from earlier applications (*wetGRID, Soft Office, obliqueWTC*).

Speakscape. Instead of making a horizontal wool-thread model with an open ring, we allowed the moving and merging lines to interact with a smooth supporting surface, a sheet of transparent Perspex, whose surface shape greatly influences the converging and bifurcating tendencies of the wool threads. We deformed the surface's shape vertically into a landscape that affected how fast the water ran off as the system was taken out of the tank after dipping. Its geography would be a mapping of collective movements of the inhabitants of the area. To acquire that information we conducted local interviews about people's language and movements, and categorized people according to their 'speak' — language, dialect, accent, jargon or the like — the languages of bankers, Arabs, skaters, girls, rap, shopping. This resulted in a

Constant
New Babylon/Ruhrgebiet, 1963

In 2001 I interviewed Rem Koolhaas about his visits to Lagos (published as 'Africa Comes First'), where photographs of flexible structures in water or huge markets along the highway show a strong interest in self-organization as part of urban design. He said, 'Yes, self-organization is important but only in combination with organization, with planning, not to replace it.' The question then becomes how these systems can cooperate with and profit from each other. Many photographs show how highways or streets can suddenly stop functioning and overflow into a field of sand or water to become something else. For this it is necessary that the borders between line-highway and field-surface are blurred and open.

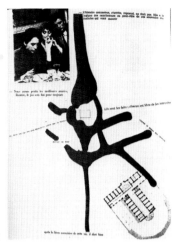

p 42

Guy Debord with Asger Jorn
Mémoires, 1959

For Debord the liquid was a momentary line-trace while for Pollock it was more structural, because the traces needed to lock into each other to form a surface-landscape. Constant, who luckily was expelled from the Situationist International by Debord, uncovered structures between rigid and liquid, between unplanned and planned. Later again, Frei Otto developed precise techniques and methodologies to generate such mixtures of open and directed, of surface and line.

p 66
p 272

Jackson Pollock
Autumn Rhythm, 1950

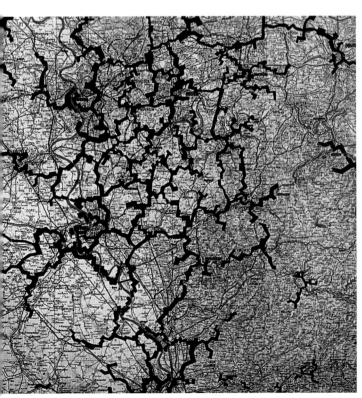

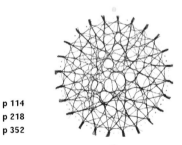

p 114
p 218
p 352

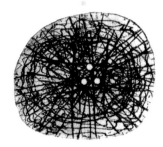

Constant
Round Etching with Three Holes,
1958

system of vectors structured between Nanterre University, La Défense, the Park and the centre of Paris.

Entangled space (mega-architecture). We placed a set of parallel wool threads in the direction of the Grande Axe and attached them at the two sides of the Perspex with an overlength of 8%. The intention was to create an enormous shopping centre of airport proportions in the middle of a historic city. The area, 5 by 2 kilometres, would connect to the La Défense area on the east side and to several highways and a bridge on the west side. We shook the system under water and took it out slowly. Whenever we found merging groups among the wool threads, we tied them up with loose ends of decreasing length. We did this in four steps, organizing the structure mainly through entanglements, spatial knots inserted to structure the 'dérivian' experience of strolling. All threads coming out of this operation were materialized as tubular buildings, like a completely curved version of Heathrow airport, with shops leading not to aeroplanes but to other shops, and more shops, an arabesque of multiple interlacing brands.

Dotted space (micro-urbanism). The system of tubular commercial buildings connected to global money flows would have a considerable effect on local land prices. The area between this shopping structure and the edge of surrounding nineteenth-century Paris should, we decided, become a conglomerate of *tax-free zones*, where local initiatives could develop freely as a self-organized system: a *terrain vague* that would not be filled up immediately by buildings but by an urbanism that would develop over time. It follows the idea of the sheet directly, because it begins as an open landscape, to be later saturated by economic pressures and desires. To turn this occupational strategy into something as structured as growth, one needs certain connective or even genetic algorithms. In our case, we chose minor rules to guide the growth: every building would be round (for all-around orientation) and accompanied by an extension of sewage, electricity, communications and road networks, each of which split off from previous branches according to certain angles.

We mapped local movements in the landscape of Paris by conducting almost a hundred interviews. We indexed their 'speak', i.e., their tendencies to form groups through the use of a hybrid French, and then plotted the vectors of these groups on the Paris map. These micro-migrations are not just of groups but also between groups.

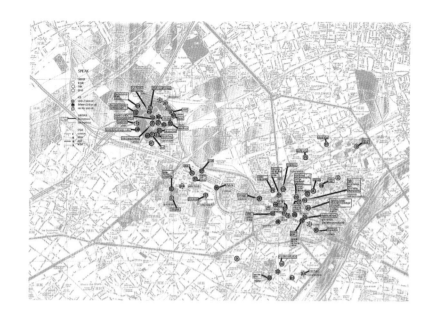

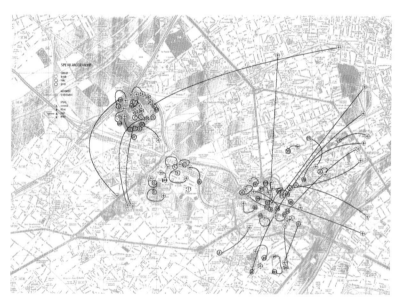

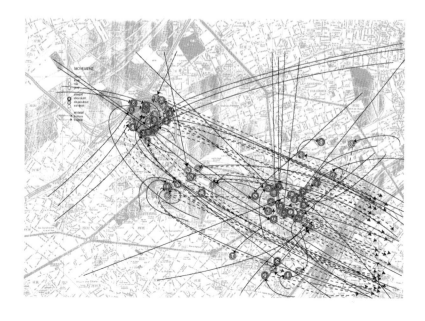

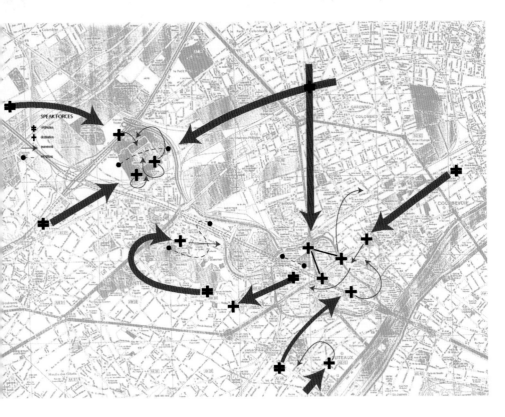

We deviated from Frei Otto's wool-thread model by mapping the local immigrations onto a sheet of transparent Perspex as a landscape of hills and valleys (see following pages). On the sheet we attached wool threads with 8% slack in the direction of the Grande Axe and connecting in the east to La Défense area. After the system is submerged in water, the water runs off the hills and directs the wool threads into connections of entanglements. This is repeated four times; each time an entanglement emerges we add a new wool thread on that point.

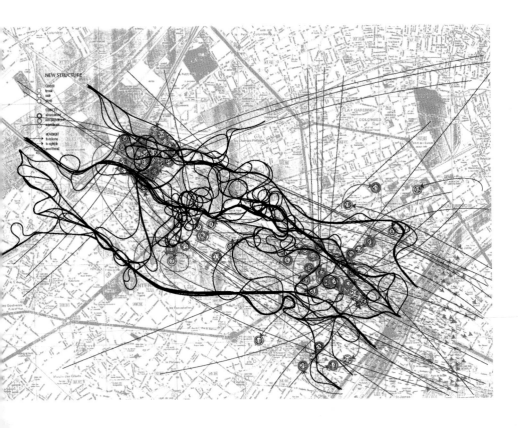

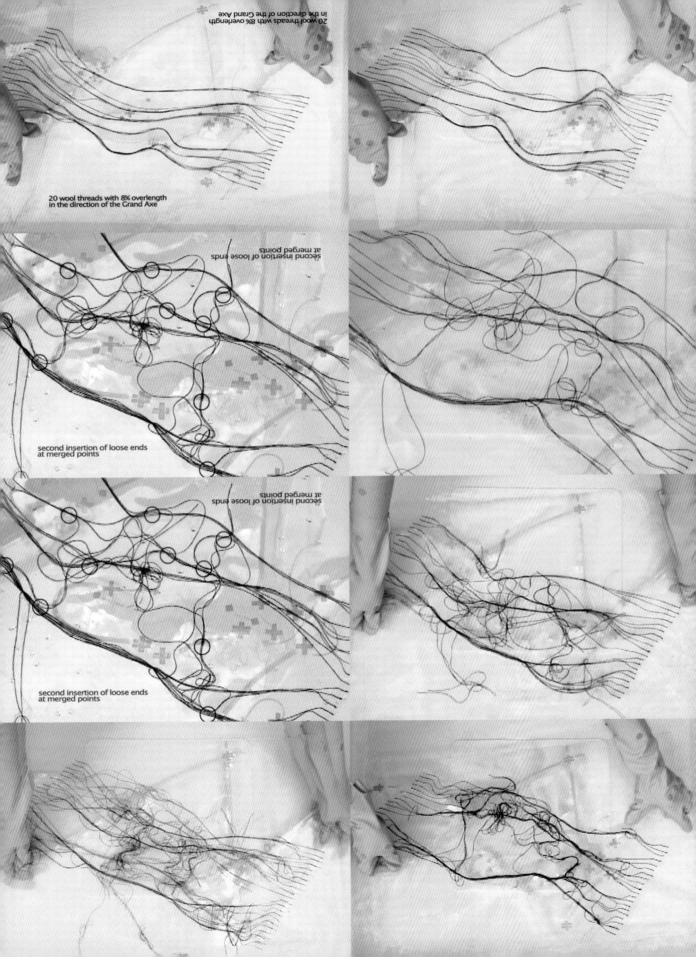

20 wool threads with 8% overlength
in the direction of the Grand Axe

second insertion of loose ends
at merged points

second insertion of loose ends
at merged points

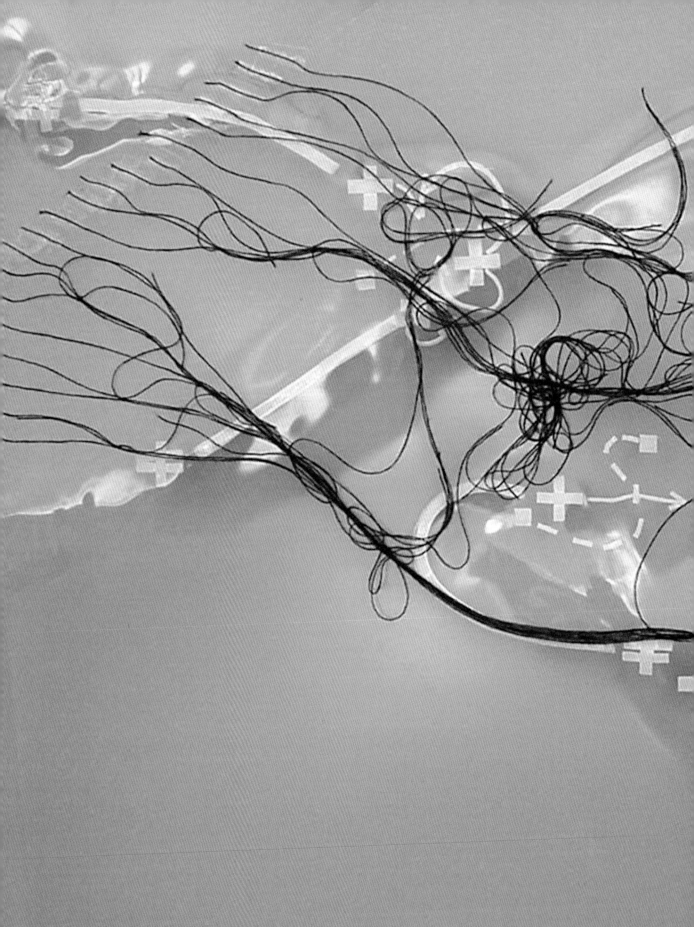

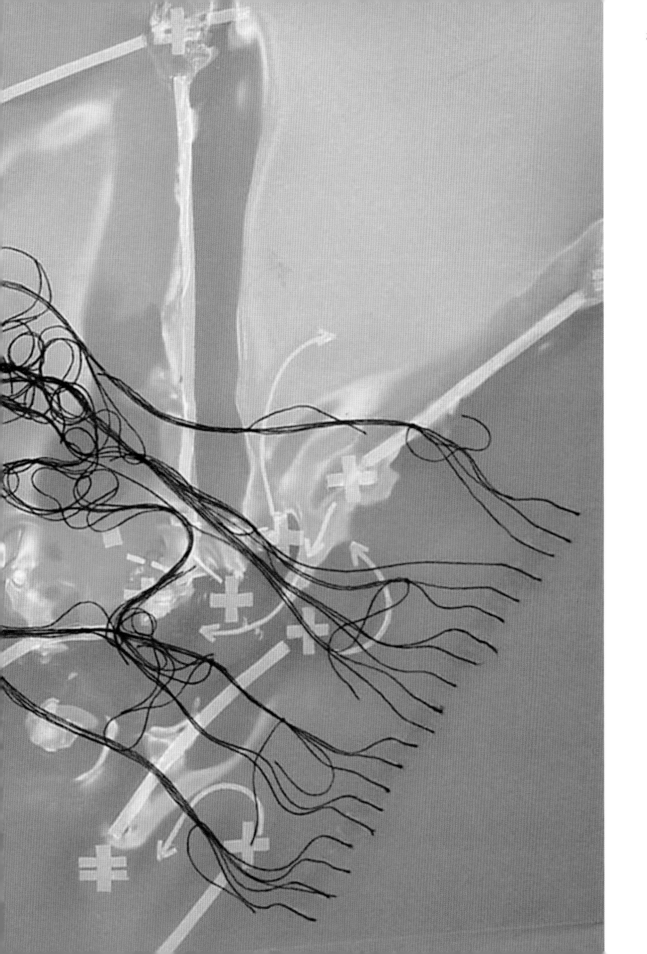

micro-urbanism

The no-man's lands between the mega-architecture and the nineteenth-century structure of
Paris are declared tax-free zones, but only for
local initiatives. There is no infrastructure, but
each building (which must be round) is obliged
to contribute its own continuation of the road
and sewage system. A network will emerge
over the years between the new mega-structure
and the historic Paris.

mega-architecture

The entanglements of wool threads are translated into
highways and tubular structures that function mainly as
shopping centres. Based on airport typologies, these
tubular structures bring peripheral strategies into the
heart of the city, which should be read as an aggressive
commercial continuation of La Défense.

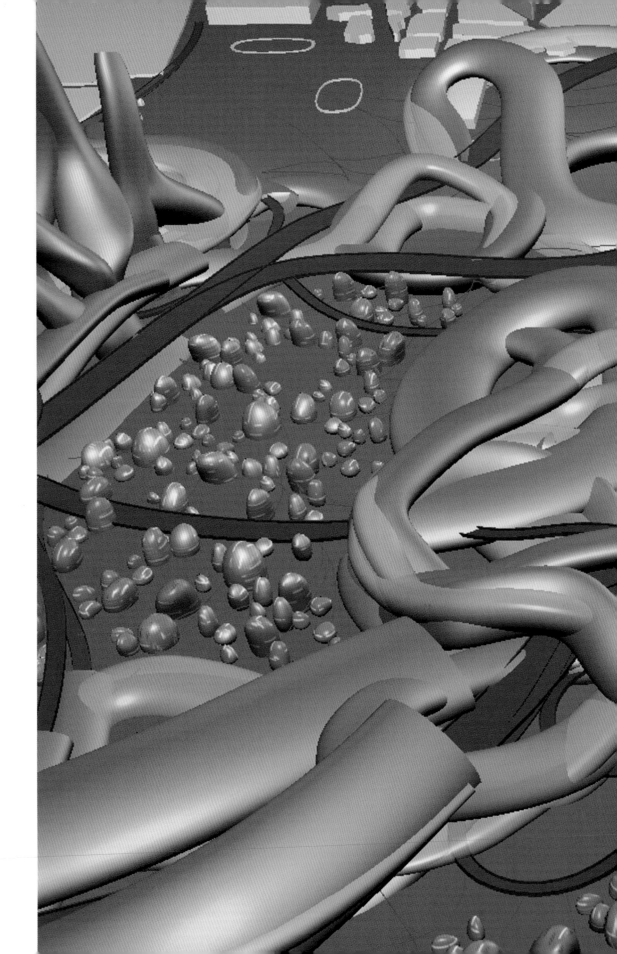

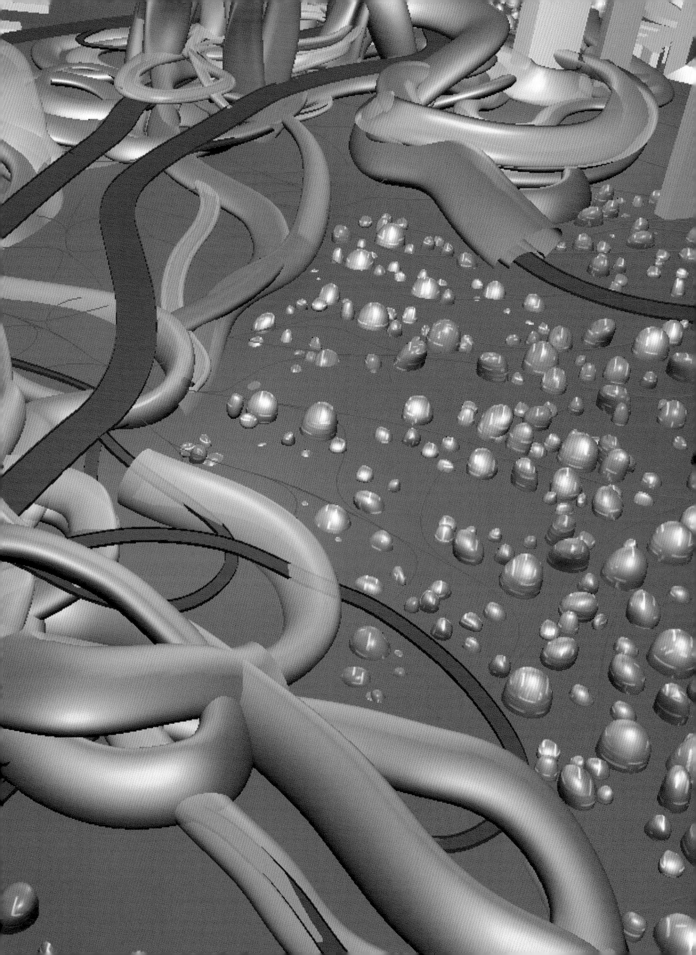

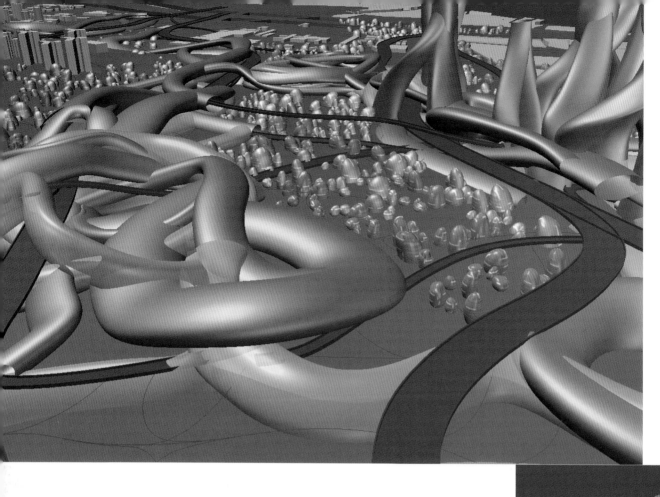

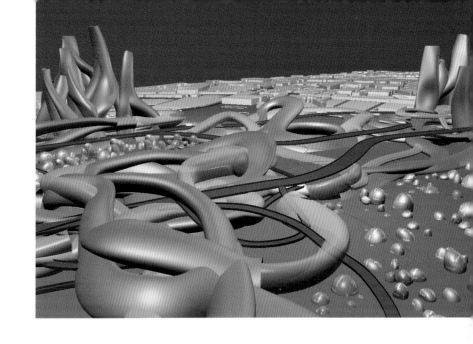

view from La Défense towards Nanterre

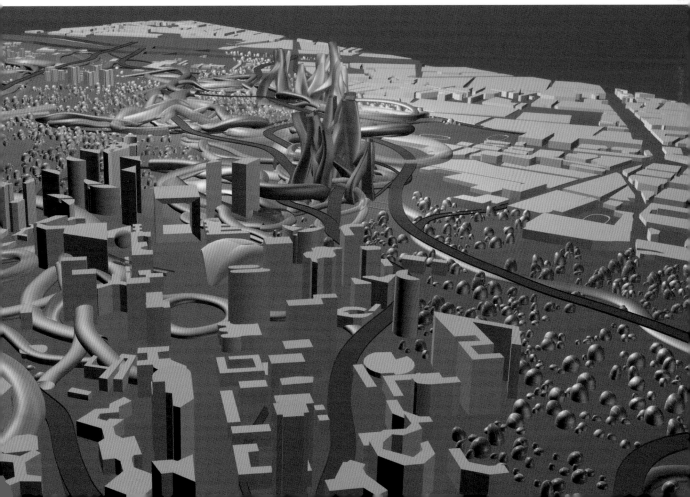

IL 35 p. 181

Varying Otto's three-dimensional wool-thread technique to generate branching column systems, we used the method for a set of flexible *cores*, where each wool thread became the centreline of a lean tower. The horizontal shaking under water should be understood as a transfer of street interaction into the verticality of a tower. The project is, therefore, more urbanist than architectural, where a network of elevators acts as a subway system.

before dipping (700 metres)

obliqueWTC

design for a new World Trade Center,
for Max Protetch Gallery,
New York, November 2001

During a short period after 9/11 we all hoped architecture would become a public matter in the United States. But America is far beyond a nation-state now: it has merged with its own global effect, a mediated atmosphere where all forces, especially socio-political, cultural and economic forces, return to earth hundredfold. In that framework I wanted to rethink the WTC as something bigger than large, more than a skyscraper.

We should try to find *urban* strategies to deal with the Huge, with global forces that work on local situations. We should be more concerned with the structure of the Huge than its size. Again using a variation on the wool-thread technique developed by Frei Otto, we took one thread for each core of the destroyed or damaged buildings on the former WTC site. As an inverted model the wool threads hang straight down under the force of gravity. When dipped into water and removed, all threads reorganize themselves into a complex network (with the cohesive lateral forces of the water now added to the gravitational system), comparable to bone structure. The structure is not formed by a simple extrusion of a plan, but is self-organized into a networked mega-structure, in which the whole is larger than the sum of its parts. We thickened each of the wool threads into a lean tower that merges and splits as it moves upwards, which enabled the structure to comply with the New York zoning law that stipulates high buildings must occupy only 25% of the total site area. In this case, however, the 25% is always positioned somewhere else, making it either a single mega-building with many (structural) holes in it or multiple thin towers that cooperate to make one huge structure. The towers sometimes act as a bridge, sometimes as a counterstructure for another one, and sometimes free themselves to become smaller subtowers.

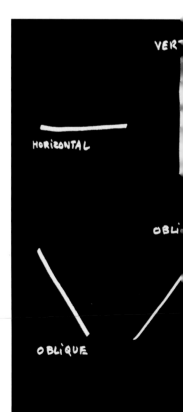

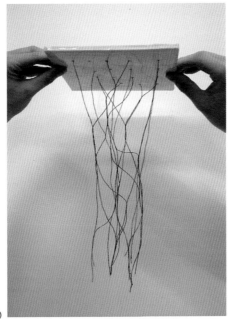

after dipping (520 metres)

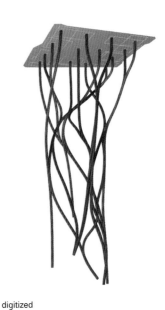

digitized

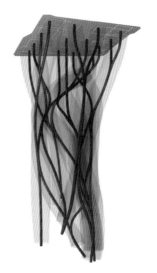

thickened

rotated

ADDITION.

MULTIPLICATION.

Virilos/66

The *oblique* was an architectural invention of Paul Virilio and Claude Parent in the 1960s. It was intended as a critique on normative orthogonality but also promised a new type of construction, since the floors were not just tilted but formed diagonals. Diagonals later became associated with *deconstruction*, which dealt only with a *critique* on modernist top-down thinking. With our WTC one should understand the complex network not as tilted but as *straight*, a bottom-up straightness, but fully *constructivist* nonetheless (see pp 358–59).

p 54
p 106
p 314

The porous tower allows for the required amount of sunlight to reach the street in accordance with New York zoning laws.

[STUDENT RESEARCH]

On page 180 in **IL 35** *there is an image in which a Mies-like grid is transformed into a branching column system through a lengthening of the wool threads and their subsequent dipping in water. In my teaching in the USA and Germany I have developed these techniques with students. Three important techniques emerged:*

A. Because all wool threads represent columns, it adheres most closely to the original Frei Otto model, but it adapts the top and bottom grid to site or programme requirements.

B. In addition to grids the model also introduced external elements into the generative technique. These can be small objects or, in this case, hooks or rings that shift the column-model into a contour-model.

C. The third technique is an entirely digital variation where the lines reorganize into centre-lines, later to be thickened as lean towers. This we call a core-model.

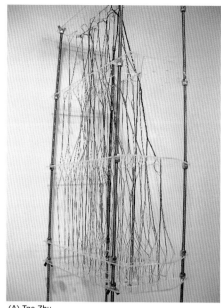

(A) Tao Zhu

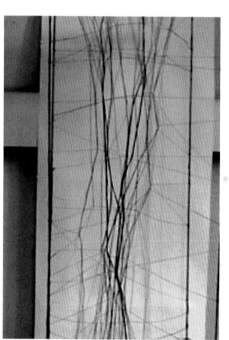
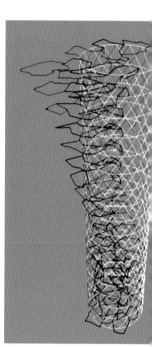

(B) Marcus Leinweber

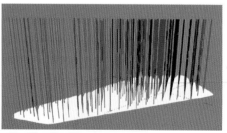
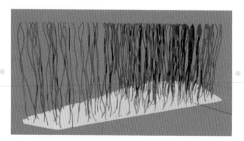
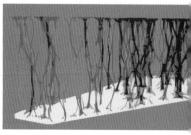

(C) Matthias Schrader-Thiet

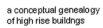
a conceptual genealogy
of high rise buildngs

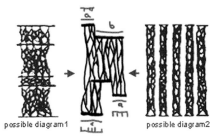

possible diagram1 → ← possible diagram2

possible diagram3

toward new diagrams

mies' seagram building → thread experiment → scaling of calculative machine ← 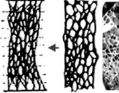 controlled 3d net cancellous bone

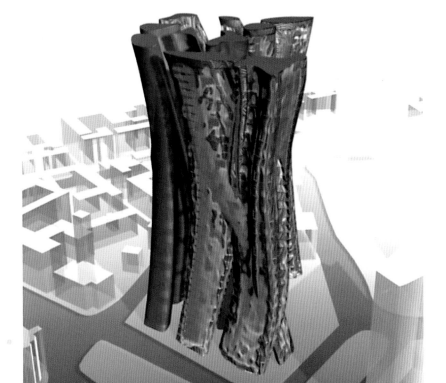

kahn's philadelphia city hall

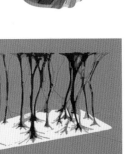

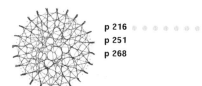

p 216
p 251
p 268

In analogue computing it is quite difficult to make a system produce pure variation without any accidental side-effects. I want to move slowly away from analogue computing and replace it with digital techniques. For time-based procedures we need to move towards programming and scripting, and for design development we need to move towards figure-configuration techniques where the movement-phase is replaced by a matrix of variable figures and the structuring-phase is replaced by configurational patterning. We will then also have the opportunity to develop it into a clearer aesthetic language.

La Tana di Alice

Alice-in-Wonderland pavilion,
'Pinopoli' – an extension to the existing Pinocchio Park in Collodi, Italy, 2001

Young Alice is caught between two mirrors of similarity, an internal one of growing up and an external one of being in a world of people who are sometimes more similar to you than you are to yourself. It's the mystery of being among others, of having brothers and sisters, but also of having a body and a face that has a future and a past. Alice is a brave child, who cleverly plays the one against the other, as she accepts the continuous changes of size as a logic in itself.

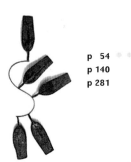

p 54
p 140
p 281

A

overlength

LEVEL 1 (x,y)

Our small *Tana di Alice* is a three-dimensional mirror, in the classic tradition of the Mirror Hall *(Sala degli Specchi)* of Nero's Domus Aurea but also found in the Baroque palaces of central and southern Europe. We translated this idea into the modern technologies of virtual reality, of interactive projection techniques where visitors have the possibility to transform in real time in front of an electronic mirror.

The geometry of the *Tana di Alice* is based on the play between two similarities, between replication and reproduction, between the idea that change emerges from the self and that it is enforced from the outside. In several operations, we split and lengthened a set of lines, similar to the idea of offspring, so that each line would contain another line and then another. This process of implication/explication results in a complex surface that consists of a series of self-similar ribs (made of epoxy), which form the actual space on the inside.

To get inside the *Tana di Alice* we have to go through a hole (like Alice), and after passing through an underground tunnel we enter the complex formed interior. In the middle is an area that unfolds to the sides, which are mostly inaccessible but visible areas. In the tunnel there are cameras where visitors can have their faces downloaded into the Replicator Program, which changes their emotion, sex and age. The new faces will be projected in real time in the Mirror Hall at several different zones in the space and the interior's highly reflective surfaces will provide an infinite number of reproductions.

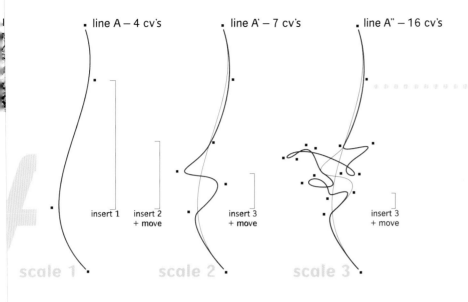

line A – 4 cv's   line A' – 7 cv's   line A" – 16 cv's

insert 1   insert 2 + move   insert 3 + move   insert 3 + move

scale 1   scale 2   scale 3

Hermann Finsterlin,
architectural sketches, 1919

Instead of working with wool threads we used digital splines and increased their length through a precise algorithm: insert three points and move only the middle one outwards, and then repeat the operation. At a certain point the curve starts containing spaces by self-intersection, different from the bifurcation techniques in *Son-O-House* and *wetGRID*, but with a similar blistering result.

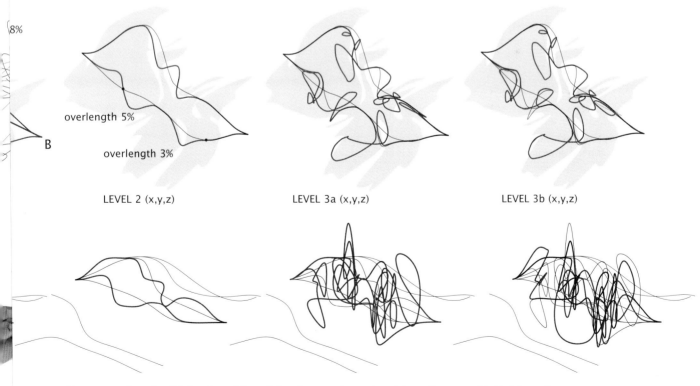

8%

B

overlength 5%

overlength 3%

LEVEL 2 (x,y,z)   LEVEL 3a (x,y,z)   LEVEL 3b (x,y,z)

The passage from A to B is lengthened through iterative curvature, where intersections are added to intersections.

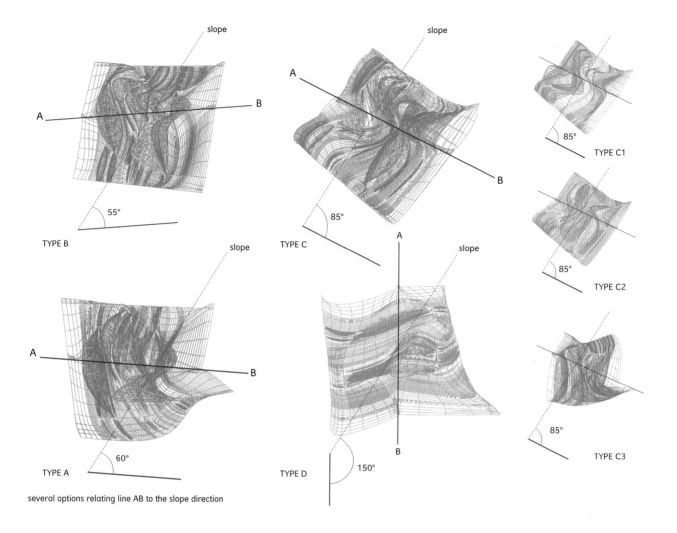

slope

A   B

55°

TYPE B

slope

A

B

85°

TYPE C

slope

A

B

60°

TYPE A

several options relating line AB to the slope direction

A

slope

B

150°

TYPE D

slope

85°

TYPE C1

85°

TYPE C2

85°

TYPE C3

The arabesque curves connecting A and B are closed or 'lofted' with the boundary of the site where the structure merges with the ground. This makes the curves higher and more spacious in the middle zone (where visitors pass) and lower towards the ends. With its duck's tails at the end and its triple paper spline in the middle area it is similar to the *Son-O-House*, but here there is no tearing, only intersecting.

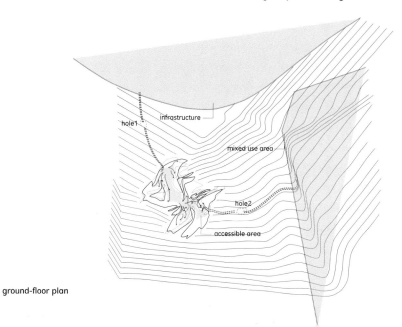

ground-floor plan

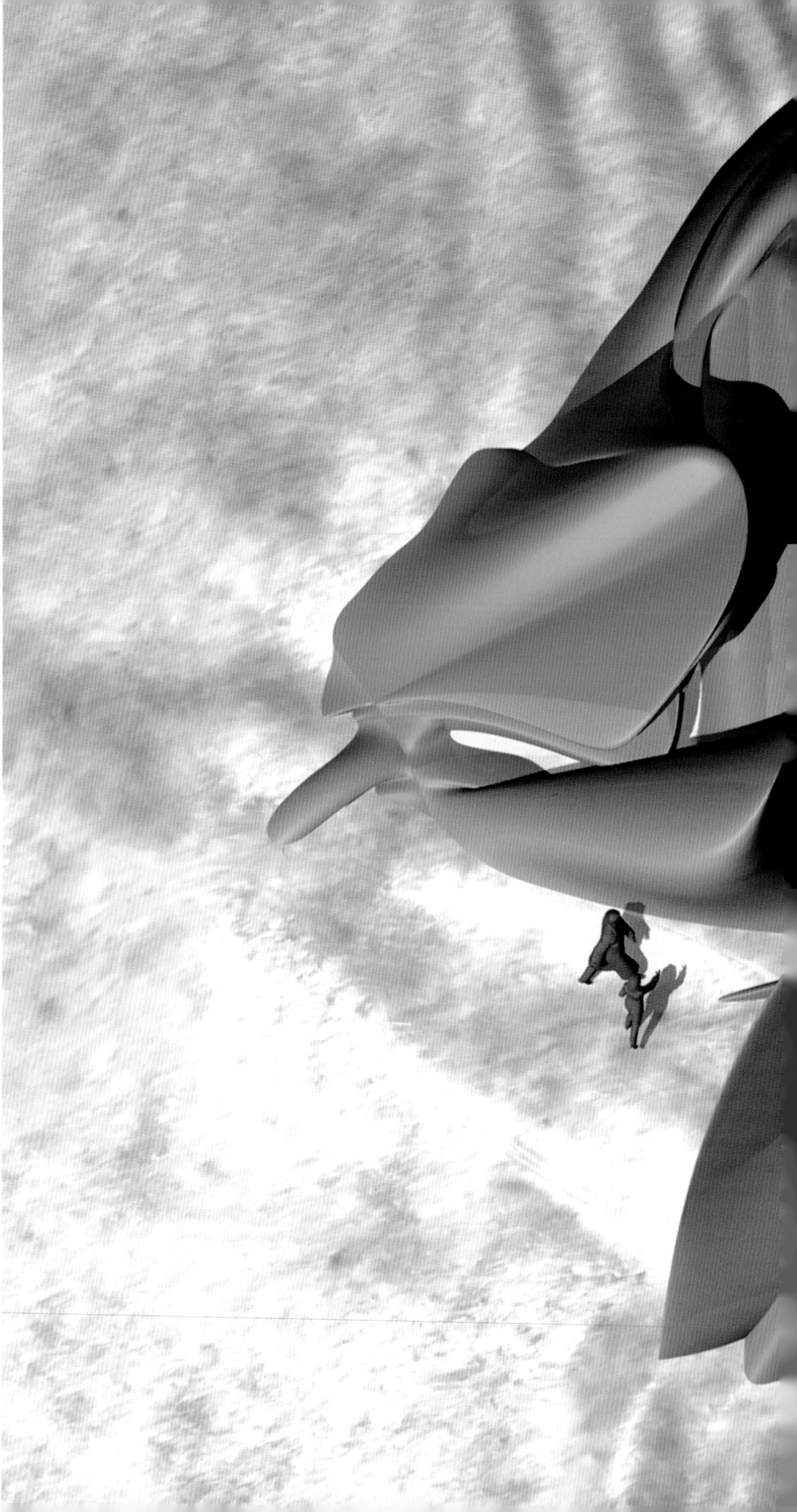

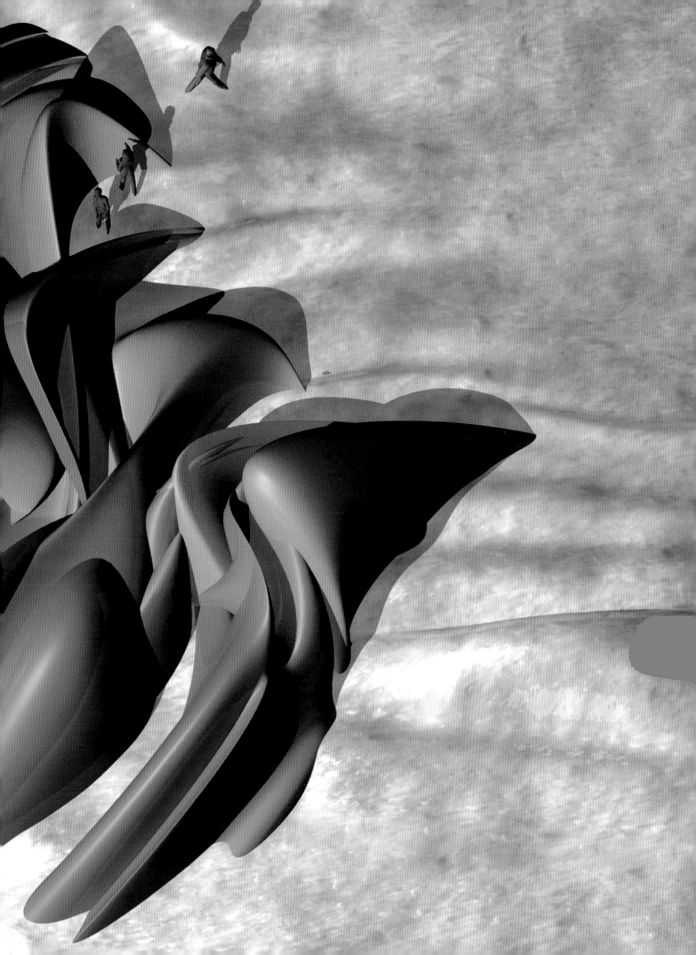

six emotions

light green surface
projection screen

aging

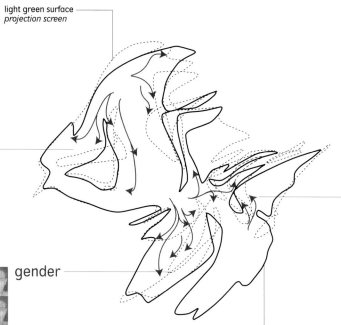

gender

dark green surface
hyperreflective mirror

The Replicator Program processes digital photos of the visitors so that they see themselves transformed. The program morphs men into women, alters the emotional expressions on their faces or changes their age.

Every exhibition should always contain the visitor. In general there are two options for such immersion: landscape and portrait. Perhaps they are interchangeable because psychological exploration of a face equals physical movement in a landscape. Every Western is based on this equation, where hours of plot are contracted into seconds of face close-ups. Involving the body of the visitor, as in H₂Oexpo or wetGRID, leans towards the landscape end of the spectrum. D-tower, with its personal messages, FACES and Tana di Alice are portrait-oriented. It is not by accident that these three are data-base projects creating huge archives, vast landscapes of faces.

p 133
p 172

p 38
p 156

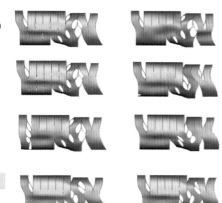

The advantage of studying analogue techniques but applying them digitally (instead of digitizing them later, as with *Soft Office*) is that the configurational aspects of interrelating the figures (here, tearing and branching) can fit much better with a programme, especially a tight one, such as this pop music centre.

FEDUROK

pop music centre CRMA, including two concert halls, a bar, library, sound studios and offices, Nancy, France, 2002

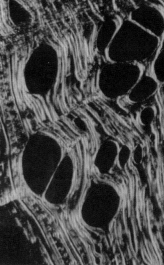

> *How can there be gaps in continuous surfaces? One might expect that in curved surfaces holes have to be cut out later; in our research we have found that it is more logical to have holes and curvature co-emerge with the form. Instead of thinking of holes as subtractions, we consider them as internal edge conditions. The hole need not be an absence but an element that adds structure.*

IL 33 p. 175

The project is a compact structure that contains two main concert halls with technical spaces and offices, as well as a restaurant-bar, library and music studios. The structure is designed as a generic system that tends towards a closed-hangar typology but submits to specifications that open up the volume towards the city and adapt the shape to local differentiation. Instead of making a strange alien spaceship that has just landed, we modulated the urban language of vertical façades, transforming the system only slightly. Where it needed to connect to the adjacent square, these transformations shifted to a more landscaped roof. In this area of Nancy – the city of Jean Prouvé – where the city changes from a stony residential neighbourhood into a steel industrial area, such a strategy is a necessity.

Though the programme is straightforward, there are distinct areas where the programme is more vague and open to transformations. Within the mechanical skeleton of the halls, studios and offices, we inserted zones whose functions vary throughout the day or evening. The bar-restaurant can be changed into a disco in the evening, the disco can be the foyer of the large hall again, the patio can be changed from a dance space into a terrace, the halls can be connected or disconnected by means of mobile partitions.

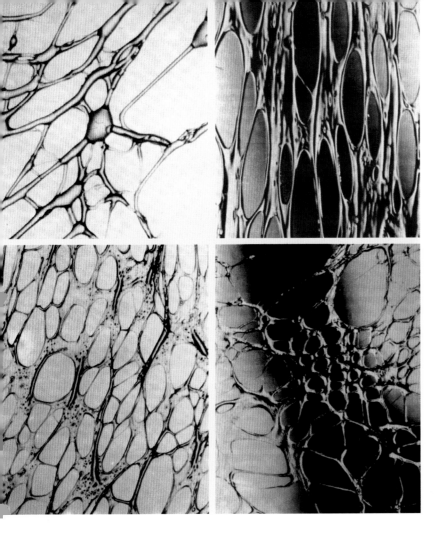

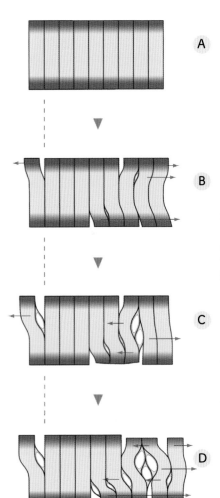

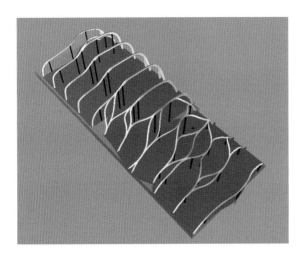

A

B

C

D

We used a system of bands (with the width of three parking places) that functioned as a portal span over the large halls or as a row of rooms connected through a corridor. The tearing procedure follows a number of steps: (A) this system contains the programme without any spaces for social interactions (2400 square metres); (B) the system opens up to the city and allows for connections (2600 square metres); (C) the openings start to affect the activities inside (2800 square metres); and (D) possible internal functions start interacting to create new social spaces, such as clubs and patios (3000 square metres).

The structure of the system is based on portals that span different lengths. While the bands are bent laterally, the portals start bifurcating and weaving into one another. The structure becomes somewhat like a shell — a more porous system that allows for entry of light.

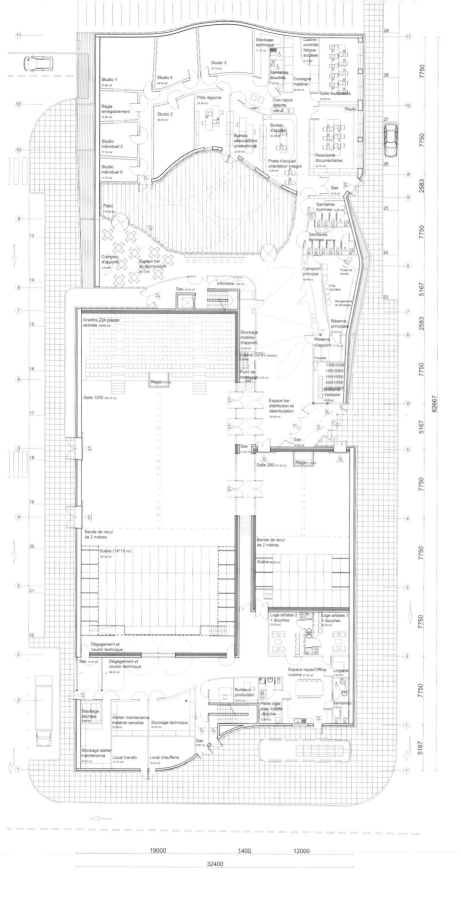

We modulated the band-structure so that it could expand to vertical façades as much as to a horizontal square.

We calibrated the structure to local views from a street, from a corner or from a large open square with trees.

A normal ruled surface (like the one for H$_2$Oexpo, see p. 18) divides both lengths of the different curves over the same number of straight lines, i.e. rulers. The rulers will never be parallel unless, by accident, the curves have the same length. Here, the material itself is made of straight rulers: corrugated steel plates, which means that after the surfaces unfold onto a flat plane, the rules need to run parallel. This special type of ruled surface is called a 'developable surface'. The corrugated sheets would never fit over the roof of H$_2$Oexpo because its geometry consists of non-parallel rulers.

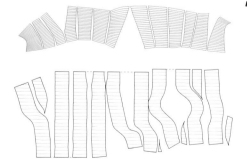

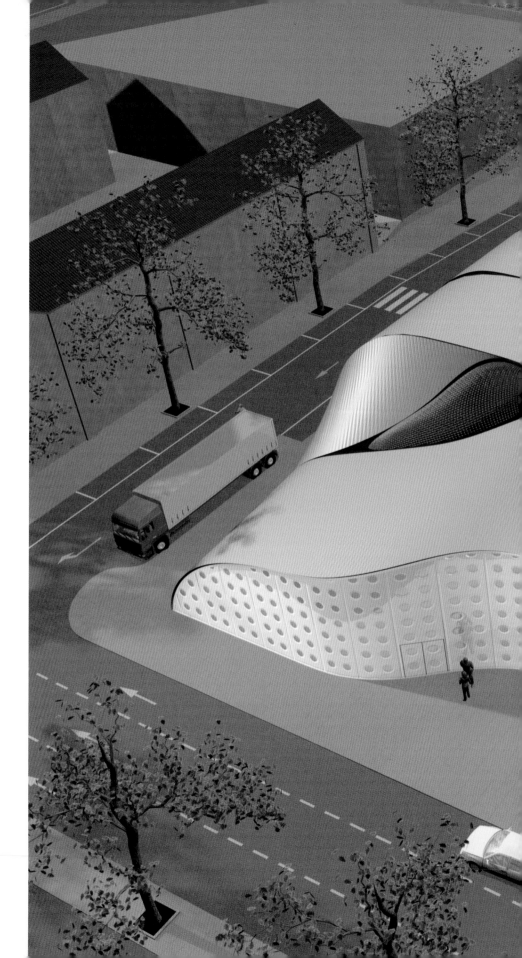

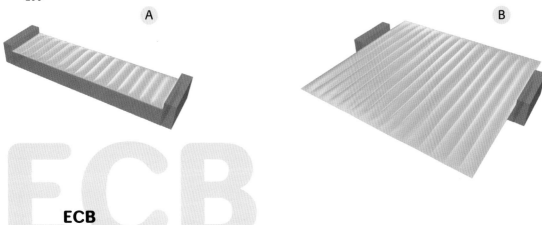

A

B

ECB

European Central Bank, headquarters offices including libraries, restaurants, landscaping, parking and sports facilities, Frankfurt, Germany, 2003

Since creating the design for the new WTC we have become increasingly interested in the use of honeycomb skins: a very powerful tool for structuring double curvature (without resorting to triangulation, which is never structural) that we know from the research of Buckminster Fuller, who only used it for domes and spheres. We can now safely develop it in a more variable direction where geometrical articulation is guided by structural variation.

We developed a design strategy that could absorb the old while extending the old to become new and innovative. Frankfurt's local Grossmarkthalle of the 1920s was to be preserved as a monument. Our design methodology is based on a concept of variable modulation: all architectural types that are needed in this programme (halls, towers, slabs) are made into a family of continuous relations. Our approach was to treat the Grossmarkthalle (A) not just as a building from a bygone period but as a tectonic structure extendible in both directions, north and south, to facilitate a dense programme of office slabs with glass atriums between (B and C). This same structure was then varied in the vertical direction to transform the typology of ribbed vaults into either the curved roof of a large hall (like the sports facilities) or a smooth parabolic tower (D). This type of tower does not require any columns. All loads are transferred downwards through both the tripod core, made up of vertical elevators and diagonal emergency stairs, and structural skin. Along the structure's edge, the skin adapts again to the environment, taking on the shape and height of the residential buildings.

The concept's uniformity is strengthened by the uniformity of the skin: a steel honeycomb structure filled with large glass panels at the outer skin and a second glass skin on the interior, ensuring natural ventilation in between. Adjustable panels between the glass surfaces regulate the flow of the warm and cold air in this shaft, and skin dissolves the traditional distinction between façade and roof. The structural hexagonal skin, based on the famous research

Ernst Haeckel
Radiolaria,
1909

C

D

IL 33

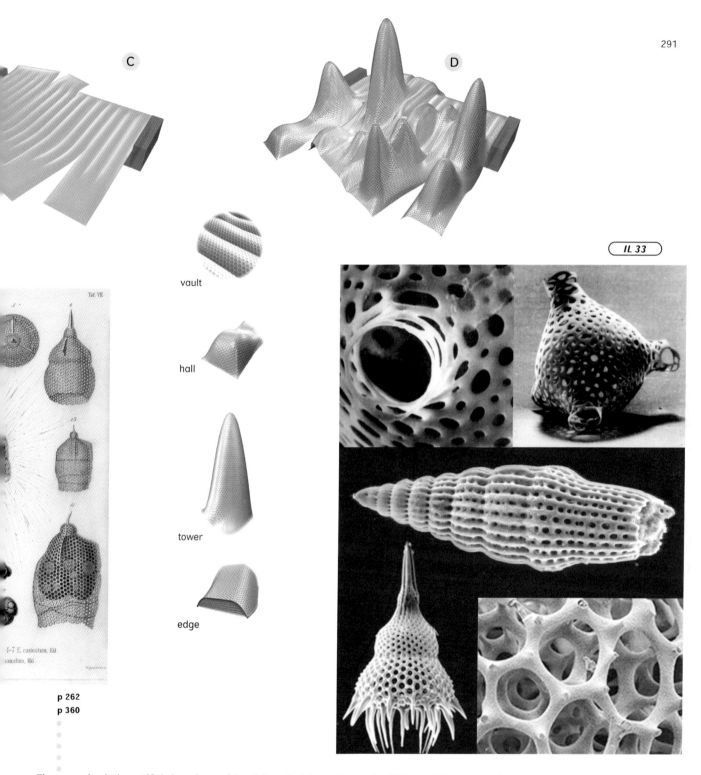

vault

hall

tower

edge

p 262
p 360

The amazingly beautiful drawings of Ernst Haeckel from the early 1900s and the research of Helmcke and Otto throughout the second half of the twentieth century show that Radiolaria (micro-organisms around 0.1 millimetres in size) are of a highly architectural nature. For these German bioconstructivists this is another argument in favour of the idea that a substantial part of the living form is non-genetic in origin. What makes the study of Radiolaria so relevant is that it teaches us that variation is a product of uniformity or, better, isomorphism; and second, that isomorphism is not fatally attracted to the Sphere but is the actual generator of ribs, spikes, creases, tubes and the like. Variation within the system can produce variation of the system (see p. 360, Detlef Mertins, 'Bioconstructivisms').

Tramway station

Main exit

ECP 1

Access to ECB parking

Green belt

Bus/press parking

Main entrance

Logistics parking

ECP 2

Sports parking

Bridge and café

S

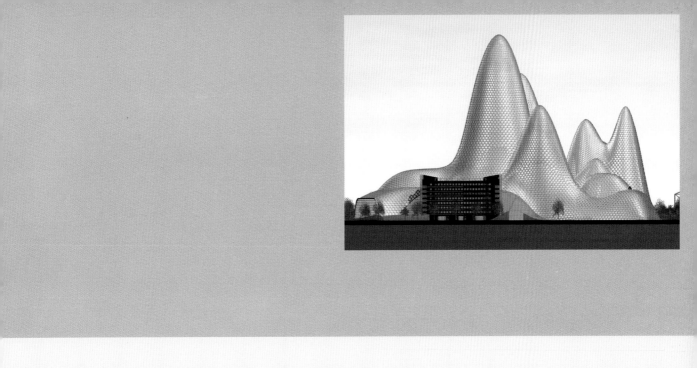

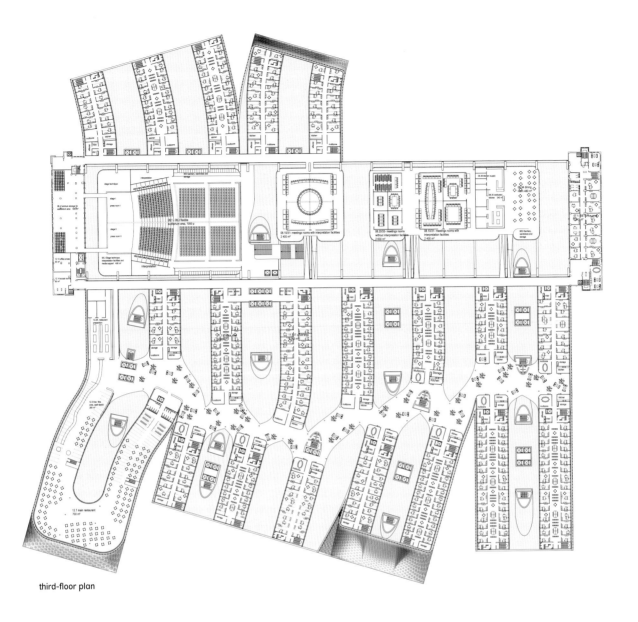

third-floor plan

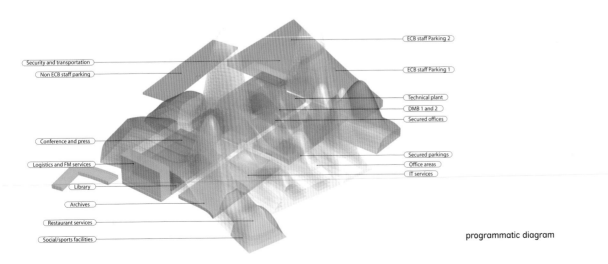

Security and transportation

Non ECB staff parking

Conference and press

Logistics and FM services

Library

Archives

Restaurant services

Social/sports facilities

ECB staff Parking 2

ECB staff Parking 1

Technical plant

DMB 1 and 2

Secured offices

Secured parkings

Office areas

IT services

programmatic diagram

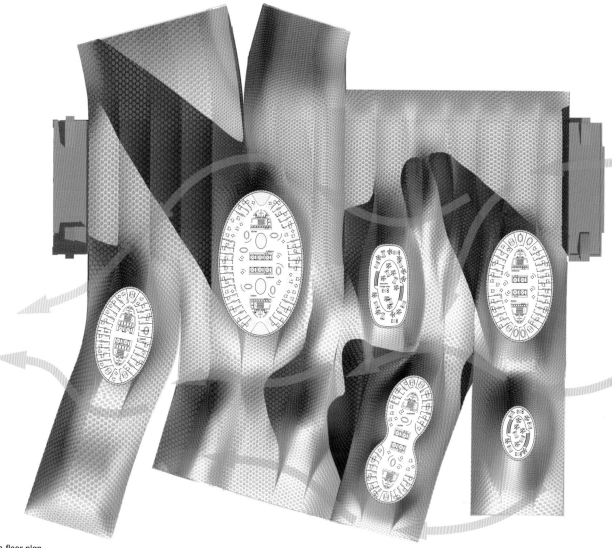

thirteenth-floor plan

The 200,000-square-metre programme accommodates five 'security levels'. The old Grossmarkthalle, almost 250 metres long, contains all the representative functions. Offices are designed in either a strip or tower typology, all bathed in daylight and naturally ventilated. A ribbed structure of combi-offices with tripod cores (straight elevators and diagonal emergency stairs) occupies the open glass atriums between the strips.

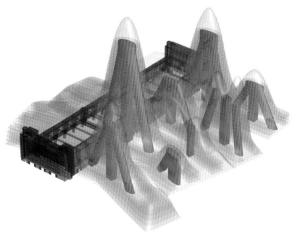

core diagram

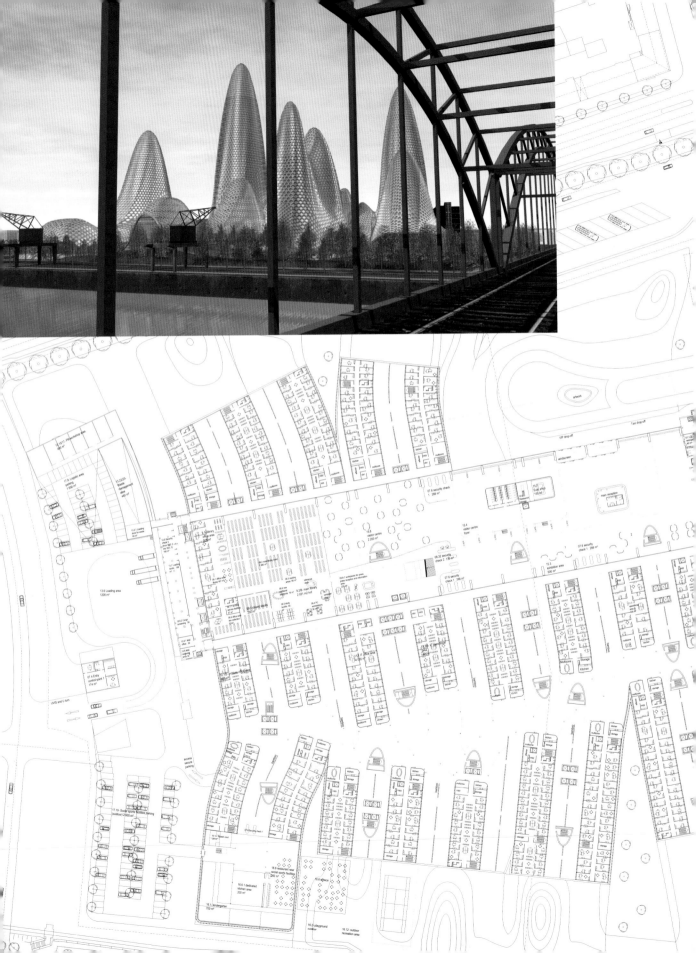

view of the entrance area

ground-floor plan

The new structure is woven into the old Grossmarkthalle (reception area with lobbies, conference and press facilities).

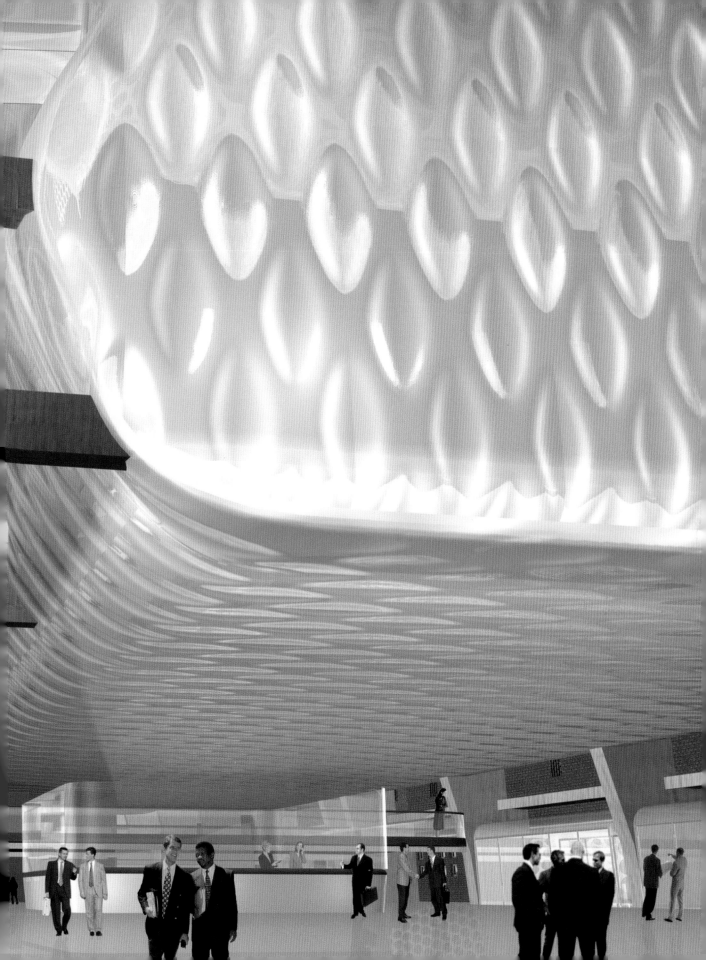

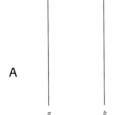
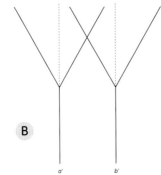
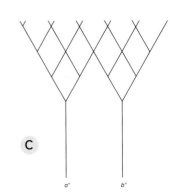

A   B   C

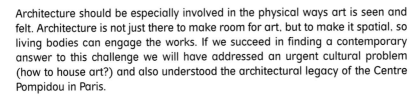

Pompidou Two

a second Centre Pompidou for the City of Metz,
invited competition,
Metz, France, 2003

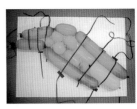

The **Pompidou Two** *presented the opportunity to escape from the futile Bilbao-sculpture-vs.-Tate-garage opposition. 'Architecture as art' or 'no architecture' are evasive answers to the question of how to root art in society, to which the answer should be: through architecture itself.*

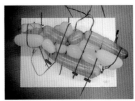

Architecture should be especially involved in the physical ways art is seen and felt. Architecture is not just there to make room for art, but to make it spatial, so living bodies can engage the works. If we succeed in finding a contemporary answer to this challenge we will have addressed an urgent cultural problem (how to house art?) and also understood the architectural legacy of the Centre Pompidou in Paris.

Urbanism

We designed a building that can be recognized worldwide as the new Centre Pompidou in Metz, that shapes the site not only by domination of a singular object on an island but also by guiding the direction of a tunnel towards the south.

The square consists of an undulating landscape, both mineral and green, which absorbs small dispersed events as well as large festivals. To the left of the entry of the CPM we project an 'art window' that draws people into the atmosphere of culture. On the roof of this space people can watch events; the landscape is more articulated where the café has its terrace. The square's boundaries are woven into the existing and projected plans by: a. accepting the eastern slope as a natural boundary; b. projecting a large pavement on the south side with terraces and kiosks to guide the orientation towards the east and the railway bridge; and c. proposing to develop the north side of the site as a fully urban edge instead of a slope to the railway tracks.

Architecture

The most spectacular feature of the architecture is that the higher zone of the *Grande Nef* develops through the building as a diagonal void that distributes diffused daylight from the top and organizes the circulation between all the museum rooms, which are connected by a loop with galleries where visitors will

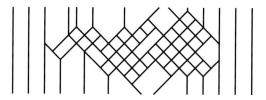

topological unwrapping of green
balloon structure

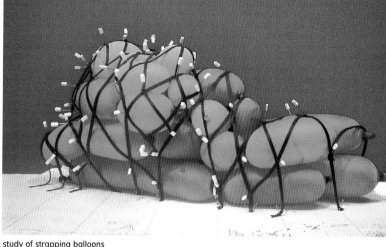

study of strapping balloons

Two

final balloon model

To develop *Pompidou Two* we followed a similar but reverse procedure to *D-tower* (p.158). Instead of working from surface to line we operated from line to surface. We started with a generic *portal* structure where tubular balloons are tied to a board by black straps (A). We twisted the tubes so they could hinge, but to strap these the portals need to bifurcate and branch out (B). The hinged tubes are then broken down into separate spheres that allow the volume to be increased considerably. For this the bifurcated portals split further to form *shells* that prevent the balloons from falling out (C). We now have a portal structure (with its typical hierarchy of primary and secondary elements) that *transforms* into a shell structure (without that hierarchy) to create local *deformations* of volume. Again, a gothic principle *pur sang*.

not miss anything of the exhibition or get lost. These loops are vertically connected by escalators.

When visitors enter the CPM they are given the space to take decisions: black box, café, bookshop, toilets, info desk, auditorium, tickets and *Grande Nef* are presented in an architectural articulation on the urban platform of the Forum. We distributed the crowd as comfortably as possible so visitors do not overlap and all programmatic elements can develop without disturbing others. This fan-shaped scheme is connected to a more utilitarian wing that contains the art reception and offices and respects the functional requirements of a modern museum.

Instead of making all the exhibition spaces into boxes with impossible corners where one cannot hang any artworks, we based the rooms on rounded geometries that allow for curatorial continuity, where sculptures and installations are as comfortable as paintings. All the light enters through a translucent ceiling where daylight is mixed with artificial light that can be regulated by sensors. The rooms are all alike but no two are the same: there is a continuous and slight modulation of all spatial effects that makes the rooms suitable for many purposes without resorting to the neutrality of dead boxes.

The building on top is almost twice as wide as below, which makes the external appearance of its entry (standing under an 11-metre overhang), the internal void and marks an easily identifiable building. On the highest level we have a terrace, a kitchen and, in a dome-like space flooded with daylight, a restaurant affording a superb view over the city.

To digitize the balloon-technique we needed a special kind of surface geometry. Generally, one works either with polygons (segmented facets, like boxes or crystals) or NURBS surfaces that are continuous. Here we used *subdivision surfaces* that have properties of both: a NURBS balloon can change with one mouse click into a creased box.

Structure

All architectural invention in this building proceeds through structural operations. While the volume transforms towards the upper middle area, the steel portals split up increasingly and weave into a shell-surface that allows in the diffused daylight, a structural transformation that guides the shift from opaque to translucent — including small transparent openings giving incidental views over the city and the *parvis*.

The structural logic is a design instrument with potential to vary between opaque and translucent, between single-curved and double-curved, or between standard and non-standard building elements. The standard building elements are all straight, flat and industrially manufactured (making up two-thirds of the exterior surface), while non-standard elements are half-products, such as epoxy, that are shaped through numerical machining techniques. Thus we have a worthy successor to the first Centre Pompidou and a museum where technology has obtained the undeniable profile of culture and cultural progression that places art back in the heart of society.

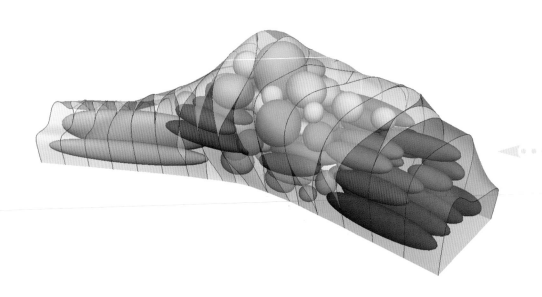

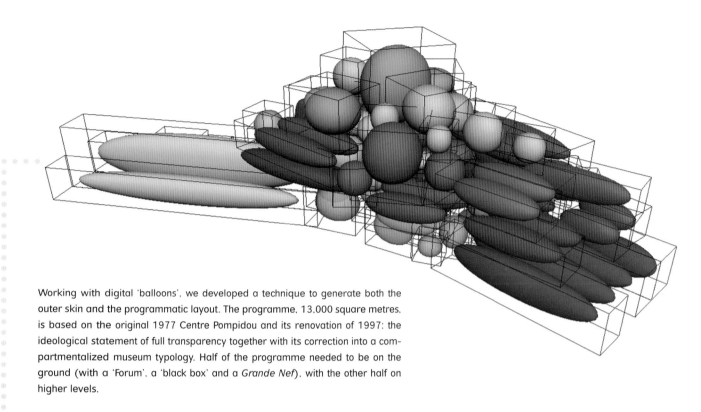

Working with digital 'balloons', we developed a technique to generate both the outer skin and the programmatic layout. The programme, 13,000 square metres, is based on the original 1977 Centre Pompidou and its renovation of 1997: the ideological statement of full transparency together with its correction into a compartmentalized museum typology. Half of the programme needed to be on the ground (with a 'Forum', a 'black box' and a *Grande Nef*), with the other half on higher levels.

For the development of the programme we translated the analogue technique into digital scripts. All scripts were based on translating deformations of a portal structure as transformations into shells.

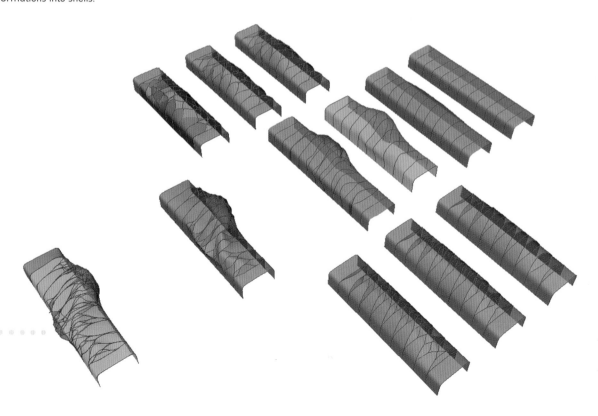

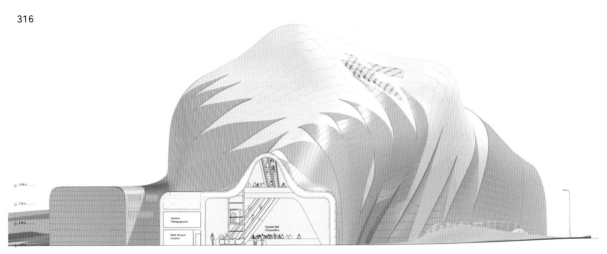

section A. cutting over the *Grande Nef*

view into the Forum area

view into the Forum area from the interior terrace

view from the top exhibition level down into the Forum

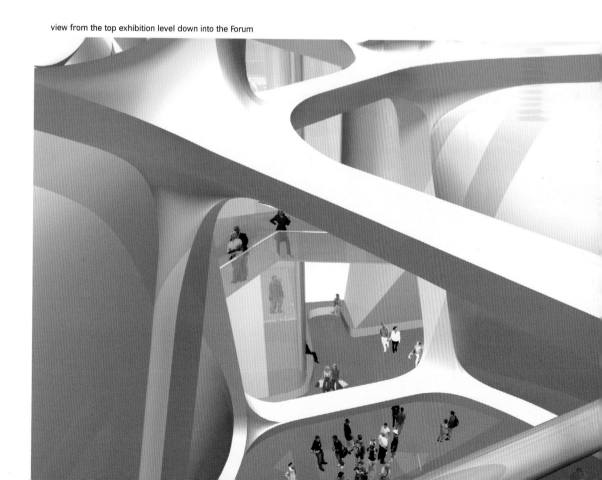

section B. cutting over the entry area

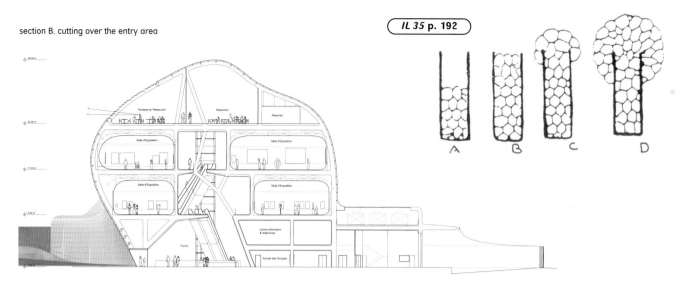

IL 35 p. 192

If the system were generated by round balloons only — with packing — one could make all the upper floors into an integrated system. Here there is a bit too much stacking (packing creates a lot of diagonals that compromise wheelchair accessibility), but potentially it is possible to span a huge void with solid foam.

view from the rue des Messageries

section C

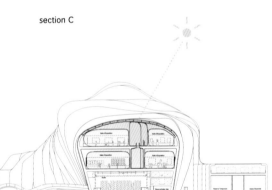

The strapping-balloons technique produces a system of double skins, for the interior volumes and the exterior volume as a whole. This creates a pocket that makes room for air-conditioning and daylight access, complemented by artificial light. Rooms are covered with white materials, translucent or reflective – the light refracts in all directions to become diffused.

Building Experience
The Architecture of Perception

Brian Massumi

1. Interview with Lars Spuybroek. Arjen Mulder and Maaike Post, eds. *Book for the Electronic Arts* (Rotterdam: V2_Organisation/de Balie, 2000).

Postponing the Image

For me the main question was: can I make the content of the paintings, the perception of them, be the architecture itself? – Lars Spuybroek[1]

In the *wetGRID* design for the Musée des Beaux-Arts in Nantes (1999–2000) Lars Spuybroek sought to extend the architectural programme of the exhibit into a meta-architectural exploration of the interconnection between perception and construction. The goal was to build the exhibit's theme by making a literal 'Vision Machine' that effectively fed the content of the photographs and paintings on display into the experience of the installation space. This was no metaphor. The aim was for the experience of the art and the experience of the building to be brought into active proximity with each other. For this to happen, a shared ground, on which there was already an implicit entwining, would have to be extracted from both sides and brought into view. It was immediately clear that this would be a 'ground' that is not a ground, and a more-than-optical 'view'.

There is no doubt in Spuybroek's mind as to where this shared ground is to be found: in movement. This may seem paradoxical at first, since movement is the last thing we normally think of as the content of still images. Naïvely, we think of the visual content of the image as representations of the form of objects. Many of us have been schooled to think beyond this common-sense approach to see the content as the acquired cultural codes enabling us to recognize arrays of paint or chemical pigments as referencing objective forms. Neither of these approaches to image-content works in this connection. Both impose an alien becoming on architecture. To meet painting and photography in representation, architecture would have to become pictorial (suggesting a centrality of decoration). To meet them in cultural coding, it would have to become language-like (suggesting a centrality of message decoding). Although this latter route was widely followed in late twentieth-century architecture, it backgrounds the undeniable role of construction as a spacing (timing, channelling, filtering) of embodied movement. Movement, not message, is the actual content of architecture. Acknowledging this, however, would seem to oblige the still image to become diametrically other than it is: moving. To work a way out of the predicament

BUILDING

a zone of proximity needs to be found where image meets architecture and where neither ceases to be itself.

Spuybroek suggests that common ground is *potential* movement. Potential movement is 'abstracted into' the architecture, he says, 'and that abstract movement loops back and relates again to people's movement'.[2] Potentials for movement are extracted from actual movement, then fed back into it via architecture. We normally think of abstraction as a distancing *from* the actual, but here potentials are being 'abstracted *into* it'. This means that elements are built into the design that trigger the movement actually under way into a state of overlap with changes in its register, with possible continuations, or with alternatives to itself. If potential movement could similarly be extracted from the still image content and hooked on the same architectural triggers, then not only would actual movement in the building overlap with potential movements, but the potentials of architecture would overlap with those of painting and photography. The clarity of the actual movements under way would be shadowed by a vagueness of what they could be, at the abstract intersection of building content and image content.

To achieve this, it is necessary to 'postpone the image'[3]: to suspend the recognition or decoding of a finally and fully determinate content by building potentializing hesitations into the predictable channelling of movement through the building.

2. Lars Spuybroek. 'Architecture of Interaction: "An Informational Form".' Interview with Im Sik Cho. *ANC (Architecture and Culture)* (no. 244, September 2001): 111.

3. Lars Spuybroek. 'Machining Architecture.' *The Weight of the Image* (Rotterdam: NAI Publishers, 2001): n.p.

Tending Perception

Our agenda should be to short-circuit action, perception and construction. – Lars Spuybroek[4]

4. See p. 358. Lars Spuybroek. 'The Structure of Vagueness'.

Take a seat, lean back, stop fidgeting. Short-circuit action. Purge your thoughts of the daily course, things done and to do. Attend to the peripheries of your vision as much as to its centre of focus. After a moment, from the heart of the visual stillness, you will start to feel a faint commotion, a hint of a pull. It is as if you were being drawn out of your recliner into the centre of your visual field. The centre is no longer a simple optical focus. It has become an attractive force. That is because the periphery is not a distinct boundary. It is cloudy ring-around: a 360-degree horizon where your vision fades into indistinctness in all directions. The peripheral fade-out gives a strange tunnel-like feel to the whole of the visual field, which funnels you towards the centre with a feeling of slight vertigo. If you try to shake the feeling by moving your head, say to the right, the effect is only heightened by the ski-jump of your nose suddenly leaping into view, no longer in its anatomically middle position, but as a promontory protruding from the peripheral vagueness and unshakeably suggesting a slalom down your legs, the only clearly visible part of your mostly occluded body. The funnel effect is also heightened by the beams of the ceiling and the pattern of the floor tiling, both of which converge towards the window to which the feet at the far end of your legs are also pointing arest their ottoman. Out the window, a path leads from your up-ended toes towards a vanishing point at the earth's horizon. The centre of visual attraction is where your feet, the window-sill and the path meet, connecting the periphery of your field to the vanishing point at its centre. The toe-point connects two horizons of different orders, the lateral horizon of the earth and circumference of your visual field, in a continuous sweep running across your incompletely appearing body through the geometry of the room. The toe—window—path convergence is an invitation to stroll. It visibly suggests a potential

James J. Gibson. *The Ecological Approach to Visual Perception* (1986): 119.

XPERIENCE

transition from the slalom of stillness into which your reclining thoughts stirred you, to a calming walk through the garden.

The garden path is what James J. Gibson calls an 'affordance'.[5] An affordance is a possibility of convergence that unconsciously exerts a pull, drawing the body forward into a movement the body already feels itself performing before it actually stirs. When it does stir, it relays between sense modes in a habitual fashion, recognizing itself in the renewal of the familiar relay, which in turn locates it along a path marked by an ordered sequence of further affordances. Each affordance governs a tendency drawing the body forward, away from where it is, further down a familiar path presenting an ordered unfolding of the variety of its experiential modalities.

The entire sequence is pre-felt, more or less vaguely, in the stirring of the tendency. A view of the garden is the already-feeling of the soles of the feet relaying from the sight of the path into tactile contact with it. It is the intervening proprioceptive pre-feeling of the flexing of the muscles and joints. It is the kinaesthetic presentiment of the flow of your body past the flowers. It is the succession of anticipated relays into pleasant new sights, which for now, from the recliner, remain occluded by the window frames and in the path. There is a familiar function to be fulfilled by the stroll down the path. That function, stress-relief, can be fulfilled in advance simply by the presentiment of it. The variety of sensings that would relay in the actual movement of the walk are already included, in germinal form, in the seated suggestion of the movement triggered by an errant glance out the window. It was the pull of their pre-inclusion, their already stirring without yet actually coming about, that made an event of that simple sitting. Sitting still is the performance of a tendency towards movement. The tendency is already a movement, without the actual movement. And it is already a sign of the fulfilment of the conventional function, without the actual fulfilment. It is the pre-performance, in potential, of the movement and its function. In potential, the movement is already in the world without yet having extended itself along its actual path. It is in intensity.

The important thing to keep in mind is that the tendency to respond determines the perception. – Lloyd Kaufman[6]

If the tendency to respond determines the perception, then holding back the response while holding onto the tendency postpones perception. The image fails to advance into its own determinateness. Its perception and the action it governs are short-circuited, held, incipiently, in their own potential. The pre-feeling of the affordances and their sequencing continues indeterminately, in intensity.

One of the ways this postponement can be achieved is by gesturing to perspective with intimations of depth while at the same time undermining its full deployment. The undermining can be achieved by bringing two of the fundamental structuring elements of the field of vision into resonance. The periphery of vision and the vanishing point can be abstractly connected, across the actual content of the image. In the recliner, this contact between the circumference of the field of vision and its central vanishing point was already established by the draw exerted by the toe–window–path convergence. Its attractive force animated the visual field with an inward activity: a funnel-effect dizzying down the nose and sweeping along the legs. This immanent activity is itself an experience of potential movement, connected to but distinct from the sequencing of anticipated garden-path variety affordances, and supplementary to the object recognition, decoding and function fulfilment associated with them. It is abstract in the sense that it corresponds to no actual

5. James J. Gibson. *The Ecological Approach to Visual Perception* (Hillsdale, NJ: Lawrence Erlbaum, 1979): 127–43.

Ernst Mach. *The Field of Vision*.(1886): 14.

6. Lloyd Kaufman. *Perception: The World Transformed* (New York, NY: Oxford University Press, 1979): 378.

BUILDING

features of the image. It is contained in the image, but is not its content. The periphery of vision and the vanishing point are poles determining an abstract, vortical, potential movement affecting the field of vision in its entirety. The ease with which they tend to join belies the stability that the field of vision exhibits when it is functioning on the familiar ground of content recognition and decoding.

The potential movement enveloped in the vanishing point towards which the toe–window–path convergence gestured has already been described. This potential movement is comforting to the extent that it brings a presentiment of the fulfilment of the soothing function of the stroll, and is attached to more or less predictable content. But it is destabilizing inasmuch as it betokens infinite continuation beyond fulfilment of that function and any particularizable content. At the limit, it extends into a smudged array of potential inter-sense relays receding indistinctly to an infinitesimal scale beyond any actual perception's powers of resolution.

The periphery of vision can also be destabilizing when it ceases to function as a framing of the field of vision and instead betokens a completion never reached. For it promises, at the mere turn of the head or a swivel of the body, a filling-in of the field of vision, whose partiality can be disturbing. But with each movement seeking its completion, the periphery and the partiality return. They persist as a draw from vision into kinesthesia and proprioception, turn and swivel. Vision is not in fact framed. At its edge lies a 360-degree horizon of potential movement, into which it is constantly advancing. But as it advances, it succeeds only in displacing this moving limit. Vision never reaches the limit – or is always already at it, in its tendency to reach beyond itself.

Vertigo is experienced when the circumferential fringe of vision swirls in on the perspectival vanishing point in a vortex of potential experience, like turbulent water around a drain. The lateral horizon towards which the vanishing point recedes, and which grounds experience on the gravitational plane of the earth, rotates chaotically with the vortex, destabilizing not only the body's station but its relation to any vertical elevation rising perpendicular to the ground.

Drawing showing the distortion of the body image. Oliver Sacks. *Migraine* (London: Faber & Faber, repr. 1995). From the British Migraine Association.

Dizziness is intensely disorienting because it is never just an experience of vertigo, but always also a vertigo of experience: a vortex sweeping away the stability of experience's very structuring and the repeatability of its recognizable functions. Even the most genteel vertigo affecting the most domestic visual field radically ungrounds the ground of experience. The variety of other-sense potential that it sweeps in from the fringe, and towards which it centrally drains, forbids reducing vision to its manifestly optical content (especially when vision is trained on the multisensory body itself).

The body-image is never a complete structure; it is never static; there are always disrupting tendencies. – Paul Schilder[7]

7. Paul Schilder. *The Image and Appearance of the Human Body* (New York: International Universities Press, 1950): 287.

Even the most smoothly strolling of experiences contains a minimal degree of vertigo. Each relay from vision to an other-sense experience such as touch or proprioception carries vision across its functional limit. This necessarily occurs at every step along any line of actual movement. When vision makes the transition, vision must be marked, however slightly, by the turbulence of passing its limit, or of its limit passing into it. There is a micro-vertigo immanent to the interconnection of the senses that accompanies all movement. Vertigo, then, is not qualitatively different from the potential for actual movement. The actualization of potential movement is a vertigo of experience, by the same token as vertigo is the experience of potential movement.

XPERIENCE

Given a number of dimensions of feeling, all possible varieties are obtainable by varying the intensities of the different elements. Accordingly, time logically supposes a continuous range of intensity in feeling. It follows, then, ... that when any particular kind of feeling is present, an infinitesimal continuation of all feelings differing infinitesimally from that is present. – C. S. Peirce[8]

8. C. S. Peirce. Nathan Houser and Christian Kloesel. eds. *The Essential Peirce: Selected Philosophical Writings* (Bloomington: University of Indiana Press. vol. 1. 1992): 323–24.

Experience always gives a number of dimensions of feeling. And it always presupposes time, in the indefinite continuation at its centre and the deferred completion at its periphery. All possible varieties of experience inhabit every vision, enveloped in movements whose actualization would take time but whose variety is already intensely present in potential. All possibilities of feeling are obtainable by varying the intensities of the different elements. This means, for example, that the degree to which the vertigo of potential movement is experienced in a built environment can be varied by varying the nature, strength or frequency of the visual cues for such things as distance, station, direction, framing and perspective that are made available for recognition and de-coding, and through the nature and allure of available affordances for familiar function. Construction can short-circuit action and perception, in the sense of feeding them into each other on the level of their potential (un)grounding. They can be extracted or abstracted from their content in such a way that their immanent activity and the movement of their potential are vertiginously abstracted *into* architecture.

Surface Depth

In *wetGRID*, Spuybroek went straight to the nub of the issue: vertigo. His strategy was to build degrees of vertigo into the experience of the exhibit in a way that connected the content of the architecture – the visitors' actual moving through – with the content of the paintings by making them meet in a common element of abstracted potential movement.

To build in vertigo as potential movement it was necessary to build out shadow, perspective and horizon, and to re-tool framing. Framing as normally used in art and architecture neutralizes the danger of the periphery by replacing its indefinite fringing with an unambiguous boundary that divides inside (content) from outside (context), forbidding the destabilization of a turbulent flow that would intermix their potentials. The horizon founds tectonics by grounding action on a perceptual plane parallel to that of the earth, in rectilinear contrast to station and vertical elevation, often consid-ered the essential dimension of architecture, whose nature is then to uplift through resistance to the force of gravity. Rather than privileging rigidifying forces of material resistance, Spuybroek seeks a 'liquid' architecture (un)grounded on potentializing forces of lived variation, abstractingly immanent to both perception and action in their constructed interconnection. He wants to build buildings in a way that is a rebuilding of experience, rather than the simple erection of a tectonic structure. Although per-spective, for its part, harbours at its centre the potential perceptual danger of the vanishing point's infinitesimal recession, it neutralizes this danger by focusing on the predictable middle distance, where one step distinctly follows the next, from one rec-ognizable object to another, the intersense relays between passifyingly yoked to familiar functions. Shadow goes hand in hand with perspective. The occlusions that shadow presupposes imply an ordering of objects in a distinct succession along a navigable perspective line receding controllably into a middle distance. Shadow presents perspectival depth, whether or not a vanishing point is manifestly operative.

Frantisek Kupka. *Conte de pistils et d'étamines* (1919–20). In the exhibition 'Vision Machine'.

BUILDING

To sidestep these conventional architectural limitations, in the design for the 'Vision Machine' exhibit Spuybroek avoided any hint of shadow and any right angles between the horizontal and the vertical planes. This divested perception of the possibility of orienting itself according to perspective, and rendered unfamiliar the culturally encoded function of the gallery space. Visitors to art galleries are accustomed to strolling on the horizontal plane of the floor and seeing on the vertical plane of the wall, on which the pictures are hung and against which they are framed. The sequential hanging on the same plane of distinctly separated, framed images governs an ordered movement of the feet in the service of the studied eye's progression through the content of the show.

In the absence of right angles between the horizontal and vertical planes of construction, it becomes uncertain where the floor ends and where the wall begins. Their sharp distinction is replaced by a continuous curve, setting the construction on the oblique. The lean of the construction makes for a lack of shadow, which in turn prevents perspectival depth. The curvilinear, semi-translucent tunnels composing the installation still clearly occupy volume. But the geometry of the volume is not graspable at a glance. It is all continuous surface, folding in and away, invaginating and exfoliating. The foldings offer a kind of surface depth, without perspective. Upon entering the gallery, it is not at first apparent whether a given portion of the surface volume is offering an affordance for feet or for eyes, or what kind of progression along the surface, into the depth of the exhibit, is being afforded. Visual perception and the action of walking enter into a disorienting zone of indistinction. They dizzyingly loop into each other, sorting themselves out over the duration only as the visitor hesitantly moves around the installation. Even after exploration, at every bend they threaten to fall back into intermixing. To gain purchase, the eyes must follow the feet, themselves assisted by the occasional touch against the structure and an unaccustomed attention to the proprioception assisting balance and posture in the unfamiliar surrounds. Different sense perceptions fold into and out of each other, as perception folds into and out of exploratory action. The threat of vertigo taking hold gives pause in each advance through the installation's experience. In that hesitation, the sense-modes are suspended in potential relay. There is an indecision as to which relay will actualize next, and whether its actualization will land with enough purchase to determine a next action. In the same hesitation, perception and action come together in constructed postponement.

What emanates from the body and what emanates from architectural surrounds intermixes. – Gins and Arakawa[9]

9. M. Gins and S. Arakawa. *Architectural Body* (Tuscaloosa: University of Alabama Press, 2002): 66.

The construction has succeeded in building in a mutual abstraction of the modes of perception, and of perception and action, in such a way that they loop into each other, meeting in their potential relays. The experience of the exhibition has been effectively placed on a vertiginous common ground of potential movement that is as much in abstraction of any particular mode of perception as it is in abstraction of any actually determinate action – all the while doublng the effective unfolding of both. The building has in fact managed to extract a common element from its lived content, in a way that enables it to loop into the still-image content of the paintings and photographs on display.

The content of many of the images is itself abstract or wilfully vertiginous, sometimes to an hallucinatory extreme. This match between the content and the context is not a mirroring or coded reflection of what lies outside the frame.

328

10. Lars Spuybroek. Interview with Arielle Pelenc in the catalogue to the exhibition 'Vision Machine'.

11. Bernard Cache. Anne Boyman. trans. *Earth Moves: The Furnishing of Territories* (Cambridge, MA: MIT Press, 1995): 109.

There is no clear distinction between inner and outer orientation ... they are integrated into one system. – Lars Spuybroek[10]

The frames of the images in the exhibit do not separate the images from their built surround. They connect them to it. Bernard Cache reminds us that a kite is a frame.[11] A kite is not separate from its turbulent milieu. It is responsive to it. It is dynamically connected to it in that it receives and visibly expresses the forces moving through it. The images toss in the turbulence of the installation's experience like kites in stormy skies, hanging, seemingly precariously, at odd and oblique angles from the curved architectural surface of uncertain definition, wall–floor. They respond to, receive and visibly express the force of the architecturally abstracted potential movement on which they toss. They offer a floating affordance, or 'landing site' in Gins and Arakawa's vocabulary, not for repeat function fuelled by habitual object-recognition, but for the architecturally induced vertigo of movement's potentializing abstraction from these. Not reflections or representations of their surrounds, they are operative analogues of the process unfolding in the built environment, into which it cumulatively feeds forward, adding itself to the properly artistic process of abstraction already at work in the frame. Transmitted into the art, other-sense movements are even more thoroughly held in potential. Only optical experience can actualize itself on the ungrounded landing site offered by the image. The non-visual senses remain potentialized, but their readiness to land, to actualize in a next relay, is radically short-circuited. The harder they press, the more deeply they are held in potential. They cannot not continue to be felt, but only in the vision, wholly invested in sight, divested of any shred of their own actuality. Other-sense potential movement is packed into opticality. Vision becomes intensely imbued with the 'infinitesimal continuation' of the non-visual senses.

The Vision Machine is the coupling of a certain architectural ungrounding with a turbulence-sensitive artistic framing that transmits the force of non-visual senses into purely optical experience, making it visible in a vertigo of potential movement at amplified intensity.

Building Experience

The exhibition architecture is literally a machine and, like all machines, has been engineered and constructed. The perceptual processes described above have been 'abstracted in' to construction during the design process, long before bodies have been in actual movement through the installation-to-come and there were wall–floors for paintings to hang on. The design would have to have the ability to address bodies on the level of their potential movement, that is, below the level of object recognition, familiar function, and cultural decoding (even if all of these must necessarily continue to operate at least sporadically or 'postponed', suspended in their incipiency). This means connecting to them on the level of force. The force would have to be at once deforming (able to separate bodies from the habitual form of their experience), transformative (converting actual movement into potential movement) and transitive (capable of being abstracted into the architecture and from there of moving into the picture frame to merge with the deforming and transformative forces native to painting and photography). In a word (Simondon's), the force would have to be transductive.[12]

12. Gilbert Simondon. *L'Individu et sa genèse physico-biologique* (Grenoble, France: Million, 1995): 29–34.

In this project, Spuybroek's approach was to make the design process itself a series of transductive steps, which can then transfer directly, machinically, to the final

construction. He began by programming abstract forces of deformation on the computer. Control vertices were connected to flat strips of simulated rubber, at their edges. The vertices were then connected to each other by strings, with virtual springs attached to the intersections of the threads. A force of rotation applied to the springs would transmit a vortical force to the attached strips, which would continuously deform into an undulation in which concave curves would appear. At places, the strips would come together to suggest a fusion into a more extended concavity, or they would split apart. The concavities, having elevation, were taken as proto-interiorities and the splits as proto-openings. This proto-architectural effect of the application of vortical force was then materialized in a model made of paper strips mapping the computer simulation. A small number of rules was applied to further the transformation in the same direction it was already taking. These manual 'algorithms' involved placing paper clips at certain strategic points to connect the paper strips in such a way as to augment the concavities and openings, taking a step further on their way to becoming (somewhat peculiar) architectural elements (non-standard rooms and entrances). The vortical effect was thus amplified and transmitted to a new material, in which it prepared the way for an analogous transformation taking further the process begun in the material of departure. The vortex was transduced. The paper model was then returned to the computer, in order to be rematerialized in a third transductive step that would take the vortical emergence of architectural form into the actual building. The model was digitized and its surface was cross-sectioned top to bottom. Segments of the cross-sections were selected to form a skeleton, then milled in wood by computer-controlled machinery. The pieces of the wood were then joined by semi-translucent cotton fabric to re-establish the continuous undulations of the curvilinear surface.

In the transduction to wood, the proto-architectural form gained the ability to be self-supporting. It could now stand as architecture. But its resistance to the force of gravity was not the motor of its design. It was an emergent property of a transmitted transformative force–effect, as were the non-standard architectural elements that finally took form. Because of this, the final structure was defined more by the imprint it bore of the nature of the abstract originating force than by any conventional architectural coding. The vortical nature of that originating force meant that the form that finally emerged across the series of transductive steps was undulatory. It had no corners between walls or between wall and floor, no edges to occlude and cast shadow, no linear vanishing points to anchor perspective. An architecturally habituated body entering it could not but feel a certain vertigo. The abstract force of the programmed vortex had been effectively transduced into embodied vertigo. It had jumped from the computer, through paper, wood and fabric, to the architecturally contained, art-enjoying human body. A common ground had indeed been found where architectural and artistic perception, action and construction dynamically meet. Potential movement had advanced all along the transductive line to find visible expression in an experience of anomalously framed viewing.

Not Determinately Nothing

Spuybroek does not design form. He guides a form-taking process that moves abstract forces through a series of transformations towards architectural embodiment. The resulting structure is a built expression of the nature of the force, whose transduced imprint it continues to bear. It also bears the abstractness of the force of departure and the flexibility of the intermediary materials through which the force

passes. The abstractness and flexibility persist as a vagueness in the structure, preventing too determinate an object identity from being pinned to it. For example, the walls of the Nantes exhibit are not formally distinguished from the floor. The columns produced by the skeletal wood sections are not processually separate from the wall. The curvaceousness of the overall form is enfolding rather than enclosing, leaving an indecision between interior and exterior. The structure is not codifiable as a traditional architectural form. But it retains an unmistakable quality of buildingness by virtue of the fact that it has been constructed, is free-standing and is at a scale at which a human body can be moved through it and be contained by it. The installation is a proto-architectural form non-standardly occupying a generic architectural place.

I materialize many undefined things. – Lars Spuybroek[13]

13. Interview with Lars Spuybroek. Arjen Mulder and Maaike Post, eds. *Book for the Electronic Arts* (Rotterdam: V2_Organisation/de Balie, 2000).

The relatively undefined nature of the final form is a derivative of the openness of its process of emergence, which was an experimental playing out of the effects of a force through successive transformations and material transfers. The playing-out of force-effects that drives the design is also a transitive thinking-through of the potential movements they carry in seed and can disseminate. The algorithms applied to the paper model make it a literal analogue computer, akin to Gaudí's Sagrada Familia suspended chain studies. The thought elaborated by the process is how to continue the experimental openness of the transductive design into the experience of the building.

Tentativeness: feeling and thinking combined. – Gins and Arakawa[14]

14. M. Gins and S. Arakawa. *Architectural Body* (Tuscaloosa: University of Alabama Press, 2002): 82.

The vagueness Spuybroek's process materially thinks through in order to build in is not a simple lack. It is the dynamic presence of Peirce's 'continuous range of intensity' in transductive thought/feeling. Although it hinges on suspending habitual action and inculcated decoding to 'postpone' the image in potential movement, it is not, for all of that, determinately nothing. It is the incipience of a something transductively to come.

> *Potential means indeterminate yet capable of determination. ... The vague always tends to become determinate, simply because its vagueness does not determine it to be vague. ... It is not determinately nothing.* – C. S. Peirce[15]

15. C. S. Peirce. Peirce Edition Project. ed. *The Essential Peirce: Selected Philosophical Writings* (Bloomington: University of Indiana Press, vol. 2, 1998): 323–24.

Determined to Be Determined

In every vagueness there is a tendency to become something determinate. In other words, vagueness is the sign of a potential movement towards definite form-taking. The vague is a positive state of intensive activity enveloping all possible varieties of experience. The tendency to take form may be suspended and held in intensity. This was the aim of the *wetGRID* project, which occupied a generic architectural function, that of housing art, with a built experience that overspilled the expectations of the genre. Traditionally, one consolidated set of possible experiences can be selected and abstracted into the design of a determinate form so that its form recognizably exhibits the conventional characteristics of its type, for example the office building, and definitely fulfils its associated function.

In his *Soft Office* project, Spuybroek seeks to invent an in-between state where a generic function is fulfilled, but flexibly. The aim is to design an office building with internal differentiations associated with different activities. But instead of mapping generic functions to rooms with forms to match, Spuybroek recategorizes

BUILDING

the activities that will be housed according to the patterns of behaviour that are involved, and extracts from this a different topography. Certain patterns of behaviour recur in relation to different functions. For example, certain functions not usually grouped together might demand an office worker to be alone, and others to group together for collaborative work. Some require sitting still before a desk, others moving about. Collaborative work may be creative or rote, movements choreographed or somewhat stochastic. There are often expected rhythms of movement between different patterns of behaviour implied in the stages required to fulfil a function. Now if, instead of mapping dedicated functions to separate rooms, you map similar patterns of movement to shared spaces, the architectural problem suddenly shifts.

The problem that the *Soft Office* project set for itself was to design a limited set of flexible spaces lending themselves to different functions sharing certain patterns of office behaviour, and then build in transitions between the flexible spaces that encourage spontaneous movements from one to another. The idea is to try to build in the creative synergy that comes from cross-connections between usually compart-mentalized activities and from chance variations in function-filling progressions. In order to achieve this, as in *wetGRID*, the design for *Soft Office* had to take the embeddedness of potential movement in perception as its architectural object, and similarly seek a zone of proximity between perception, action and construction. However, more determinate affordances would have to be built in for a more limited set of possible experiences than was the case in Nantes. The affordances would in addition have to be more stably attainable, in order to limit the scope for the vertigo inherent in inter-sense relay making the architectural experience fly off its axis or lose too much perspective (not usually desired for office workers). A certain vagueness would be retained. But, in the words of Gins and Arakawa, it would have to present a 'plausible indeterminacy'[16]: in other words, one determined to be determined as leading profitably to the development of saleable product (in the area of media and entertainment).

For *Soft Office*, Spuybroek employed a similar technique as in *wetGRID* but involving in the analogue computing stage a lacquer and rubber-string apparatus adapted from Frei Otto. The resulting proto-architectural curvilinear forms embodied the same form-taking process as in Nantes, but the determination of the form had to be taken one step further. More definite programme elements had to be mapped to the resulting spaces, given the commercial development research function of the building.

Soft Office prolongs *wetGRID* in a way that adapts Spuybroek's experimental design process to the requirements of commercial architecture, without changing the basic nature of the process. It is in fact a transduction of *wetGRID* as a whole that transforms its motive force of vertigo into a force of functional flexibility, and transmits that flexibility to an existing genre of building conventionally lacking in creative form and creatively lived content. *Soft Office* is part of a transductive dissemination of the creative form-taking process Spuybroek developed in such projects as *Vision Machine*. It expands the range of the building types it can plausibly occupy and of the archi-tectural functions it can fulfil.

16. M. Gins and S. Arakawa. *Architectural Body* (Tuscaloosa: University of Alabama Press, 2002): 97.

The Object of Interactivity

Arjen Mulder

Architecture is a stable medium, just like painting and sculpture, the written and the printed word, photography and film. Because it deals with space, architecture's closest relative is sculpture, even though a considerable body of architecture exists on paper only, in which case it is more closely related to the art of drawing (either digital or not). Over the past thirty years hybrid forms have emerged, mixing classical sculpture and technical media. This led to the video installation – basically little more than moving images on monitors in a structure drawing attention to (the status of) these images. Next came the interactive installation – a technical-sculptural set-up that requires some sort of intervention by the spectator to evoke the art experience: if you remain inactive, nothing happens. The walk-through art of sculpture called architecture shows a similar hybridization with technical media. On the one hand there is an architecture that adorns itself with monitors, not just for decorative purposes or to intensify the experience of its users, but also to relay commercial messages and other information and to facilitate routing, security and so on. On the other hand we see the emergence of a type of interactive architecture where either the building activates its users or the users have to activate the building in order to gain access to some event or other. It is this interactive architecture I wish to discuss here from the viewpoint of media theory and art theory. The other hybridization of architecture – that of the digital techniques moving the design process from the drawing board to the computer – I leave aside here.

Interaction and Autonomy

We may call any system interactive if it is flexible enough to adapt itself to the use that is being made of it and if, vice versa, it changes its users through the changes these users cause within the system. In other words: when two systems are linked to each other and change each other via this link, we speak of inter-activity. Say an animal changes its surroundings by digging a hole and then adapts its lifestyle to the shelter this hole offers – for instance by taking only those routes through the landscape that lead directly to the hole or that lead as far away from it as possible, and when as a result of this paths are formed

THE OBJECT OF

in the landscape that in the rainy season are filled with water and carry off branches and loose soil, and if this creates a niche for pioneer plants, which are then visited by butterflies or bees that hitherto had no business at this location, leading to the arrival of caterpillar-eating tits, which themselves are a prey for sparrow-hawks and other small birds of prey that will build holes and nests and will now and again rob a young from the animal that first dug the hole at that spot – we can then summarize this long, gradual, complex process as inter-activity between the animal and the landscape. Interactivity is the default state of any living system, because life means linking yourself to other systems and in doing so making alterations to yourself and others through feedback loops.

Twentieth-century Modernism aimed to get out of this natural state and produce systems (works of art) that would not be changed by the use that was being made of them and which also left their users complete freedom in the way they wished to use them. Modernism stemmed from the primal experience that each movement is made up of many stationary moments and from this it deduced the principle that if you could create just one such moment, both art itself and the audience would coincide with themselves. Autonomous art is art that has managed to escape from the order of interactivity. The body fuses with its own functioning and forms a closed system. Complete alienation offers the only escape from the pressure to change and be changed that life imposes on us; all feeling must be eliminated, every tie to an outside world must be severed. Modernist art represents nothing but itself, presents nothing but the isolation of itself. The only change that Modernist art wished to inspire in its users was freedom, defined as the experience of nothing.

The reason that a certain category of art works is currently defined as interactive art – whereas every system on earth is basically interactive, includ-ing art – is that we have only recently put Modernism and its Postmodern version behind us. Only within the context of Modernism and Postmodernism can it be considered peculiar that some art wishes to interact with the audience instead of refusing to reach out to it at all. From a Modernist point of view, to call art interactive implied a condemnation, as interactive art is by definition not autonomous or sovereign but aims only to cause an effect, both in the audience and, via the audience, in itself. After prolonged Modernist schooling the audience is thoroughly trained in 'interpassive' art consumption: a silent reflec- tion on works of art that give back nothing of themselves. Art that explicitly wants to break through this lethargy, indeed, does not even exist as long as the audience remains passive – i.e. interactive art – then becomes something special indeed. Art that succeeds in seducing the audience to evoke itself, the art itself, can be easily distinguished from all other arts that attempt to create an audience for themselves. In short, interpassive art creates an audience, interactive art creates itself through an audience.

Virtual Life

Like all art, interactive art has its own object, its own defining illusion that can be evoked only by this particular art form and by no other. Every type of art dis-tinguishes itself from other art forms and from all non-artistic forms because it

evokes a specific illusion that is regarded by the audience as authentic (if not, it is bad art). It is this illusion that is authentic about art, that legitimizes the very existence of this particular art form. It is what invites us to reflect on life, as every illusion evoked by art is a symbolic expression of an aspect of our biological existence that can be subjected to reflection only via this symbolic approach, instead of being experienced just in a direct, non-symbolic way. The word 'reflection' here means neither being silently absorbed in a work of art in order to partake in the ineffable – the aim of Modernism – nor the critical positioning and decontexualization of the artwork that was at the heart of Postmodernism. It rather refers to a process of realization that addresses all human faculties – perception, feeling, intuition, instinct, taste, will, conscience, self-awareness, memory, imagination, sense – in order to extend the reach of these abilities. Reflection implies expanding your inner self by looking at something external (listening to it, touching it, smelling it, tasting it) and deepening your view of the world by contemplating your inner self. The insights thus gained may be expressed in words, but also in gestures, practices, world views, in emotional processes that are faced and not avoided, in short (brace yourself): in love.

The above train of thought is based on the work of American philosopher Susanne K. Langer (1895–1985), who is currently, and not just by me, being rediscovered as the greatest thinker on art and feeling of the twentieth century. Her work is a source of comfort for anyone who after the postmodernist confusion is searching for clarity in what should be to us the most precious of all artificial endeavours of mankind: the arts. Susanne Langer has defined the illusion that all forms of art evoke as the 'virtual object' that is present in these artworks and which actualizes itself as it is experienced by the viewers, listeners or users of that art. In her masterpiece *Feeling and Form* (1953) Langer has described the virtual object of all forms of art known to her: not just of the visual arts, but also of literature and the performing arts. While Langer must have gone through her own process of understanding art during the heyday of Modernism, her work is neither supportive nor apologetic of it. The philosopher regards Modernism as just one way of evoking in various forms of art the thing that is at the centre of all art, i.e. 'virtual life'.

Virtual life is life that is actualized by the beholder of art through the living experiences he or she carries within his or her own person. Virtual life has many aspects, both in space and in time, and each of the arts has appropriated one of them. Every art form evokes the illusion of being precisely what it is not. In painting, an illusion of space is created by arranging shapes and colours on a flat plane. This is the virtual space of painting. The virtual object of sculpture is the kinetic volume surrounding the sculpture, the empty space wherein the sculpture appears to be moving, even if it is standing still. Architecture evokes a virtual ethnical domain: it turns any arbitrary location into a site for a people, a company or a family. Sculpture and architecture, being related media, complement each other: the virtual kinetic volume is a symbolic representation of the personal space surrounding each individual, whereas the virtual ethnical domain is a symbolic representation of the shared social environment of which everyone is part. Dance contains virtual powers: the powers by which dancers seem to attract and repel each other while in reality being able to move freely in any direction. Music's virtual object is the controlled, intensified passage of the present, of time that seems to come alive in rhythm and melody, even as it progresses in the same inanimate way as ever. And so on. Each element, each building block of a work of art should express the illusion of life, i.e. the virtual object of which the work of art is the carrier: art is 'living form'. To understand art means to understand what its virtual object is: to understand which shape this object takes within a specific work of art and to understand which specific abilities and experiences it excites in the beholder, however individual these may have seemed before they were stimulated by a work of art. To understand art therefore means to understand how specific our general human abilities function and how general our individual experiences are.

Our brains and our bodies do not contain two separate systems of experience, where the one can be activated only by real experiences and the other only by media. Medial experiences are as real as immediate ones and the accompanying feelings are just as authentic. The only difference between them is their source. We truly see depth in the canvas, as the painting stimulates the depth-experience we all carry within ourselves. Yet we do not confuse a painted space with a space outside, because in everyday space we do not construct our experience of depth by vision alone but also by touch, movement and resistance, by hearing sounds from close up and from far away and voices that fade away and echo. A painted space, however, is purely visual. The very reason why art exists is that we humans are full of experiences and feelings that cannot be wholly expressed in words – our everyday instrument of reflection. Painting, photography, sculpture, architecture, music, dance, theatre, even poetry, novels and essays are about other things and contain other insights from those we can express through logical reasoning. Discursive knowledge can be put into words, written down, analyzed, abstracted, reasoned and criticized. Discursive knowledge is all knowledge that is pursued by philosophy and science. Presentational knowledge cannot be immediately captured and described in concepts because it is still too new, too unknown. This knowledge is therefore described or indicated by images and metaphors; it presents itself. A metaphor or presentational image does have meaning but this meaning can as yet be expressed only by this particular image. The word 'image' here should be interpreted in the same broad sense as is customary in modern neurology; an image may also be evoked by a melody, a dance, a building, a poem or an essay. It is impossible to tell what a presentational image presents exactly, as there are no other examples yet that present the same thing: we cannot yet distinguish between the image and its meaning. A presentational image is different from a depiction as the latter is representational in nature and has a recognizable meaning.

The D-tower

Art is presentational knowledge. Each form of art triggers one specific type of presentational knowledge. Each form of art contains a specific virtual experience that actualizes itself within the viewer, listener, reader, visitor or

INTERACTIVITY

'toucher' of art. Each time, the virtual object triggers an emotional range that is not subject to internal investigation by any other form of art. It appeals to feelings and experiences we recognize, but also to feelings that we have never had before. A work of art therefore does something, it actively has an effect on its beholders; but as they are being changed by the art experience, the beholders also do something to the work of art: they bring it to life. They turn something that was only virtual into something that is actual by connecting it to their bodies and all of the abilities, emotions and experiences that are part of it. This brings me to *D-tower*, the project in the Dutch town of Doetinchem by Lars Spuybroek and Q. S. Serafijn. This project – in part a tower-like sculpture, in part illumination, in part website, in part permanent survey – takes both mutually influencing parts of art, meaning the virtual and the actual, the object and the feeling, absolutely literally. In doing so, *D-tower* problematizes the idea of inter-activity in such a way that we can now envisage a possible answer to the question: what exactly is the virtual object of interactive art and which modalities, experiential content and emotional values may that object hold?

D-tower consists of a visible sculpture that includes a virtual kinetic volume: the tower itself, which is of such a shape that it looks as if at any moment it may lumber off on its insectoid or mollusc-like legs. The tower is not a building: it cannot be lived in or otherwise be occupied, although it does have a function in the urban planning here as a beacon or landmark. Because of its shape the tower is above all a sculpture; its virtual life, however, does not lie in the fact that this shape comes across as an organic one but rather in the fact that it is incomprehensible as a standing figure while at the same time the beholder appreciates the necessity of its shape in the sense of 'conforming to the laws of nature'. No matter where one stands around the tower, it always looks different: there is no ideal position from where the tower reveals the secret of its shape or from where the entire image can be seen at its best (like, for instance, the front–right position with the sculptures of Ernst Barlach). Walking around and underneath the sculpture, you realize that you are not looking at an image made by man but one made by natural forces. You are not actually looking at a tower, a standing structure, but at a splotch of something that has freed itself from matter and now hangs from the earth, holding on by slimy strings. The shape, in other words, is vague. It is structurally vague (because it is impossible to tell where the columns end and the dome starts), formally vague (because it is impossible to tell whether the tower hangs, spins or stands) and socially vague (because it is impossible to tell whether the tower stands in the most public or the most private of spaces). And therefore it is 'plastically inter-active', in the words of Spuybroek. That is to say that the shape is not utilitarian, it is charged with affect, evoking feelings associated with gliding, falling, caressing, sliding, rising, swaying. There is a lot of movement in the tower, even though it is stationary. The tower is not a motion that at some point was arrested and became a building but rather a sculpture that has continued to virtually contain its motion within its kinetic volume, which actualizes itself daily in all of the bodies and vehicles that move around it.

And yet this sculpture is not an autonomous work of art, as the tower denies its sculpturalness by primarily functioning as the medium for a light

THE OBJECT OF

show. It has no intrinsic meaning but enables a different medium to produce meaning: the four colours that illuminate the tower and represent the dominant mood of the inhabitants of the city surrounding the tower. Blue stands for happiness, green for hatred, yellow for fear, red for love: the colours of fire. At night, the illuminated tower is the city's virtual fireplace. The tower's colour is computed – by a computer program that statistically processes the answers given by a representative sample of Doetinchem's population in a continuous survey of their emotional condition – as a value that corresponds with a general emotional value, which in turn corresponds with one of the four colours being projected (from within) onto the tower's exterior. In this way the virtual kinetic volume surrounding the sculpture appears not only in the real void around and underneath the tower but is simultaneously evoked in the virtual (or digital) domain of the city's inhabitants who take part in the website's survey. The town expresses its feelings through *D-tower*. Its residents use the tower to present themselves and in this sense they turn the tower into the work of art they wish to see (this is why the autonomous sculptural nature of the tower must be denied, which is achieved with the illumination). At the same time the illuminated tower, showing to the world the emotional state of the people of Doetinchem, in turn influences this emotional state: how do people start to feel when the tower beams into the night in glaring green (hatred) or, alternatively, reassuring red (love)? The tower robs these feelings, privately expressed on the website, of their authenticity and innocence by forcing the citizens into action: make sure the tower shines a different colour if you dislike this one or make sure it keeps its present colour if this one makes you feel good. So, via the associated website, the tower interacts electronically with its surroundings. Just as the virtual object of any type of art is actualized by the emotions invested in it by its beholder, the emotions of the people of Doetinchem control the actual appearance of their object, their beacon, their landmark in the city. Just as the sculpture of *D-tower* in its plastic interactivity suggests an elusive motion of gliding and caressing, of rushing on and sliding away, so its electronic interactivity conjures up the suggestion of a continuous emotional movement among the citizens: suggestion or, put more bluntly, illusion, as these movements are being triggered in no small part by the colours of the sculpture themselves. The colours of the tower do not depict the residents' emotions, they do not represent them: they present these emotions, for no one can ever tell what their 'real' emotions are and which emotions are reactions to the actual colour value of the tower.

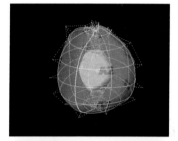

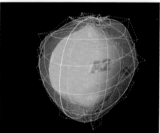

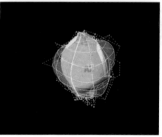

Digital animation of contracting and expanding forces on a sphere. NOX, *D-tower*, 1998–2004

Slow Interactivity

Let's just take a step back here. We actualize the experience of the virtual dimension of a work of art with the aid of previous, other experiences. However, these already present experiences are often so powerful that they superimpose themselves, as it were, over the newly seen or read work, rendering it literally invisible. If art is to evoke a living experience with its audience, it should not address specific feelings but rather the general human ability to have feelings and the general human ability to perceive these feelings within ourselves from

INTERACTIVITY

some distance. Art should raise this question with the audience: where does this feeling within me come from? Only then will the viewer, reader or listener really be prepared to look, read and listen – for a second time. In beholding art there is a moment of delay; art cannot be taken in in one go and in real time, as it always and at the earliest hits home at the second encounter and often only at the umpteenth confrontation. This necessary delay has been used by traditionally inclined art critics as an argument for placing interactive installations outside of the domain of art, because in interactive art the immediate response is almost always essential. It is just like that in computer games: one moment of reflection and your avatar dies. *D-tower* proves that this immediacy is not always necessary. Here is an interactive work of art whose changes in audience and object could stretch out over days, weeks, maybe even years and decades.

What then is the defining illusion of interactive art? Which virtual object is actualized in the visitor or user? Which presentational image in interactive art defies a discursive approach while at the same time it is absolutely real – living knowledge? How do we think or what thinks within us when we are open to interactive art? Interactive art isolates our ability to react from all other human abilities: an interactive work of art contains virtual behaviour. By interacting with it we actualize this behaviour within ourselves. Therefore interactive art makes it possible to reflect on what we do automatically without the need or indeed the power to think about it. The interaction between a visitor and an interactive installation does not create any confusion as to whether the visitor's actions are real. The installation isolates our behaviour from the rest of the world as does the frame round the picture, the pedestal under the statue, the façade of the building, the paper under the poem, the physical book with the novel, the stage for the theatre. The interactive visitor's behaviour is symbolic, as in a sense it takes place in a vacuum. Each element of an interactive installation – software, hardware, ambience, interface – must be an expression of the virtual behaviour that is to be actualized in the visitor in order to initiate the art experience and facilitate reflection-in-the-widest-sense-of-the-word. This reflection is brought about by the manner in which the interactive system responds to the visitor's behaviour. Because visitors see, feel or hear the results of their behaviour, this behaviour becomes the subject of closer inspection – quick as lightning at times, but speed is not a defining attribute of interactive art. What is defining is the virtual behaviour, the behaviour of both visitor and work of art itself – the visitors' behaviour at the website as well as the behaviour of the light on the sculpture in the case of *D-tower*. An interactive installation breaks with standard behaviour and in doing so gives us insight into human and machine-like behavioural mechanisms, with each reaction that is triggered by the system for a second time, with each intervention by the user that is doubled in the installation. *D-tower*'s tower therefore is not so much a sculpture that shows the emotional state of the residents of Doetinchem as it is an installation that enables them to understand, expand and deepen their emotional life. The realization that people not from Doetinchem can see this inner fire flare and flicker by watching the shifting colours of the tower makes us outsiders also an active part of the process of interaction.

THE OBJECT OF

The Interactive Experience

Tommy. Designed by Spuybroek as a sort of vase it is in reality more like a hollow object that invites its owner to pick it up, put it onto his or her lap and caress and finger it (it contains several orifices, supposedly to put flowers in). The same undefined shape as the sculpture in the *D-tower* project, the same seemingly organic artificiality or artificial organicity, and as a result the same plastic interactivity. The same impossibility of finding an ideal point outside of the object from where it might be viewed in all its perfection or misshapenness. This is not an object to look at, but rather one to feel up in an indecent manner. The vagueness of its shape appeals directly to the body that finds itself defenceless against it. In the hands of its owner the vase itself becomes a body, an obscene delicacy, a polymorphous perversion to blindly yield to, as sight itself is clueless here. *Tommy*'s functionality – that it is a vase for flowers – is a mere excuse, something to legitimize our giving in to illegal or at least indecent pawing. With *Tommy* in your lap you get the urge to thrust, but into what exactly, and what with? In short, *Tommy* is more than just a beautiful or ugly shape, more also than just a functional or non-functional object: it is an animate object, a living thing, containing something that directly touches and brings to life the body of its owner. However, the problem is that no one has ever had sex with this kind of body: its shape is found neither in the wild nor in the laboratory. *Tommy* evokes an eroticism that did not exist prior to the moment that the owner placed it on his or her lap. *Tommy* expands the erotic ability, the erotic urge of its owner to a range the human body is not yet ready for.

Art contains virtual experiences, virtual emotions. In art, an animistic view of objects (including sounds) has persisted that dates from mythical pre-historic times and has never been replaced nor can be replaced by any rational or scientific view of life whatsoever, simply because our senses and brain are so extremely keen to discern meaning in everything and see traces of life in anything. Meaning is an object's property that lives, or has lived and is now dead. But what is living about an object? This: *the virtual feeling that is actualized in humans and that comes to life within us.* To live is to feel you are alive. Feeling is the basis of consciousness, including rational thought and scien-tific methods. All art objects contain a virtual feeling, a designed feeling that has been virtualized in its design and therefore can be actualized again – if not so much as an experience but rather as something that potentially may be experienced. Works of art, like the myths from the animistic stage of human history, are symbols of feelings that must be expressed symbolically in order to get a grip on them, either to prevent oneself from being overwhelmed by them or to prevent them slipping away once and for all. These feelings may be cat-egorized by type of art – as witnessed by the virtual objects described above – but each type of art may have a whole range of manifestations, for instance that of the kinetic space experience in sculpture or the experience of the ethnical domain in architecture. To feel the life in a sculpture is to be aware of the life in the haptic volume surrounding it, of the potential life around the objects; it is having a true experience of motion while knowing full well that the object or project in front of you was created intentionally to give you that experience.

INTERACTIVITY

The feeling that interactive art evokes and makes accessible to reflection is the feeling that you do not end where your skin ends, that you are more than just a body with senses and a brain. That life means continual expansion outside yourself. That your body is always open and you are living outward-bound. That the outside world for a large part is what you yourself are and that in this outside world you are overlapping with other people, other systems — both living ones and virtually living ones. Just as you are in considerable measure your own vehicle when driving a car or riding a bicycle. Just as you are in considerable measure the city in which you live, because it functions as one huge external memory that partly relieves your internal memory and partly suppresses it. You find out when you are on holiday and suddenly remember all sorts of events that never came to mind when you were at home. People are as intelligent as they manage their environment to be and as sensitive as they manage their environment to be, because they are as much their environment as they are themselves.

Just like all other living beings, we are distributed cognitive systems, distributed memory systems, acting systems, emotional systems. Our feelings spread over our surroundings in the form of virtual experiences that we localize in objects, routes and persons. This is why we avoid certain streets or neighbourhoods, why we will sit next to certain people and not next to others on a train or in a waiting room, why we like some restaurants better than others, why we feel at ease with one neighbour and uncomfortable in the company of another neighbour, and so on. It is this whole vague cloud of intangible feelings and parts of ourselves that we experience outside of ourselves that interactive art exploits and opens up to exploration, expansion and deepening. Interactive art teaches us why we react how to what and why the outside world reacts to this. Interaction designers design interactive behaviour in such a way that the user never has to think about it (unless an error occurs within the system). Interaction artists let virtual behaviour design itself, let it develop in such a way that we experience and acknowledge all the incomprehensibility of our behaviour, and consciously allow it to be created by others, just as we create the behaviour of others. The goal is (brace yourself again) love/love.

THE OBJECT OF

INTERACTIVITY

Notes on the Surfacing of Walls:
NOX, Kiesler, Semper

Andrew Benjamin

Openings

When architecture, in seeking an analogy to understand its own use of notation, deployed the relationship between choreography and dance, there was a temptation to concentrate on the movement and not on the surface on which the dance took place. Choreography and its resultant activity provided a prompt in the same way that conceptualism is often understood to have prompted a type of architecture. The prompt, however, is not just external to architecture's materiality; once the logic of the prompt is pursued then materiality may fail to figure as a site of architectural experimentation and research. And yet, the danger inherent in distinguishing, in too simple a sense, between the dance and the surface on which it takes place is that reducing dance and choreography to the role of a prompt within architecture may lead to an evocation of the surface – the literal surface, the surface independent of any effects, the surface *tout court* – as evidence of materiality. (The material is then identified with the empirical.) As such, the surface would be no more than what is given in opposition to the conceptual. What has to occur is the freeing of the surface from this opposition in order that it be repositioned within the practice and theory of architecture. Bodies and surfaces can find a way of connecting only if the material presence of architecture – architecture as a material presence – comes to define its reality.

Before this can happen, however, a further possibility has to be distanced, namely the tradition of architectural thinking that takes Ruskin and Pugin as the points of departure – a tradition resulting in Postmodernism as an architectural style – which attempts to distinguish between ornament and 'edifice' (Ruskin's term) such that the architectural effect will always be located in either the ornamental or the symbolic. Any concern with the surface would be almost immediately subsumed. Surfaces would have become either the bearer of ornament or would be construed as merely ornamental. The counter argument is that what has to occur if the surface's materiality and not just its empirical presence is taken as significant is, once again, the repositioning of the surface outside its location within an opposition between the ornamental and the structural. The surface has to be incorporated in what will be described as a material event. This material event is the moment at which geometry, programme and the work of materials are interconnected. And yet, that cannot be all. Once the term 'event' is introduced then what has to be acknowledged is the possibility of singularity. Not the singularity of the idiosyncratic, but a conception of the singular in which the specific interconnection between geometry, programme and materials resists any form of generality except as an abstraction and thus as a diagram. Understood in this sense the material event can define architecture's autonomy as much as its potential for criticality. Architecture becomes the work of matter.

Contemporary concerns with the surface in architecture are already positioned beyond the hold of traditional oppositions. The practice of criticism therefore has to contend with a new series of constraints. The point from which any departure and thus this 'contending' has to be made is the work of Gottfried Semper.[1] Semper's significance resides in his insistence on rethinking architectural practice in terms of textiles and materials. It will be in relation to that positioning that recent architectural works – in this instance projects by NOX – can be taken up. It is, however, vital to be clear here. The argument is not that there is a sustained historical development leading from Semper to the present. The inherent historicism of such a position overlooks the vital fact that it is the presence of contemporary work that activates the potential in Semper. The actuality of his work lies in the way geometry and matter working together open up architectural possibilities.

In general terms the work of Gottfried Semper continues to exert a hold on a range of architectural activities. While the work is of genuine historical importance – e.g. no adequate historical account of the Ringstrasse can be given that does not engage with Semper's *Kunsthistorisches Museum* – the contention here is that there are significant elements of his writings that can be understood as addressing issues within contemporary design practice.[2] While a beginning will be made with Semper – a beginning that will lead in terms of a narrative via Kiesler's *Endless House Projects* of the 1950s and then to NOX – the implicit argument, as has been intimated, is that it is only because of the presence of works by Kiesler and NOX that the potential in Semper can come to the fore. Starting from the centrality of textile it becomes possible to argue for the primacy of the surface within Semper's project. The surface thought in terms of its material presence – in Semper's specific case, textile as the interrelation of geometry and matter – opens up as a question how the wall is to be understood. Although this is a general argument, what is also true is that different textiles will have different geometrical implications.

Semper

In the 'Prolegomenon' to his great work on style (*Der Stil*) and during a survey of the different approaches to art (art including architecture), Semper makes the following claim: 'Art in its highest exaltation hates exegesis; it therefore immediately shuns the emphasis on meaning.' (p. 195/XX–XXI) The passage moves on to a concern with materials. However, and prior to any more detailed consideration of the way such a concern unfolds, the significance of this comment needs to be noted. The immediate question that emerges is what the hating of 'exegesis' entails. The straightforward answer is that this resistance amounts to the privileging of the material or tectonic nature of architecture over archi-

1. References to Semper will be to the following editions. In each instance the pagination, English preceding the German, will be given in the text. Gottfried Semper. *The Four Elements of Architecture and Other Writings* (translated by Harry Francis Mallgrave and Wolfgang Herman). Cambridge University Press. Cambridge. 1989. *Vier Elemente der Baukunst*. Braunschweig. 1851. *Der Stil*. München. F. Bruschmann. 1878–79.

2. If there were the space, attention could be given to the interior of Semper's *Dresden Synagogue* as an exercise in the relationship between programme and cladding.

NG OF WALLS

tecture's symbolic presence. A concern for meaning is often equated with symbols or expression. While it will always be true to argue that architecture, by virtue of being built form, will have an ineliminable symbolic dimension, such a claim does not take account of architecture in its totality. On one level the presence of a symbolic dimension cannot be denied. Architecture will always stand for something, and yet this is not the central point. Rather, the force of the claim is that it announces a shift in emphasis. The move, whose effect is to distance a concern with architecture as a site of meaning, involves emphasizing both the relationship with the building's inherent materiality and the connection between material presence and function.

Now, while the issues involved are clearly more nuanced than is allowed by a simple opposition between meaning and materials, it is nonetheless the case that to write of the shunning of 'meaning' is already to tie questions of the work's activity to what is realized through material presence. And yet, in the same section of *Der Stil*, Semper is critical of the positions held by those whom he identifies as the 'materialists'. He argues that they

> can be criticised in general for having fettered the idea too much to the material, for falsely believing that the store of architectural forms is determined solely by the structural and material conditions, and that only these supply the means for further development. The material in fact is subservient to the idea and is by no means the only decisive factor for embodying the idea in the phenomenal world. Although form, the idea becoming visible (*Die Form, die zur Erscheinung gewordene Idee*), should not be in conflict with the material out of which it is made, it is not absolutely necessary that the material as such becomes an additional factor in the artistic appearance. (p. 190/XVI)

What here is meant by 'idea'? The term 'idea' is Semper's. The mistake of the 'materialists' is that they thought they were opposed to any sense of idea, precisely because they conflated ideas and meanings; the idea had to have a transcendent or transcendental quality for the built form to express a meaning. The issue therefore is not with the idea in and of itself. Rather, it is how the idea is understood. That there can be ideas is not incompatible with an architectural strategy that insists on materials and the realization of function through material effects. What has to be distanced is thus what could be described as an idealist conception of the idea. The idea, rather than being external and thus regulating from outside, is bound up with the presence of the object as architecture.

To develop his position Semper drew on and then redeployed the distinction between *Kernform* (core form), *Werkform* (structural member) and *Kunstform* (art form) established by Bötticher.[3] For Bötticher, *Kunstform* was the outward projection of the structural presence of the object. Ornamentation therefore was not an addition. It was given within that relationship. While Bötticher would link that interrelation of the different types of form to 'universal unities of beauty and truth', that was not a necessary connection. The important point was that the idea — the architectural work's ideational content — was bound up with its structural and material presence. If there had to be a sense of propriety or adequation then it was not given by the architectural object's having either a symbolic or expressive quality such that the object stood for an idea. Adequation was always defined internally. It was the relationship between

3. The most sustained introduction to Bötticher's work is Mitchell Schwarzer. 'Ontology and Representation in Karl Bötticher's Theory of Tectonics'. *Journal of the Society of Architectural Historians* (vol. 52. September 1993): 267–80.

THE SURFACI

materials and their outward presence. To hold to this relationship was, of course, to hold to a version of architectural autonomy. The force of this position can be seen in Semper's quasi definition of form as the 'idea becoming visible'. To pursue the connection between autonomy on the one hand and the interrelationship between the three types of form on the other, what we shall take up is Semper's treatment of the wall. The wall, as an object of architectural consideration, is present from the earliest writings on polychromatic antiquities to the final writings on style. The wall, however, needs to be understood as surface positioned as much beyond the opposition between surface and depth as beyond any reduction to a flat screen. The wall as surface – surface as wall – has for Semper an already given textile quality. The wall does not have a tectonic dimension as an addition; it is tectonic from the start.

The point of entry has to be the approach to the wall as presented in *The Four Elements of Architecture*. While an integral part of the overall historical importance of Semper is the way that these elements – hearth, roof, enclosure and mound – provide a way of dealing with the question of the origins of architecture, by far the most significant for contemporary concerns is the account of the emergence of the wall from the enclosure. Indeed, it may be that the '*Wandbereiter*' is the proto-architect of today. (Semper more or less concedes the same in §63 of *Der Stil*.) His claim that 'wickerwork was the essence of the wall' is well known. Its importance, both historically and for the present, resides in its giving to the wall the quality of a textile that is already the tectonics of the surface. The surface has therefore a geometry of construction that will open the way in which the building's overall geometry will work.

This formulation needs to be connected to the related argument that establishes a distinction between the wall (involving, of course, the essential function of the wall) and load bearing. Walls, for Semper, cannot be separated from the activity of spatial disclosure. From a Semperian perspective, space is not a given that is then divided. The contrary is the case. Space is a result. Hence, the wall is that which brings about spatial enclosure. In general terms, therefore, space is the result of the surface's operation. The detail of his position is formulated in *The Four Elements of Architecture* in the following terms:

> Hanging carpets remained the true walls, the visible boundaries of space. The often solid walls behind them were necessary for reasons that had nothing to do with the creation of space; they were needed for security, for supporting a load, for their permanence and so on. Wherever the need for these secondary functions did not arise, the carpets remained the original means for separating space. Even where building solid walls became necessary, the latter were only the invisible structure hidden behind the true and legitimate representatives of the wall, the colourful woven carpets. (p. 104)

The importance of this formulation is that it moves the wall away from being simply a structural element to having a clearly defined function within (or as part of) an overall structure.[4] While for Semper there needs to be an accord between the outward appearance of structural elements and the nature of that function, such a relationship cannot be understood straightforwardly in terms of a theory of ornamentation. What has to be opened up is the potential in Semper's conception of the wall.

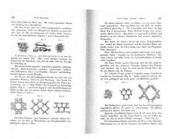

Pages 186 and 187 from the original first volume of Gottfried Semper's *Der Stil in den technischen und tektonischen Künsten* (1860–1863).

4. This position is argued for in considerable detail in §62 of *Der Stil*. In that context walls are described as 'spatial concepts' (*raümliche Begriffe*) (255/214). There is the important addition that concerns for load bearing were 'foreign to the original idea of spatial enclosure (*das Raumsabschloss*)'. While this formulation holds to a distinction between wall and structure, it allows for the development of materials in which wall – again as an effect – and structure come to be interarticulated.

Semper's project can be understood as the attempt to identify within the history of architecture – specifically Hellenic art in this context – a principle that could be extracted. In a sense it is, for example, the nature of Semper's relation to Quatremère de Quincy that should inform a contemporary response to his own work. The value for Semper of Quatremère's writings on ancient sculpture is that they provide an opening. In Semper's terms it lay in their 'practical tendency'. He continues:

> In line with this tendency the work does not as it were parade the form before us as a finished product according to the lessons of aesthetic ideality, but lets us see the artistic form and the high idea (*die Kunstform und die hohe Idee*) that dwells within it; it considers and shows how both were inseparable from the material and technical execution and how the Hellenic spirit manifested itself in the freest mastery of these factors, as well as the old, sanctified tradition. (pp 249/207)

The significance of the formulation lies in the differentiation of form from what is termed 'aesthetic ideality'. Form and ideas could not be separated from materials, materials' presentation and questions of technique. Semper undoes the opposition between form and idea by incorporating both as material possibilities. Any vestige of that metaphysical opposition is displaced by emphasis that has been given to materials and techniques. Once the idea is no longer understood as external, then the building cannot be understood as the idea's symbolic presentation. Hellenic style therefore involved an interrelationship of all these elements. This explains why, in addition, art-form and decoration cannot be separated. They are, in Semper's terms, 'so intimately bound together by the influence of the principle of surface dressing (*das Flächenbekleidungs-prinzip*) that an isolated look at either is impossible'. (pp 252–53/211)

What emerges from this way of giving centrality to materials is the possibility of arguing that materials are what they effect. When, as has already been noted, Semper argues that 'wickerwork' was the original wall, it was because it was the 'original space divider'. This realization of division defined the 'essence' of the wall. What this means is that any consideration of the wall has to do with the way in which materials realize their effect. This accounts for the move in the same text to the claim that the wall 'retained this meaning when materials other than the original were used' (p. 104). (It should be noted, if only in passing, that the connection is between meaning and materials and not meaning and symbolic determination.) The history of the wall therefore becomes the history of the way materials realize the wall effect. The wall effect is spatial division, though only ever as a result. Hence, it becomes possible to question the quality of the space produced, since it is produced (effected) by the work of specific materials. (While it cannot be pursued here, emphasizing the fact that space is not given but produced indicates the need for another understanding of the decorative and thus the body's relation to 'ornamented' walls.) There is a further result that also can be noted. Once it can be argued that the definition of the wall has to do with spatial enclosure and is not reducible to the presence of literal walls – a possibility also evident in Loos's letting the intersection of the *Raumplan* and the work of cladding produce volumetric difference, hence the effect of the wall – it then follows that the wall is not given

THE SURFACE

in opposition to the floor.[5] This point can be extended, since if the wall/floor opposition no longer defines the work of the wall – but the wall *is* the wall effect, i.e. spatial division – this will necessitate a reconsideration of the corner, since the corner is defined by the intersection of an already determined floor/wall relation. Thence the relation between wall, floor and corner can be rethought. A form this can take is the rearticulation of that relation as a surface, not just a surface as a flat exterior but also a surface as tectonic entity, the reciprocity of materials and geometry. Furthermore, programmatic demands requiring that the elements of architecture have a distinct quality can locate that difference as individuated by a surface.

Finally, therefore, the function of the wall is not only internal to the architecture in question – thereby generating a sense of autonomy, a sense reinforced by the move from an externally orientated symbolic meaning to an internally regulated system of activity – it also cannot be thought outside its relation to materiality. Semper's work dissolved the distinction between structure and ornament. The wall was given an integrity that came from its definition in terms of the effecting of spatial enclosure while at the same time locating that realization in the operation of materials.

Kiesler

While Kiesler's work is linked, rightly, to the history of surrealism and often discussed in relation to Duchamp, there is an inherently architectural dimension that should not be neglected. In 'A Brief Note on Designing the Gallery', Kiesler outlines some of the positions resulting in both the *Surrealist Gallery* and the accompanying *Studies for Perception*.[6] Fundamental to the project – the gallery design – is a rethinking of the place and the placing of the frame. The framed work has to move beyond the duality of 'vision' and 'reality'. The 'barrier' separating the human world and the world of art needs to be overcome. Kiesler argues that

> the barrier must be dissolved: the frame, today reduced to an arbitrary rigidity, must regain its architectural, spatial significance. The two opposing worlds must be seen again as jointly indispensable forces in the same world … It is up to the architectural technician of today to invent, in terms of his techniques, a means by which such unity can again be made possible.[7]

The distinction between vision and reality touches on the distinction between wall and floor. Any detailed consideration of Kiesler's gallery spaces has to start from the position that it is not simply the projection of the framed works into space, it is the projection that, once understood in connection to the curving of the wall, has an effect on the body and therefore on the floor/wall relation. The interconnection between these projects and those taking place under the heading of the *Endless House Projects* could be described as the move from a potential to an actual vanishing of the corner. Writing of his own project, Kiesler defined it in the following terms:

> The Endless House is not amorphous, not a free-for-all form. On the contrary its construction has strict boundaries according to the scale

5. This relationship between *Raumplan* and cladding is at its most emphatic in *Haus Müller*.

Gallery, New York, 1942. In *Frederick Kiesler, Art of This Century* (1996): 107.

6. The images of these projects as well as the text 'A Brief Note on Designing the Gallery' can be found in *Friedrich Kiesler: Art of This Century* (Friedrich Kiesler-Zentrum Wien, 2002).

7. Kiesler. Ibid: 34.

8. F. Kiesler. *The Endless House* (Thames & Hudson, London, 1985): 43.

of our living, its shape and form are determined by inherent life forces, not by building code standards or the vagaries of décor fads. Space in the Endless House is continuous; all living areas can be unified into a single continuum.[8]

Many questions arise. Two are central. The first has to concern the relationship between the 'single endless continuum' and the wall. The second is to explain what is meant by 'life forces'. Part of that explanation involves arguing that giving a determining centrality to these 'life forces' will entail that the body — that which moves, sees, in sum inhabits — has a different place within architecture. It is a place that is structured as well as structuring. Defined in these terms, the body will lose both its singular and exemplary status. Part of what these 'forces' denote therefore is bodies (plural and therefore different) in the place of an idealization of the body (singular and therefore always the same; the body of myth).

And yet, the argument cannot just be that a different sense of programme has been invented and thus experimentation in architecture will have no more than a discursive quality, will amount to experimentation purely on the level of meaning.[9] Another form of invention is necessary. Kiesler identifies it in terms of the development of 'techniques'. In fact, what Kiesler's work, taken into conjunction with his own project descriptions, makes clear is that rearticulating the relationship between the wall and the floor into the continuous surface occurs as the result of an architectural practice necessitating the creation of techniques proper to its potential built realization. The interruption of the relation between wall, corner and floor by the projection of art into a volume, thereby redefining both art's spatiality and the viewing of objects, is an end that is linked to this possibility. Techniques delimit specific architectural interventions. They are therefore inseparable from material possibilities. Kiesler's project — in architectural terms — needs to be understood as a diagram that demands realization as a material event. Such a move would bring to Kiesler the tectonic dimension that the presentation of the projects so clearly lacks.

Frederick Kiesler, *Endless House*, 1959

9. What is opened up here is the general problem of what counts as experimentation and research in architecture. It might be necessary in order to answer this question to distinguish between experimentation *for* architecture and experimentation *in* architecture. In regards to the former it is clear that experiments by engineers and software manufactures, working together, have created a range of materials that makes an important addition to architecture. The question of the nature of that addition, or the incorporation of such developments, becomes a way of understanding the role of experimentation in architecture. Furthermore, it indicates why collaboration between engineers and architects is fundamental rather than creating the expectation that the architect can resolve in advance questions of materials. Equally, it indicates, or this would be the argument, that the second form of experimentation is inextricably bound up with what has been identified here as the material event.

10. The *Son-O-House* is a public artwork undertaken in collaboration with the composer Edwin van der Heide.

NOX

The *Son-O-House* recalls Kiesler and allows both Bötticher and Semper to be evoked.[10] Before engaging with its specificity I must make a point about representation. Architecture is as much bound to its varying means of representation and thus what these means make possible as it is to material possibility. There is, of course, an important connection between them. As has already been noted, the limitations inherent in the work of Kiesler — limitations only ever discovered afterwards — have to be located in the way in which the project was represented. It is not simply that the computer — and more precisely animation programs — has altered the means of representation. This has occurred. Of greater significance is that the use of these representational tools has altered the nature of the 'representation'. Moreover, the process of what Kiesler referred to as 'life forces' can now be calibrated. The body can play a role as a design tool. This capacity of the body plays an important role in the production of the *Son-O-House*. What needs to be identified therefore is the way the initial experimentation took place. It is not as though the result is explicable simply in terms of its origins. Nonetheless, the significant point of departure was the way

THE SURFAC

the tracing of bodily movement could then be traced in the production of volumes. Their initial shape bears a direct correlation with the movement of bodies. What this means is that movement is not a metaphor. Nor do bodies function in a way that would be analogous to the operation of the architecture. The object has not been choreographed. In sum, analogy and metaphor no longer determine architecture's relation to the body.

The reason for insisting on the absence of choreography – or at least choreography as conventionally understood, namely as anticipating movement – is because of the role of what Lars Spuybroek describes as analogue-computing models. While Bötticher wanted to link architecture to its realization through the inherent property of materials – a position that reappears in Semper – in this instance the intermediary use of models enables their material presence to have an effect on the construction of the project. The studies of the movement of bodies – studies involving filming and the subsequent digital registration of the results – are transferred to strips of paper. Cuts within these strips refer to different aspects and intensity of movement. The paper strips are to be understood not only as lines, but also lines conveying information. The lines are not representational in any direct sense. They already have two intrinsic properties. They are informed. In addition, however, the material of construction – 'paper' – has its own qualities. As the informed strips are stapled together, they begin to form a complex arabesque, which has the potential to yield wall, floor and corner relations. Those relations emerge out of the interconnection of the vaults implicit in the analogue-computer model but which are only truly actualized once the model is digitized. In addition, the digitization of the models gives rise to further developments – ones with their own important consequences. Digitization allows, via a movement from surface to line, each of the vaulted sections its own discreet termination. In other words, surfaces reach their own termination in a line. This occurs because of the move from one form of modelling to another. The potential of paper is actualized through digital transformation.

One of the aspects of this overall project delimiting its particularity is the temporality of construction, i.e. the stages of its realization. The conventions of spatiality always see movement and by extension circulation as the result of construction. While it is possible to establish circulation diagrams before construction and thus to give priority to circulation and materials as defining the logic of the building, its actual occurrence is always after the event of construction. (An example here would be Mendelssohn's use of glass in the 1927 Stuttgart Department Store to locate and house circulation.) In the case of the *Son-O-House* movement is diagrammed directly onto material. The intermediary step is excluded. In addition, as has been noted, the very fact that these materials – here paper – have their own properties is what enables them to function not as scale model, in any direct sense, but as analogue-computers. (There is an interesting representational question here concerning what is 'seen' in these paper models.) Materials, already informed, yield geometry as a consequence of the nature of their materiality.[11] Movement, working through modelling – both analogue-computer and digital – is what makes construction possible. Construction becomes the place of movement, although it was movement's relation to materials that was the generator of the initial process.

As a result of the methods used to create the vaults, they function by refusing any straightforward distinction between column and wall. It is the

11. The distance of the relation between NOX and Semper occurs at this point. The latter was interested in materials as given by the distinction between *Werkform* and *Kunstform*. Part of the interest for NOX lies in the geometric possibilities inherent in material. This accounts for the role of Frei Otto's work within the projects and therefore situates the references to him and the Institute for Lightweight Structures occurring elsewhere in the book.

JG OF WALLS

12. I have discussed this aspect of time in a number of contexts. In sum it draws on Freud's conception of *Nachträglichkeit* (a term I understand as 'iterative reworking'). For Freud this means that in regards to two occurrences the second charges the first with a quality that reveals the potential within it. Allowing this to become a way of thinking about historical time gives repetition a fundamental role. However, it is repetition that has to be thought within the movement in which something is given again by its having been brought into relation. See Andrew Benjamin, *The Plural Event* (London: Routledge, 1993).

process of their integration that yields the wall. However, the way that occurs means that the melding of what are traditionally taken to be fixed distinctions — vault, column, wall — establishes what could be described as an openness in relation to functional designation, with the result that the attribution of precise determinations will have the same quality as fixing a static point on a dynamic surface. The surface yields fixity. The steel ribs touch the ground, creating edges. Nonetheless, the internal dynamic of the way this occurs means that the edges that are created will have a complex relation to the ground. (Ground is understood as an architectural condition, as well as implicated in the conventions marking the history of the corner.) There are corners and walls, yet the nature of the walls dissolves already determined distinctions between them, compounding thereby the project's complexity. An inherent part of that complexity is that these relations (wall/floor/corner, and so on) are unpredictable within the way such relations are generally conceived in the history of modernist architecture. There is another side to this complication, a side that addresses how the unpredictable allows for the retroactive creation of sites of prediction.[12] It will be essential to return to this point after taking up, albeit briefly, programmatic concerns.

The *Son-O-House* is an art project staging the relationship between movement and sound. The built work houses sound that is produced by movement through the building. However, this does not occur as the result of a simple correlation between position and sound production. In the same way as the building's structuration — the process of its acquiring structure — is linked to movement, the internal operation of the building links sound to movement. Differing modalities of bodily position have an effect on the production. The curvature of the wall positions bodies in different ways. The potential in Kiesler's 'life forces' now has another life, an architectural *Nachleben* ('afterlife') occurring through having realised the potential in materials. (It was, of course, precisely this state of affairs that was lacking from Kiesler's initial projects.) However, the life involved, much like the bodies, will be defined by different ways of being present. The curvature of the wall and the manner in which spatial enclosure is effected are implicated in how sound is produced. Instead of a simple process of interaction where sound production would be the direct result of crossing thresholds, here sensors register movement and that registration provides a patterning in relation to which composition occurs. The movement diagram created by the building's occupants scores the music. There is therefore an intermediary step. What this recapitulates is, of course, the original diagram of construction. Movement led to construction. However, the direction was not literal. The initial registration of movement gave rise to the analogue-computer, which allowed material possibilities to be worked out — what emerged was that the 'truth' of steel could be discovered in paper. This was because of the material quality of the paper. The move to the digital and the adaptation of the paper model in the process have to be understood as shifts. What enables them to occur, however, is the use of material as sites both of the registration of research and of that which occasions research. Materiality, in both instances, is central. Materiality cannot be reduced to simple tectonics. It incorporates both tectonics and the geometry inherent in differing materials.

Given this level of description — and the intention has been to identify the presence of the project in terms of a material event — the final element that remains to be addressed concerns the object's relation to Semper and Kiesler.

THE SURFAC

This has already been identified in terms of the relationship between the unpredictable and the history of architecture. In regards to developing an understanding of the connection between Semper and NOX, the argument is that the movement of historical time can be understood as working in a more complex direction than is usually assumed. In other words, historical time is not the linear progression from past to the present. The connection between the projects and the undoing of the insistence of linear time can be accounted for by the connection having been given in both instances through the retained centrality of textile and materials. Neither term should be simply generalized and thus viewed as abstract. Differing materials, like textiles, will have differing potentials. The *Son-O-House* emerges therefore as singular. There are two interrelated aspects to singularity. The first is that what is meant by the singular object is one that cannot function as a prototype but only as a diagram. This entails emphasizing the building's capacity to generate further architectural propositions that have to do with its presence as a material event rather than its presence as an image. The second aspect of singularity is that such an object has the capacity to cause a retroactive movement in which connections are established. This move occurs because the basis of the connection cannot be adequately provided by the image. On the contrary, any connection will be given by the object's organization, i.e. the intrinsic qualities of the object. Organization has to be understood therefore as diagrammatic. No longer being defined by the image – and thus reduced to the status of an image – it can then have a generative capacity. What are generated are representations. And yet, they occur precisely by insisting on the abstract quality of the material event. Indeed, it is only once work such as the *Son-O-House* is thought in terms of its presence as a material event that it then becomes possible to identify similar states of affairs. They exist beyond the simplifying hold of appearance. (Similarities and dissimilarities constructed simply on the level of the image are just that, similar and dissimilar images.) Identifications beyond the hold of the image are retroactive connections. Their construction has the effect of securing history within theory and therefore winning history for the practice of design.

Son-O-House, see p. 174.

JG OF WALLS

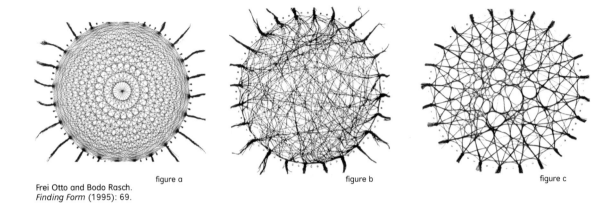

Frei Otto and Bodo Rasch.
Finding Form (1995): 69.

figure a   figure b   figure c

The Structure of Vagueness

Lars Spuybroek

In the early 1990s, Frei Otto and his team at the Institute for Lightweight Structures in Stuttgart studied what they called 'optimized path systems'. This research followed experimentations with material systems for calculating form, similar to the chain modelling technique Gaudí used for the Sagrada Familia. Each of these material machines was devised so that, through numerous interactions among its elements over a certain time span, the machine re-structures or, as Frei Otto says, 'finds [a] form'. Most consisted of materials that process forces by transformation, which is a special form of analogue computing. Since the materials function as 'agents', it is essential that they have a certain flexibility, a certain amount of freedom to act. It is also essential, however, that this freedom is limited to a certain degree by the structure of the machine itself. In classic analogue computing most movement is contained in gears, pistons or slots, or often in liquids held by rigid containers, but in Otto's machines nearly all materials are mixtures of liquids and solids, or begin as liquid and end up rigid. The interactions frequently result in a geometry that is based on complex material behaviour of elasticity and variability: sand, balloons, paper, soap film (including the famous minimal surfaces for the Munich Olympia Stadium), soap bubbles, glue, varnish and wool threads. This last material was used to calculate the shape of two-dimensional city patterns, three-dimensional cancellous bone structure and branching column systems. The wool thread machines are similar vectorized systems that minimize the number of paths, meaning they share geometries of merging and bifurcating. This technique follows a three-step algorithmic procedure:

STEP 1 (figure a): Map all the targets of the system (in this case, houses) on a board. For simplicity's sake these are arranged here in a circle, which could be on a supporting surface or an open ring. Connect each point to every other using a wool thread. This ensures the basic connectivity of the system: each house is connected to another by a road. This stage of the system consists only of crossings; it is a typical surface model, a wire frame that makes up a neat surface.

Lord Kelvin, tide predictor from the early 1870s. It was one of the first large-scale analogue computers.

THE STRUCTUR

STEP 2 (figure b): Give each wool thread an overlength of 8%. Because no single road ever leads straight to a single house, we are always forced to take detours in cities. The figure of 8% is generalized: this amount of detouring need not be averaged down to a single figure for the whole and can be differentiated throughout the system.

STEP 3 (figure c): Dip the whole system in water, shake it carefully and remove it so that it breaks the surface slowly. Wet threads have a tendency to stick together, and as threads start to merge they lose this capacity at other positions, since merging means elimination of available overlength. All overlength is thus processed out of the system by a surplus of stickiness. Since the paths are coming from all directions, the mergings also come from all directions, which results in a system organized by gaps, rounded holes, surrounded by thick mergings of threads, sometimes more than eight, and smaller fields of crossings.

The first step contains only geometry, no materiality; then materiality takes over and the procedure comes to a halt in a state of full geometry again, a geometry not, however, imposed on a material but the result of material interactions. It starts out explicitly Euclidean, but it doesn't finish as such, because in the end there is no longer a clear segmentation of dimensions. While we could call the system's first step a geometrical surface, a system where all directions are equally present, the final stage of the model is much more complex, because it consists of patches of crossings, mergings and holes. The crossing-patches consist of two dimensions, which means in these areas many directions are still available in the system – lines keep criss-crossing each other as in the initial state. The merging-patches consist of only one dimension, where the system takes on a single direction – many lines adhere to form a main artery. And the holes are areas where all dimensions and directions are lost. While the first stage consists of homogeneous tiling, the last stage consists of heterogeneously nested patching.

The end result (figure c) is based on looseness, but is itself not loose, not weak, but rigid and completely tight (when attached on an open ring it comes out of the water straight and horizontal). It is a strategy of flexible, individually weak elements cooperating to form strong collective configurations. What emerges is complex or *soft rigidity*, very different from the top-down, simple or *frozen rigidity* of the first stage. We should resist the idea that the first stage is a rigid order and the end result is just a romantic labyrinth or park. The arabesque order of the end result is in fact as rigid as the first gridded stage, but more intelligent because it optimizes individual necessities in a collective economy. Yet it is not an easily readable and clear form of order, but a *vague order*; it is barely possible to distinguish between surface areas, linear elements and holes. Surfaces can function as linearities, lines can cooperate in surfaces, and holes can exist at all scales. Everything between the dimensions is materialized, and though the dimensions are singularities arranging the system (the mergings into thick lines are like the ridges of dunes, which orient the sand surface to the wind forces), it is continuity that makes them emerge. The order

OF VAGUENESS

is vague but very precise, because nothing is left out. There is no randomness, there is only variation.

The truly amazing feature of this system is that it is structured by holes; the nesting of holes is the driving force behind its formation. Architects are trained to think that holes are, at the end, subtracted from a system but this machine operates not on subtraction or addition but on multiplication, in the classic sense of early systems theory, which states that a whole is always larger than the sum of its parts. Here porosity is an emergent property. The first stage is basically drawn, in contrast to the end stage, which is processed by a machine, calculated. All effects that co-exist in the final result, all the curves, mergings and holes are interrelated, nothing can be changed without affecting the arrangement of the whole. All lines are mobilized simultaneously, whereas drawing is serial, one line being drawn after the other. A drawing is always created in the visual field, while the analogue machine follows a partly blind and informational logic where the image is the end product of the process. And though this technique should be considered as a hybrid of the top-down and the bottom-up, the drawn and the generated, its intelligence lies in the fact that nothing is 'translated'; the drawn is not 'translated' into the real: it works 1:1. In that sense it is not even a model. This *direct proportion* is one of the main features of analogue computing, which simulates not by numbers but by an empirical rescaling of the real. In the case of our optimized path system it is the materialization of the ink as wool *beforehand* that makes it work.

The organizational and informational stage is material, not immaterial, as is so often put forth. It is the material *potential*, the material's distributed intelligence that sets the machine in motion, a transfer of water-turbulence to wool-curvature. Then it is the stickiness, the hairiness and the curvability of the wool thread, together with the cohesive forces on the water surface, that bring it to a halt and inform the end result. It is simply impossible to do this in ink. It is an intensive technique within an extensive system, and though the quantities (surface area, number of houses and so on) are given beforehand, the quality emerges through the interaction and multiplication of different parameters. Generally, the intensive is a deformational property (like heating), but here it also becomes a transformational property (like boiling): the threads restructure and reorganize to 'find form'. The system as a whole passes a critical threshold such that the degrees of freedom of deformation, which are more like extensive movements within an internal structure, become intensive, qualitative changes of 'that' structure.

Wet Grid vs Dry Grid

The classic Greek grid is a system that separates infrastructural movement from material structure. Simply put: the structure is solid, while movement is liquid. We must consider the orthogonal grid as a frozen condition, because its state of geometrical homogeneity relates directly to a material, crystallized state of frozenness. Frozen states are simple and were therefore the first to be mastered by the geometers, but to understand complex states we need to develop complex geometries. We are taught to think geometry is the higher, the more abstract and pure form of materiality, which is a misconception because

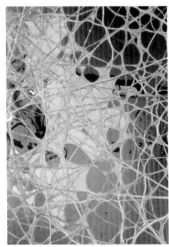

Experimental model produced in our office based on Frei Otto's two-dimensional optimized path system. For *Soft Office*, 2001.

THE STRUCTUR

though geometry strives for exactitude, it is totally imprecise. Any geometer comes after the event, when everything has dried up, and deals only with the extensive state of the material, measuring length, width and height. The wet grid, Frei Otto's grid, is one in which movement is structurally absorbed by the system, where the intensive and the extensive are combined as flexibility and motion. The geometry does not follow the event, it co-evolves with materiality through analogue, wet computing. One might call the organization of the final stage wet and its structure dry. While it itself is not moving any more, it has attained an architecture of movement.

Movement must be viewed as information, as pure difference, because we all know when 'information' does not cause any change it is superfluous. It simply did not in-form, it did not enter the form. Movement in itself is not enough to be called information, it must be internally processed as a (temporary or permanent) transformation. The physical displacement of movement must be processed as a structural change. Freezings of movement are merely traces, momentary stoppages of a bygone present, they are not structured through time, they are not paths that allow for movement to be run over and over again and slowly consolidate and evolve. On the other hand they are not roads either, which, with their precise distinction between surface and line, prevent the system from reconfiguration and adaptation. Each state of pathforming should function as the analogue computer of the next one. There should be enough solidifying for registering and enough plasticity to enable changes. This brings the optimized path systems of Frei Otto close to the contemporary multi-agent computing devices based on ant colonies with their pheromone distribution.

For a real-time, analogue computing model we need two things: first, a system that is internally structured (or else it cannot process information), and second, external flows of information. This means that simple states and complex states co-exist, in gradation. Higher states of information can happen only in lower states of information; they co-exist hierarchically but within a continuum, not next to each other. The generic and the specific share the same continuous topological space as do the standard and the non-standard. One is always engulfing the other. We need to start from a state of equilibrium that already contains information through its structure, then we need disequilibrium to increase the amount of information, then we need equilibrium again to memorize it. The brilliance of the Frei Otto model is that the flexibility is taken literally and materially, that real movement of water-flow becomes abstract movement of wool-structure, which results in a coherent language of 'bending', 'splitting', 'curving', 'nesting', 'aligning', 'merging'. All arabesque figures in the final state immediately relate to complex configurations.

To understand that complexity, however, it is necessary to understand the nature of a curve. For Aristotle any curve could be described as a mixture of straight lines and circle segments, arranged in different orders. The later curve of differential calculus virtualizes the straight line and the circle as the tangent and the approximative circle that remains an important indication for curvature. In seventeenth-century shipbuilding, however, the control of curvature was based on material intelligence, not on geometry. Curves for ships' hulls were 'lofted' 1:1 with so-called 'splines', thin slats of wood bent into shape by heavy leaden weights. The spline is present today in all 3D-modelling software, and

Plan of Milete, fifth century BC.

Ethiopian village demonstrating an energy-optimized network with minimal detours. Frei Otto and Bodo Rasch. *Finding Form* (1995): 36.

OF VAGUENESS

Curved wooden spline held in place by five weights.

though it now exists in different forms (Bezier spline, B-spline, NURBS), it is always based on the important notion of materiality. A digital spline starts out as straight and becomes curved by feeding information to it. The at-start straight spline has an internal structure of control vertices or 'cv's' and by moving these sideways it takes on curvature. The number of cv's on the line is therefore the indication for the type of curvature: how far it is off from straightness or how close it is to circularity. In short, a *geometrical* straight line going from A to B doesn't have enough structure to be moved into a state of higher complexity: moving either A or B results only in a rotation of the same straight line. The spline's prestructuring through the range of control vertices makes it *parametrical*. The only difference between a material and a digital spline is that in the material version the 'overlength' is external and in the computerized version it is internal. In the Frei Otto model the wool thread going straight from A to B in the initial state (figure a) is in its final state (figure c) charged by a whole field of other influences and directions, from C to D and from F to G and so on. The line is taken up in a field of potentials that make it an intensive line, which is simply a curve. A curve is an intelligent, better-informed straight line.

Remembering that Frei Otto's model is a path system, we should read a curve as a road with variable openness, on which one can partly return to one's footsteps, change one's mind, hesitate or forget. It is not labyrinthine, causing you to lose your way completely; no: it complicates your way, makes it multiple and negotiable. Likewise, a curve is a complicated straight line, it still goes from A to B, it still has overall direction, it still takes you somewhere, but it manages many other subdirections (tangents) along the way. It negotiates difference; it is differential precisely through connecting, through continuity. The dry grid is always segmented and Euclidean, while the wet grid is always a continuous network, topological and curved.

In architecture flexibility is usually associated with the engagement of the building with events that are unforeseen, with an unpredictable or variable use of space. During Modernism that flexibility often resulted in an undetermined architecture, in an averaging of programme, an equalization, even neutralization, of space. A generalized openness, we must keep in mind, always has the effect of neutralizing events and being unproductive, because the type of space is not engaged in the emergence of events themselves. General Miesian openness is suitable only when all desired events are fully programmed in advance, by strictly organized bodies, as in the case of a convention centre, a fair or a barracks. It is flexible, of course; it is open, yes; but it is totally passive. All activity is assigned to the institutional body. The architecture itself, however, is not involved in the way events and situations emerge. It is indifferent, as if life is merely the effect of decisions taken behind the scenes, of acts that are repetitions of previous acts, in which intentions are completely transparent. The Cartesianism doesn't just apply to its spatial geometry but even more so to the neuropsychology of the homunculus. The dry grid is not very different in its ambitions from, say, that Miesian box or hall in architecture: finding a structure, a tectonics that can absorb life, chance and change, while the structure itself must last and persist over time, to span the unforeseen with the foreseeable.

THE STRUCTUR

It is true that much of what we do is planned, and a lot of what we intend is transparent – we script and schedule ourselves – but to engage in the unforeseen need not imply that these are just accidents happening to our schedules.

The fundamental question thus becomes a study of the relationship between flexibility and movement: how does the body's flexibility relate to architecture's flexibility? I believe that extensive body locomotion is possible only when it is intensive first, both in the body and in the system. There is always a direct relationship between the system of motion and the internal mapping of movements in the body. In the dry grid that means the body is acting as if it is in an archive, constantly picking movements off the shelf, every act a re-enaction – the body itself is a dry grid. The wet grid views the body as a complex landscape of tendencies and habits that form grooves (lines) or so-called chreodes in less defined areas that are surfaces. All modern neurology describes the body as a wet computer, constantly evolving, adapting, practising, managing, coping and scripting. The problem of flexibility is not so much 'to open up space to more possibilities', but to open up the concept of the possible. An event is only ever categorized as possible afterwards. The possible as category lacks the internal structure to relate the variations; it does not produce variation by itself – it is without *potential*. The choice has always been between determined functionalism and undetermined multifunctionalism, between early and late Modernism, between the filled-in grid and the not-fully-filled-in grid. But potential is something else: 'Potential means indeterminate yet capable of determination … The vague always tends to become determinate, simply because its vagueness does not determine it to be vague … It is not determinately nothing.'[1]

Vagueness comes before the situation; neutrality comes afterwards. If it comes before, it neutralizes the forces making up the situation. *We must replace the passive flexibility of neutrality with an active flexibility of vagueness.* In opposition to neutrality, vagueness operates within a differentiated field of vectors, of tendencies, that allow for clearly defined goals and habits and for as-yet undetermined actions. It allows for both formal and informal conduct. But more importantly, it also relates them through continuity, it places them in a tense situation of elasticity. The informal doesn't come out of the blue, it emerges precisely from the planned, but only because of intensive elastic planning. It is a structural Situationism. It allows for *dérives* and *détournements* as structural properties: the transparent intentionality of planning and habit is stretched by the sideways steps of opaque intentionality. It does not mean the unforeseen is now successfully tamed and reckoned with, but the structuring of the foreseen can now produce the unforeseen and the new. Why? Because all linearity is embedded within fields of non-linearity there is an enormous surplus of information in the system, a *redundancy* that allows behaviour to develop in multiple ways. This redundancy is opportunistic and pragmatic, offering multiple ways towards a goal, but it does not afford anything to happen at any place. Non-linearity does not mean a breaking of the line, nor does it mean a relaxation that can stretch infinitely: it means a fundamental bendability, a looping, a feeding back of the line.

1. C S Peirce. Nathan Houser and Christian Kloesel, eds. *The Essential Peirce: Selected Philosophical Writings*. (Bloomington: University of Indiana Press, vol. 1, 1992).

OF VAGUENESS

A Soft Constructivism

The techniques invented and suggested by Frei Otto have been diverse, ranging from the application of already invented techniques to ongoing projects to fundamental research into material form-finding. Not surprisingly, his optimized path system machine is unique within the whole of his research because he hardly ever had to deal with horizontal structures. His research was essentially in the complexity of the elevation, the structure, not the plan. He was often invited to cooperate with architects who had already developed the plan, and his contribution was subsequently in the engineering stages, afterwards. Our agenda should be different. Patterning effects, configurational emergent effects happen at all stages, from the plan to the elevation. Instead of following the plan-floor and extrusion-wall method we should opt for a method where elevation and plan are intertwined and co-evolve into structure. For centuries the order within the design process has been plan (action), then structure at the corners (construction), which is finally filled in with walls (perception), where the latter two have been part of the splendid Semperian distinction between tectonics and textile.

Our agenda should be to short-circuit action, perception and construction. Having weak textile threads teaming up into rigid collective configurations is a direct upgrade, or inversion, of the Semperian paradigm. But threads should be three-dimensional from the start; plan-threads can twist and become wall-threads. These techniques already exist in textile art, where complex interlacings occur in crochet, weaving and knitting. The art of the arabesque is as old as architecture, it has just never been conceived at the scale of the building – and that is certainly because of technological reasons. The arabesque has always been achieved by manual labour while straight extrusion was necessarily associated with standardization and industrialism.

This is changing with non-standard architecture, however. But we should be careful not to mistake the non-standard for 'free-form architecture', for the amorphous or even the streamlined. We should strive for a rigorous non-standardization, rethinking repetition within sets of variability, reconceiving structures within ranges of flexibility. The more we move towards the non-standard, the more articulation must become an issue. If there is no technology of design, a technology of manufacture becomes nonsensical. With machines under numerical control we need the design process itself to be an informational procedure, with clear stated rules and scripts to generate a structure of vagueness.

Starting with the soft and ending with the rigid will offer us much more complexity in architecture, not in the sense of Venturi's linguistic complexity (of ambiguity), but in a material complexity (of vagueness). The science of complexity has produced many diagrams of the soft, and these have often been superimposed on rigid architectural structures or typologies. Though *deconstructivism* proved to be successful in breaking down most of architecture's top-down ordering tools (contour-tracing, proportion, axiality), it proved to be incapable of instrumentalizing complexity itself as a tool to produce architectural form. It understood every act of building as an implicit counter-act, as a negation – meanwhile, the engineers silently repaired it. We should understand all objects and bodies as part of a process of emergence, *the made as being part of the making, not the unmade.* Our goal must be *constructivism*, or emergence, and anything that emerges should co-emerge: the way we see, the way we move around, the way we act in relation to others, to our habits, to our memories. All these emergent patterns should co-emerge with material structure. This makes the agenda one of a post-industrial constructivism, a non-standard constructivism. All behaviour is material, all structure is material. How do we orient? How do we feel? How do we group or ungroup? All these questions should be posed simultaneously, together with, How does it stand up? There have been numerous attempts to borrow 'images of complexity' that were arti-ficially fed into circulational, formal or structural diagrams — Klein bottles, weather maps and the like — interesting ideas but not enough. We should feed circulation into structure, feed structure into perception, and feed perception into circulation. It doesn't matter where we start as long as we are looping a flexibility of action (affordances) into a flexibility of structure (vagueness) into a flexibility of perception (atmosphere), looping non-standard behaviour into non-standard structure into non-standard architecture.

OF VAGUENESS

Bioconstructivisms

Detlef Mertins

On meeting the German structural engineer Frei Otto in 1998, Lars Spuybroek was struck by the extent to which Otto's approach to the design of light structures resonated with his own interest in the generation of complex and dynamic curvatures. Having designed the Freshwater Pavilion (1994–97) using geometric and topological procedures, which were then materialized through the exigency of a steel structure and flexible metal sheeting, Spuybroek found in Otto a reservoir of experiments in developing curved surfaces of even greater complexity by means of a process that was already material – that was, in fact, simultaneously material, structural and geometric. Moreover, Otto's concern with flexible surfaces not only blurred the classic distinctions between surface and support, vault and beam (suggesting a non-elemental conception of structural functions) but also made construction and structure a function of movement or, more precisely, a function of the rigidification of soft, dynamic entities into calcified structures such as bones and shells. Philosophically inclined towards a dynamic conception of the universe – a Bergsonian and Deleuzian ontology of movement, time and duration – Spuybroek embarked on an intensive study of Otto's work and took up his analogical design method. A materialist of the first order, Spuybroek now developed his own experiments following those of Otto with soap bubbles, chain nets and other materials as a way to discover how complex structural behaviours find forms of their own accord, which can then be reiterated on a larger scale using tensile, cable or shell constructions.

This curious encounter between Spuybroek and Otto sends us back not only to the 1960s, but deeper in time. The recent re-engagement of architecture with generative models from nature, science and technology is itself part of a longer history of architects, engineers and theorists pursuing autopoiesis, or self-generation. While its procedures and forms have varied, self-generation has been a consistent goal in architecture for over a century, set against the perpetuation of predetermined forms and norms. The well-known polemic of the early twentieth-century avant-garde against received styles or compositional systems in art and architecture – and against style per se – may, in fact, be understood as part of a longer and larger shift in thought from notions of predetermination to self-generation, transcendence to immanence. The search for new methods of design has been integral to this shift, whether it be figured in terms of a period-setting

BIOCONSTI

revolution or the immanent production of multiplicity. Although a history of generative architecture has yet to be written, various partial histories in art, philosophy and science may serve to open this field of research.

In his landmark cross-disciplinary study, *Self-Generation: Biology, Philosophy and Literature around 1800* (1997), Helmut Müller-Sievers describes how the Aristotelian doctrine of the epigenesis of organisms – having been challenged in the seventeenth century by the rise of modern sciences – resurfaced in the eighteenth century, as the mechanistic theories of Galileo, Descartes and Newton foundered in their explanations of the appearance of new organisms. Where figures such as Charles Bonnet and Albrecht von Haller held that the germs of all living beings had been preformed since the Creation – denying nature any productive energy – a new theory of self-generation gradually took shape. An active inner principle was first proffered by the Count de Buffon and then elaborated by Caspar Friedrich Wolff, explaining the production of new organisms through the capacity of unorganized, fluid material to consolidate itself. Johann Friedrich Blumenbach transformed Wolff's 'essential force' into a 'formative drive' that served as the motive for the successive self-organization of life forms, understanding this as a transition from unorganized matter to organized corporations.[1] The biological theory of epigenesis came to underpin the theory of autonomy in the human sphere – in art, aesthetics, philosophy, politics and social institutions such as marriage. As Müller-Sievers has noted, Blumenbach's epigenesis provided a direct model for Kant's deduction of the categories, on which his shift from metaphysics to epistemology relied: 'Only if they are self-produced can the categories guarantee transcendental apriority and, by implication, cognitive necessity and universality'.[2]

In a similar vein, but looking to mathematics and its influence, rather than biology or aesthetics, the philosopher David Lachterman characterized the whole of modernity as 'constructivist' and traced its origins further back to the shift in the seventeenth century from ancient to modern mathematics. Where the mathematics of Euclid focused on axiomatic methods of geometric demonstration and the proof of theorems (existence of beings), modern mathematics emphasized geometrical construction and problem-solving.[3] As Lachterman put it, a fairly direct line runs from the 'construction of a problem' in Descartes through the 'construction of an equation' in Leibniz to the 'construction of a concept' in Kant.

Rather than reiterating ontologies of sameness, modern mathematics produced difference through new constructions. In this regard it is telling that, as Lachterman points out, Euclidean geometry arose against a Platonic backdrop that understood each of the mathematicals as having unlimited manyness. According to the doctrine of intermediates, 'the mathematicals differ from the forms inasmuch as there are many "similar" [*homoia*] squares, say, while there is only one unique form.' Lachterman continues: 'The manyness intrinsic to each "kind" of figure as well as the manyness displayed by the infinitely various images of each kind must somehow be a multiplicity indifferent to itself, a manyness of differences that make no fundamental difference, while nonetheless never collapsing into indiscriminate sameness or identity with one another.'[4] A Euclidean construction, then, does not produce heterogeneity, but rather negotiates an intricate mutuality between manyness and kinship, variation and stability. It is always an image of this one, uniquely determinate specimen of the kind. 'There is no one perfect square, but every square has to be perfect of its kind, not *sui generis*.'[5]

The quest for autopoiesis has been expressed, then, in a variety of oppositional tropes – creation versus imitation, symbol versus rhetoric, organism versus

1. See Helmut Müller-Sievers. *Self-Generation: Biology, Philosophy and Literature around 1800* (Stanford: Stanford University Press, 1997).

2. Ibid: 46.

3. David Rapport Lachterman. *The Ethics of Geometry: A Genealogy of Modernity* (New York and London: Routledge, 1989): vii.

4. Ibid: 117–18.

5. Ibid: 118.

mechanism, epigenesis versus preformation, autonomy versus metaphysics and construction *sui generis* versus reiteration of forms. In the nineteenth century, such binary oppositions came to underpin the quest for freedom among the cultural avant-garde. In his *Five Faces of Modernity* (1987), Matei Calinescu recounted that the term 'avant-garde' was first introduced in military discourse during the Middle Ages to refer to an advance guard. It was given its first figurative meaning in the Renaissance, but became a metaphor for a self-consciously advanced position in politics, literature and art only during the nineteenth century. In the 1860s, Charles Baudelaire was the first to point to the unresolved tension within the avant-garde between radical artistic freedom and programmatic political campaigns modelled on war and striving to install a new order – between critique, negation and destruction, on the one hand, and dogma, regulation and system, on the other. An alternative interpretation of what Calinescu calls the *aporia* of the avant-garde – one that sharpens the implications of this problematic, both philosophically and politically – is suggested by Michael Hardt and Tony Negri's account of the origins of modernity in their book, *Empire* (2000). Their history is even more sweeping than those reviewed above, summarizing how, in Europe between 1200 and 1400, divine and transcendental authority over worldly affairs came to be challenged by affirmations of the powers of this world, which they call 'the [revolutionary] discovery of the plane of immanence'. Citing further evidence in the writings of Nicholas of Cusa among others, Hardt and Negri conclude that the primary event of modernity was constituted by shifting knowledge from the transcendental plane to the immanent, thereby turning knowledge into a doing, a practice of transform-ing nature. Galileo Galilei went so far as to suggest that it was possible for humanity to equal divine knowledge (and hence divine doing), referring specifically to the mathematical sciences of geometry and arithmetic. As Lachterman suggested using somewhat different terms, on the plane of immanence, mathematics begins to operate differently from the way it operates within philosophies of transcendence where it secures the higher order of being. On the plane of immanence, mathematics is done constructively, solving problems and generating new entities. For Hardt and Negri, 'the powers of creation that had previously been consigned exclusively to the heavens are now brought down to earth.'

By the time of Spinoza, Hardt and Negri note, the horizon of immanence and the horizon of democratic political order had come together, bringing the politics of immanence to the fore as both the multitude, in theoretical terms, and a new democratic conception of liberation and of law through the assembly of citizens.[6] The historical process of subjectivization launched an immanent constitutive power and, with it, a politics of difference and multiplicity. This in turn sparked counterrevolutions, marking the subsequent history as 'an uninterrupted conflict between the immanent, constructive, creative forces and the transcendent power aimed at restoring order'.[7] For Hardt and Negri, this crisis is constitutive of modernity itself. Just as immanence is never achieved, so the counterrevolution is also never assured.

The conflict between immanence and transcendence may also be discerned in architecture, along with efforts to resolve it through the mediation of an architectonic system for free expression or self-generation. Critical of using historical styles, which were understood as residual transcendent authorities no longer commensurate with the present, progressive architects of the early twentieth century sought to develop a modern style that, in itself, would also avoid

6. Michael Hardt and Antonio Negri. *Empire* (Cambridge. MA: Harvard University Press. 2000): 73.

7. Ibid: 77.

BIOCONSTI

the problem of predetermination, which had taken on new urgency under the conditions of industrialization and mass production. Such a style was conceived more in terms of procedures than formal idioms. For instance, in a piece of history that has received inadequate attention, a number of Dutch architects around 1900 turned to proportional and geometric constructions as generative tools. Recognizing that not only classical, but also medieval and even Egyptian architecture employed proportional systems and geometric schema, they hoped to discover a universal mathesis, both timely and timeless, for a process of design whose results were not already determined at the outset. The validity and value of such forms were guaranteed, it was thought, by virtue of the laws of geometry, whose own authority was, in turn, guaranteed by their giveness in nature. Foremost among a group that included J. H. de Groot, K. P. C. de Bazel, P. J. H. Cuypers, and J. L. M. Lauweriks, was H. P. Berlage, whose celebrated Stock Exchange in Amsterdam (1901) was based on the Egyptian triangle.

In lectures and publications of around 1907 – synopses of which were translated and published in America in 1912 – Berlage articulated his theory of architecture based on the principles and laws of construction. Taking issue with the growing pluralism of taste-styles, he sought an objective basis for design – including the peculiarities of construction and the arrangement of forms, lines, and colours – in the laws of nature. He described these as 'the laws under which the Universe is formed, and is constantly being reformed; it is the laws which fill us with admiration for the harmony with which everything is organized, the harmony which penetrates the infinite even to its invisible atoms.'[8] He went on to argue that adherence to nature's laws and procedures need not lead to mindless repetition and sameness, since nature produces a boundless variety of organisms and creatures through the repetition of basic forms and elements. Similarly, he considered music a paradigm, since here too creativity appeared unhampered in the adherence to laws. Citing Gottfried Semper, Berlage extended this analogy to suggest that even evolution is based on 'a few normal forms and types, derived from the most ancient traditions'. They appear in an endless variety that is not arbitrary but determined by the combination of circumstances and proportions, by which he meant relations or, more precisely, organization. For Berlage, this led directly – for both practical and aesthetic reasons – to mathematics in art as in nature. He wrote:

> I need only remind you in this connection of the stereometric–ellipsordic forms of the astral bodies, and of the purely geometrical shape of their courses; of the shapes of plants, flowers and different animals, with the setting of their component parts in purely geometrical figures; of the crystals with their purely stereometrical forms, even so that some of their modifications remind one especially of the forms of the Gothic style; and lastly, of the admirable systematicalness of the lower animal and vegetable orders, in latter times brought to our knowledge by the microscope, and which I have myself used as motive for the designs of a series of ornaments.[9]

It is worth noting that, as Berlage was putting forward a constructivist cosmology of architecture, Peter Behrens in Germany drew on some of the same proportional systems but with a more conservative agenda, reiterating the transcendent claims of classicism through a neo-Kantian schematism. For Behrens, geometry con-

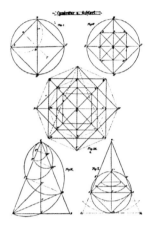

H. P. Berlage. Diagrams of quadrature (*The Western Architect*, 19, 1912).

8. H. P. Berlage. 'Foundations and Development of Architecture (Part 1)'. *The Western Architect* (vol. 18, no. 9, September 1912): 96–99. Part 2 (vol. 18, no. 10, October 1912): 104–08. These articles were based on his *Grundlagen der Architektur* (Berlin: Julius Bard, 1908), which compiled five illustrated lectures delivered at the Kunstgewerbe Museum in Zurich in 1907.

9. Berlage. 'Foundations' (Part 1): 97.

10. H. P. Berlage. *Grundlagen der Architektur* (Berlin: Julius Bard, 1908): 7, 16, 38–39.

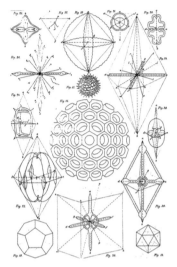

Basic polyaxon and homopolar forms. Plate II in Ernst Haeckel, *Generelle Morphologie der Organismen* (vol. 1, 1866).

11. Ernst Haeckel. *Report of the Deep-Sea Keratosa [collected by H.M.S. Challenger during the years 1873–76]* (London: Eyre & Spottiswoode, 1889): clxxxviii.

12. Ernst Haeckel. *Kunstformen der Natur* (Leipzig and Vienna: Verlag des Bibliographischen Instituts, 1904). Translation by author.

13. D'Arcy Wentworth Thompson. *On Growth and Form* (New York: Dover, 1992). Published originally in 1917 and revised in 1942.

14. Ibid: 645.

15. Ibid: 691.

16. Ibid: 695.

17. Ibid: 698.

stituted an a priori architectonic system that was to be applied across buildings, landscapes and furniture to raise the material world to the higher plane of *Kultur*, while for Berlage architecture was based on a living geometry, in itself heterogeneous rather than homogeneous, with which to produce novel astylar forms that belonged to this world.[10] Behrens's pursuit of the 'great form' – symbol of the transcendence of pure mind and spirit – privileged architectonics over construction and maintained a clear hierarchy between the material and the ideal. In contrast, for Berlage architecture was at once geometric, material, technological and biological. He understood beauty to be immanent to the self-actualization of material entities, contingent only on the rational (*sachlich*) use of means and the laws of geometry.

In citing the 'admirable systematicalness of the lower animal and vegetable orders', Berlage alluded to the microscopic single-cell sea creatures studied by the German zoologist Ernst Haeckel in the 1880s and popularized in his book of 1904, *Kunstformen der Natur [The Art Forms of Nature]* as well as other writings, including his *Report of the Scientific Results of the Voyage of H.M.S.* Challenger (London, 1887), which was later often cited. Haeckel estimated that there were 4,314 species of radiolarian included in 739 genera found all over the world, without any evident limitations of geographical habitat.[11] He also noted that the families and even genera appear to have been constant since the Cambrian age. This uni-cellular species of organisms became an exemplar for those interested in learning from the way in which self-generation in nature could produce seemingly endless variety – if not multiplicity per se – in complex as well as simple forms of life. Haeckel hoped that knowledge of Ur-animals (protozoa such as radiolarians, thalamophorians and infusorians) and Ur-plants (protophntoa such as diatomians, rosmarians and veridienians) 'would open up a rich source of motifs for painters and architects' and that 'the real art forms of Nature not only stimulate the development of the decorative arts in practical terms but also raise the understanding of the plastic arts to a higher theoretical level.'[12]

In his own landmark book, *On Growth and Form* (1917), the Scottish biologist D'Arcy Wentworth Thompson developed science's understanding of form in terms of the dynamics of living organisms, their transformation through growth and movement.[13] In considering the formation of skeletons, he recounted Haeckel's theory of 'bio-crystallization' among very simple organisms, including radiolarians and sponges. While the sponge-spicule offered a simple case of growth along a linear axis – their skeletons always begin as a loose mass of isolated spicules – the radiolarians provided a more complex case among single-cell organisms, exhibiting extraordinary intricacy, delicacy and complexity as well as beauty and variety, all by virtue of the 'intrinsic form of its elementary constituents or the geometric symmetry with which these are interconnected and arranged'.[14] For Thompson, such 'biocrystals' represented something 'midway between an inorganic crystal and an organic secretion'.[15] He distinguished their multitudinous variety from that of snowflakes, which were produced through symmetrical repetitions of one simple crystalline form, 'a beautiful illustration of Plato's *One among the Many*'.[16] The generation of the radiolarian skeleton, on the other hand, is more complex and open-ended, for it 'rings its endless changes on combinations of certain facets, corners and edges within a filmy and bubbly mass'. With this more heterogeneous technology, the radiolarian can generate continuous skeletons of netted mesh or perforated lacework that are more variegated, modulated and intricate – even irregular – than any snowflake.[17]

BIOCONSTI

For enthusiasts of biocrystallization, one of the key features of radiolarians was the apparently perfect regularity of their form or, more precisely, of their skeleton and the outer surface layer of froth-like vesicles, 'uniform in size or nearly so', which tended to produce a honeycomb or regular meshwork of hexagons. The larger implications of this regularity were made explicit in scientific cosmologies of the early-twentieth century, such as Emmerich Zederbauer's *Die Harmonie im Weltall in der Natur und Kunst* (1917) and Ernst Mössel's *Vom Geheimnis der Form und der Urform des Seines* (1938). Supported by the evidence of ever more powerful microscopes and telescopes, these authors sought to confirm that the entire universe was ordered according to the same crystalline structural laws — establishing continuity from the structure of molecules and microscopic radiolarians to macroscopic celestial configurations, between organic and inorganic, nature and technology.

Two radiolarians, the *Reticulum plasmatique*, after Carnoy, and the *Aulonia hexagona*, as depicted by Haeckel. D'Arcy Thompson, *On Growth and Form* (1942).

Perhaps the most sweeping statement of Platonic Oneness at mid-century — embracing industrialized structures as well as natural ones — was provided by R. Buckminster Fuller when he wrote that the 'subvisible microscopic animal structures called *radiolaria* are developed by the same mathematical and structural laws as those governing the man-designed geodesic and other non-man-designed spheroidal structures in nature'.[18] This similarity of underlying laws gave the radiolarians, like the geodesic domes that Fuller designed, the character of an exemplar for fundamental structures, which, he explained, were not in fact things but rather 'patterns of inherently regenerative constellar association of energy events'.[19] As if to substantiate Fuller's point, Paul Weidlinger illustrated his own account of the isomorphism in organic and inorganic materials as well as microscopic and macroscopic events, by comparing Haeckel's drawing of a radiolarian with magnified photographs of soap bubbles, the stellate cells of a reed and one of Fuller's geodesic domes, replete with tiny spikes that reinforce its resemblance to the radiolarian.[20]

18. R. Buckminster Fuller. 'Conceptuality of Fundamental Structures.' In Gyorgy Kepes, ed. *Structure in Art and in Science* (New York: George Braziller, 1965): 66–88. Quotation is on p. 80.

19. Ibid: 66.

20. Paul Weidlinger. 'Form in Engineering.' In Gyorgy Kepes, ed. *The New Landscape in Art and Science* (Chicago: Paul Theobald, 1956): 360–65.

Yet Thompson's lengthy effort to account for the diversity of the tiny creatures ultimately ran aground because of the impossible mathematics of Haeckel's theory of bio-crystallization. Not only did Thompson find it necessary to acknowledge and examine less perfectly configured specimens, such as the *Reticulum plasmatique* depicted by Carnoy, but in comparing them with Haeckel's *Aulonia* — 'looking like the finest imaginable Chinese ivory ball' — he invoked Euler to explain that '*No system of hexagons can enclose space*; whether the hexagons be equal or unequal, regular or irregular, it is still under all circumstances mathematically impossible … the array of hexagons may be extended as far as you please, and over a surface either plane or curved, but *it never closes in*.'[21] Thompson pointed out that Haeckel himself must have been aware of the problem for, in his brief description of the *Aulonia hexagona*, he noted that a few square or pentagonal facets appeared among the hexagons. Thompson concluded from this that, while Haeckel tried hard to discover and reveal the symmetry of crystallization in radiolarians and other organisms, his effort 'resolves itself into remote analogies from which no conclusions can be drawn'. In the case of the radiolarians, 'Nature keeps some of her secrets longer than others.'[22]

Ernst Haeckel, Aulographis, Plate 61, *Kunstformen der Natur* (1904).

21. Thompson: 708.

22. Thompson: 732.

23. Phillip Ritterbush. *The Art of Organic Forms* (Washington: Smithsonian Institution Press, 1968): 8. See also Donna Jeanne Haraway. *Crystals, Fabrics, and Fields: Metaphors of Organicism in Twentieth-Century Developmental Biology* (New Haven and London: Yale University Press, 1976): 11.

During the 1960s, armed with evidence from more powerful microscopes that the surface meshworks of radiolarians were in fact irregular, Phillip Ritterbush underscored the problem of regularity and biaxial symmetry when he suggested that Haeckel had altered his drawings of the radiolarians 'for them to conform more precisely to his belief in the geometric character of organisms'.[23] Ritterbush pointed

UCTIVISMS

out that Haeckel's appreciation of the regularities and symmetries of the skeletons of living organisms – and by extension, Fuller's conception of geodesic domes as manifesting patterns of constellar associations – relied on a permutation of the analogy with the crystal, which had been employed in biology since the seventeenth century. Nehemiah Grew (1628–1712), for instance, was an early plant anatomist who regarded regularities in natural forms as evidence that the processes of growth consisted of the repetition of simple steps, in which forms might be successfully analyzed.

Assuming that the modular regularity of the radiolarians demonstrated the existence of a universal transcendental order, Fuller reiterated it in the combinatorial logic of irreducible struts and universal joints that comprised his geodesic domes. In contrast, the botanist and popular science writer Raoul H. Francé had already in the 1920s interpreted the radiolarians within a cosmology of composite assemblages that understood all of creation to be constructed not of one Ur-element but of seven. In his *Die Pflanze als Erfinder* [The Plant as Inventor] (1920), Francé argued that the crystal, sphere, plane, rod, ribbon, screw and cone were the seven fundamental technical forms employed 'in various combinations by all world-processes, including architecture, machine elements, crystallography, chemistry, geography, astronomy, and art – every technique in the world'. Comparing what he called the 'biotechnics' of maple keys and tiny flagellates moving through rotation with ships' propellers underscored the isomorphism between human and natural works, inspiring the Russian artist–architect El Lissitzky to denounce the fixation with machines in the early 1920s in favour of constructing 'limbs of nature'.[24] Francé was read enthusiastically in the mid-1920s by artists and architects whom we associate with 'international constructivism' – not only El Lissitzky, but also Raoul Hausmann, László Moholy-Nagy, Hannes Meyer, Siegfried Ebeling and Ludwig Mies van der Rohe. So extensive was this reception of biotechnics or 'cosmobiotechnics', as Hausmann put it, that we may well refer to this orientation within constructivism as 'bioconstructivist'. Looking back, we may also recognize Berlage as providing an earlier iteration of bioconstructivist theory.

Lissitzky paraphrased Francé in his 'Nasci' issue of *Merz* in 1924, which he co-edited with Kurt Schwitters. It was there that Lissitzky gave a constructivist – and now scientific – twist to the idea of becoming that had saturated the artistic culture of Berlin after the Second World War, associated with both expressionism and dada. The word *nasci* is Latin for 'becoming' and approximates the German *Gestaltung*, which was used in technical discourse as well as aesthetics and biology and referred simultaneously to form and the process of formation. It implied a self-generating process of form-creation through which inner purposes or designs became visible in outer shapes. Having reiterated Francé's theory of biotechnics in their introduction to the journal, Lissitzky and Schwitters then provided a portfolio of modern artworks that can be interpreted only demonstrations of the theory. What is remarkable in this collection is the diversity produced with the seven technical forms. Beginning with Kasmir Malevich's Black Square, the folio then features one of Lissitzky's own Prouns; additional paintings by Piet Mondrian and Fernand Léger; collages by Schwitters, Hans Arp and Georges Braque; sculpture by Alexander Archipenko; photograms by Man Ray; and architecture by Vladimir Tatlin, J. J. P. Oud and Ludwig Mies van der Rohe, and several phenomena from nature. The sequence concludes with an unidentified microscopic image punctuated by a question-mark, suggesting something of the formlessness from which all form emerges or, perhaps, to which biotechnics might lead.

24. El Lissitzky and Kurt Schwitters, eds. 'Nasci,' *Merz* 8/9 (April/July 1924). See translation of text in Sophie Lissitzky-Küppers. *El Lissitzky: Life, Letters, Works* (London: Thames & Hudson, 1992): 351.

BIOCONSTI

By the 1960s, scientists sought to come to terms with the limitations of the crystal metaphor for living phenomena. While Kathlene Lonsdale, for instance, attempted to shore up the transcendental authority of the crystalline by defining it more broadly as arrangements of atoms in repeating patterns,[25] the animal geneticist Conrad Waddington turned to other concepts to account for irregularities. Waddington used the radiolarians to discuss not the similarities between organic forms and technological objects but the difference between them, characterizing man-made objects as reductive, simplistic and mono-functional in relation to the complex, varied and multi-purpose nature of living organisms. For him, organic form 'is produced by the interaction of numerous forces which are balanced against one another in a near-equilibrium that has the character not of a precisely definable pattern but rather of a slightly fluid one, a rhythm.'[26] Invoking Alfred North Whitehead's conception of rhythm to address the irregularities that Thompson had already struggled with, Waddington wrote:

> It is instructive to compare the character of the variations from the ideal form in an organic and in human creation. The shell of the minute unicellular organism *Aulonia hexagona* is one of those animal structures whose functions are simple enough for it to approximate to a simple mathematical figure, that of a sphere covered by almost regular hexagons (fig. p. 365). It will be seen that the hexagons are in practice not quite regular; they do not make up a rigidly definable pattern, but rather a rhythm, in the sense of Whitehead, who wrote: 'A rhythm involves a pattern, and to that extent is always self-identical. But no rhythm can be a mere pattern; for the rhythmic quality depends equally upon the differences involved in each exhibition of the pattern. The essence of rhythm is the fusion of sameness and novelty; so that the whole never loses the essential unity of the pattern, while the parts exhibit the contrast arising from the novelty of the detail. A mere recurrence kills rhythm as surely as does a mere confusion of detail.'[27]

Like Waddington, the French–American structural engineer, Robert Le Ricolais – a pioneer of the space frame – insisted on distinguishing natural and man-made objects and on the limits of instrumental knowledge. While 'amazed' by the coherence and purity of design that the radiolarians represented, he also characterized it as 'frightening'. 'What man makes,' he wrote, 'is usually single-purposed, whereas nature is capable of fulfilling many requirements, not always clear to our mind.'[28] Where engineers had been speaking about space frames for only twenty-five or thirty years, the radiolarians were, he explained, three hundred million years old. 'Well, it's not by chance, and I'm glad that I saw the Radiolaria before I saw Mr. Fuller's dome.' Acknowledging that analogies with natural phenomena could help resolve some problems, he held that 'it's not so important to arrive at a particular solution as it is to get some general view of the whole damn thing, which leaves you guessing.'[29] Le Ricolais's use of material experiments was consistent with such scepticism, privileging specificity and concreteness over universal mathesis. Fascinated by the 'fantastic vastitude' of the radiolarians, neither Le Ricolais nor Frei Otto treated them as synecdochic for the entire universe.[30] They were merely one among many phenomena from which an engineer could learn.

During this period, Frei Otto also took up the notion of self-generation and the analogy between biology and building, but eschewed the imitation of nature in

25. Kathlene Lonsdale. 'Art in Crystallography.' In Gyorgy Kepes, ed. *The New Landscape in Art and Science* (Chicago: Paul Theobald, 1956): 358.

26. C. H. Waddington. 'The Character of Biological Form.' In Lancelot Law Whyte, ed. *Aspects of Form* (London: Lund Humphries, 1951, 1968, 2nd edn): 43–52.

Robert Le Ricolais, Trihex dome, 1967–68 (From Peter McCleary, exhibition catalogue: *Robert Le Ricolais: Visions and Paradoxes*, 1997).

27. Waddington: 26. Waddington's citation of Whitehead is from Alfred North Whitehead, *The Principles of Natural Knowledge* (Cambridge, 1925): 198.

28. Interview with Robert Le Ricolais. 'Things themselves are lying, and so are their images.' *VIA 2: Structures: Implicit and Explicit* (University of Pennsylvania, 1973): 91.

29. Ibid: 91.

30. Le Ricolais used the term 'vastitude' in describing the variety of radiolarians.

UCTIVISMS

Frei Otto, Cover, *IL 33, Radiolaria: Shells in Nature and Technics II* (1990)

31. The 1990 issue of the journal of the Institute for Lightweight Structures, *IL 33*, was dedicated to explaining the self-generation process in some skeletons of radiolarians.

European Central Bank by NOX, see p. 292.

favour of working directly in materials to produce models that were at once natural *and* artificial. At the same time, he also eschewed their translation into a universalizing mathesis. Rather than focusing on form or formula, he took the idea of analogy in an entirely different direction, preferring to stage experiments in which materials find their own form. Where the theory of *Gestaltung* in the 1920s posited the unfolding of an essential germ from within, understanding external form as an expression of inner purpose, in the 1960s, autogenesis was redefined through cybernetics and systems theory, as a function of dynamic, open systems of organization and patterning. In this context, Otto's experiments in the form-finding potential of material process sidestep purist essentialism to open up a world in which unique and complex structures result immanently from material exigencies, without being subject to any transcendent authority, either internal or external. Otto's analogical models involve iterations at different scales and in different materials, but without positing an overarching totality, reductive universality or optimized homogeneity. Open to the air, rambling and polycentric, Otto's tensile structures operate demonstrably outside the terms of physiognomic and formal expression, leaving behind the problematics of inner–outer identity, closure and unity that had been integral to the modernist conception of the autonomous organism and of autopoiesis in human works.

It is telling that an entire issue of the *IL* journal of Otto's Institute for Lightweight Structures has been devoted to the radiolarians, whose composite of pneumatic and net structures intrigued Otto and his research group just as they did Le Ricolais. But unlike other admirers, Otto's group did not take these creatures as models for engineering, but rather sought to explain their self-generation with analogic models. Situated between natural phenomena and engineering, the isomorphic character of Otto's analogical models gives them not only instrumental value for new constructions but also explanatory power for natural phenomena.[31]

Spuybroek too is fascinated by the ways in which complex surfaces in nature result from the rigidification of flexible structures, a process so intricate as to elude precise theoretical or mathematical analysis. Like Otto, he uses a varied repertoire of analogical material models that are deceptively simple but remarkably effective for generating complex structures and tectonic surfaces. In his hands, the radiolarians are no longer emblems of universal order, their imperfections corrected into the perfect regularity of crystalline spheres. 'What is so interesting,' he writes, 'about radiolarians is that they are never spheres, though they tend towards the spherical. They are all composite spheres – tetrahedral, tubular, fan-shaped, etc.' Focusing on examples different from the perfect spheres singled out by Fuller, Spuybroek sees radiolarians not as homogeneous forms but as material technologies that produce hybrid tectonic surfaces – part pneumatic, part net structures – which are flexible in contour and shape. The rhythmic variability of these surfaces is achieved by changes in the size of openings and the thickness of the net fibres between them. With this shift from form to surface, Spuybroek leaves behind the modernist quest for the supposed self-same identity of the organism in favour of a surface that can be modulated to assume different shapes and sizes, but also architectural roles – from façades to roofs and from towers to vaults, halls and edges. While Spuybroek's bundle of interwoven towers for the World Trade Center in New York demonstrates the flexibility of radiolarian technology, the more recent project for the European Central Bank realizes its potential to operate simultaneously in a multitude of ways. More importantly still, Spuybroek's radiolarian tectonic surface is but one of an increasing repertoire of analogical models with which he works. Like Berlage and Francé, his organon of techniques is heterogeneous and divergent rather than homogeneous and convergent. Unlike them, however, he is no longer concerned with the elemental in any way, nor with unifying underlying laws, be they mathematical or biological or both. Although he employs the radiolarian technology to achieve what he calls 'a strong expression of wholeness and pluriformity at the same time', his ECB is radically asymmetrical and irregular, polycentric and contingent. And while its pattern-structure implies repetition and extension, the buildings produced with it remain singular entities.

In taking over Otto's method, Spuybroek uses it as an abstract machine, understanding this term – and the broader pragmatics of which it is a part – through Gilles Deleuze and Felix Guattari.[32] In discussing regimes of signs in *A Thousand Plateaus: Capitalism and Schizophrenia* (1987), they isolate four components of pragmatics: the generative, the transformational, the abstract machine and the machinic. The generative, they say, 'shows how the various abstract regimes form concrete mixed semiotics, with what variants, how they combine, and which one is predominant.'[33] The transformational component, on the other hand, 'shows how these regimes of signs are translated into each other, especially when there is a creation of a new regime.'[34] But, they foreground the abstract machine, with its diagrammatic mode of operation, since it deterritorializes already established semiotic formations or assemblages, is 'independent of the forms and substances, expressions and contents it will distribute'[35] and plays a 'piloting role' in the construction of new realities. The machinic component, they conclude, shows 'how abstract machines are effectuated in concrete assemblages'.[36] While their understanding of the generative is recombinatory and thus avoids implications of beginning from nothing, rethinking the generative impulse of the historical avant-garde in terms of the abstract machine helps to discharge any residual transcendentalism that continues to attend narratives of self-generation, which appears so anachronistic when reiterated by architects today. It offers a stronger and sharper version of *Gestaltung*, detaching process now entirely from form and dynamic organization from *Gestalt*. Alternatively, we could say, with Zeynep Mennan, that it could lead to a *Gestalt*-switch, a new theory of *Gestalt* that would be adequate to complex, rhythmic and modulated forms of heterogeneity.[37] Rather than settling chaos into an order that presumes to transcend it, Spuybroek generates an architecture that is self-estranging and self-different, in which identity is hybrid, multiple and open-ended. If cosmological wholeness is an issue at all, it may now be assumed as given, no longer something lost and needing to be regained, as the romantics thought. Art need no longer dedicate itself to the production of wholeness, since it is inherently part of the cosmos, whatever limited understanding of it we humans may achieve. As Keller Easterling has argued in another context, we need no longer worry about the One, but only the many.[38] There is no need for closure, unity or system that assimilates everything into One. Extending the bioconstructivism of Berlage, Francé, Lissitzky and Otto, Spuybroek now engages only in endless experiments with materials, their processes and structural potentials. What he repeats are not entities or forms but techniques, developing a new *modus operandi* for acting constructively in the world. Rather than seeking to overcome the world or to assimilate difference to the sameness of underlying laws, he works to produce new iterations of reality, drawing on the potentials of matter for the ongoing production and enjoyment of heterogeneous events.

32. Gilles Deleuze and Félix Guattari. *A Thousand Plateaus: Capitalism and Schizophrenia*. Translation and foreword by Brian Massumi (Minneapolis: University of Minnesota Press, 1987).

33. Ibid: 139.

34. Ibid: 139.

35. Ibid: 141.

36. Ibid: 146.

37. Zeynep Mennan. 'Des formes non standard: un "Gestalt Switch".' In exhibition catalogue, *Architectures non standard* (Paris: Centre Pompidou, 2003): 34–41.

38. Keller Easterling presented this argument in a lecture at the University of Pennsylvania on November 19, 2003. See her forthcoming book, *Terra Incognita*.

Materiality: Anexact and Intense

Manuel DeLanda

The importance of order, from a purely mathematical standpoint, has been immeasurably increased by many modern developments. Dedekind, Cantor, and Peano have shown how to base all Arithmetic and Analysis upon series of a certain kind … Irrationals are defined … entirely by the help of order … Projective Geometry [has] shown how to give points, lines and planes an order independent of metrical considerations and of quantity; while descriptive Geometry proves that a very large part of Geometry demands only the possibility of serial arrangement. — Bertrand Russell[1]

1. Bertrand Russell. *Principles of Mathematics* (New York, NY: W.W. Norton, 1903): 199.

With these words, published in 1903, Bertrand Russell summarized the great achievements of the nineteenth century in the reconceptualization of space. The concept of *order*, he argued, had slowly come to be viewed as more important than that of *quantity* in many different branches of mathematics. Just what Russell means by this can be explained if we focus our attention first on one-dimensional spaces, that is, on series. There are two different types of series, one referred to as 'cardinal', exemplified by the series of integers 'One, Two, Three, Four …', the other labelled 'ordinal' and illustrated by the series 'First, Second, Third, Fourth …'. While the definition of the former implies that we already have a notion of numerical quantity, the second is more abstract, demanding only the existence of asymmetrical relations between abstract elements, relations like that of *being in between* two other elements. Only the order of the sequence matters, not the nature of the elements ordered. This difference has consequences for the kinds of comparative judgments one can make about series, particularly if they are dense series, that is, if between any two elements there is always another one. While in the case of two cardinal series, each already subdivided into quantities, one can judge by exactly how much one is larger or smaller than the other, in the case of two dense ordinal series one can rigorously judge that one is greater or smaller but not by exactly how much. In other words, while two spaces already subdivided into identical units can be exactly compared, two spaces without this subdivision allow only for *anexact yet rigorous* comparisons.[2]

2. The phrase 'anexact yet rigorous' is used on several occasions by Deleuze to refer to a style of thought, but also to a characteristic of topological manifolds themselves. One occasion is the discussion of Bertrand Russell's concept of 'ordinal distances' in:Gilles Deleuze and Felix Guattari. *A Thousand Plateaus* (Minneapolis: University of Minnesota Press, 1987): 483.

The importance of anexact yet rigorous thought has only increased since Russell wrote those words. Philosophers such as Gilles Deleuze have made this kind of non-quantitative thought a cornerstone of their world-views, while architects and structural engineers are starting to exploit the morphogenetic potential of anexact spaces. (Lars Spuybroek refers to them as 'vague', while Cecil Balmond uses the term 'informal'.)[3] To understand how the rigorously vague plays a role in the design space of form we need to understand how anexact spaces are *morphogenetically prior* to exact ones. Russell realized that the former have a logical priority over the latter, since the concept of order does not presuppose that of quantity, but it is only with the work of Deleuze that we can begin to understand how cardinal series and the very notion of quantity emerge in a morphogenetic way from ordinal series. It is thanks to this morphogenetic priority, thanks to the fact that the vague or anexact may be said to engender the accurate, that these spaces can be profitably used in the generation of form during the design process.

As Bertrand Russell realized, the distinction between the cardinal and the ordinal is only a special case of that between geometrical spaces that are *metric*, that is, spaces in which the notion of a rigid length is conceptually crucial, and spaces that do not rely on the notion of length and which are referred to as non-metric. Russell mentions the space of projective geometry as an example in the quote above, but those of differential geometry and topology are also examples of non-metric spaces. A space in this mathematical sense is characterized not only by a set of points but more importantly by a definition of *proximity* between points, in other words, by the relations that define a given subset of points as a neighbourhood. If proximity is defined via a minimum length (e.g. all points less than a given distance away from a centre form a neighbourhood) the space is said to be metric (whether flat, as in Euclidean geometry, or curved, as in the non-Euclidean versions). If some other criterion is used to specify what points are nearby other points, the space is said to be non-metric (as in projective, differential or topological geometries). What other criterion of proximity can be used? In differential geometry, for example, one takes advantage of the fact that the calculus operates on equations expressing rates of change and that one of its operators (differentiation) gives as its output an instantaneous value for that rate of change. The points that form a space can then be defined not by rigid lengths from a fixed coordinate system (as in the metric case) but by the instantaneous rate at which *curvature* changes at that point. Some parts of the space will not be changing at all, other parts may be changing slowly, while others may be changing very fast. A differential space (a manifold), in effect, becomes *a field of rapidities and slownesses*, and via these infinitesimal relations one can specify neighbourhoods without having to use rigid lengths.

As historian of mathematics Morris Kline has noted, non-metric geometries are logically prior to metric ones, a fact that became established during the nineteenth century as geometrical spaces of different kinds began to be invented, not only the non-Euclidean versions of metric spaces (themselves the source of a revolution since for centuries Euclidean geometry was thought to be the unique geometry of space) but also non-metric ones. Of the latter,

3. Cecil Balmond. *Informal* (Munich: Prestel Verlag, 2002).

projective geometry had been around for a while but its humble beginnings in mapmaking and painting had kept it from enjoying the prestige that its logical priority should have granted it. All that changed as the nineteenth century unfolded. As Kline writes:

> Prior to and during the work on non-Euclidean geometry, the study of projective properties was the major geometric activity. Moreover, it was evident from the work of Von Staudt that projective geometry is logically prior to Euclidean geometry because it deals with qualitative and descriptive properties that enter into the very formation of geometrical figures and does not use the measures of line segments and angles. This fact suggested that Euclidean geometry might be some specialization of projective geometry. With the non-Euclidean geometries now at hand the possibility arose that those ... might also be specializations of projective geometry.[4]

4. Morris Kline. *Mathematical Thought from Ancient to Modern Times* (vol. 3. New York, NY: Oxford University Press. 1972): 904.

But how does one go from a relation of logical priority, a purely conceptual relation, to a morphogenetic priority? In what sense can metric spaces, where rigid lengths allow for exact comparisons, be said to be engendered from non-metric ones, where only rigorous but anexact comparisons are possible? To answer this question I need to introduce another concept, the concept of *symmetry*, also the fruit of nineteenth-century mathematical invention and also the source of major conceptual revolutions in the twentieth century. Although the technical idea cannot be explained here, one can roughly define it as the degree to which an object lacks detail: the more bland or less detailed the object the more symmetry it has. This idea can be made more mathematically precise via the notion of a group of transformations, a set of operations (having very specific properties), which when applied to a geometrical object change some of its properties while leaving others unchanged. Take for example the set consisting of rotations by 90 degrees (that is, a set containing rotations by 0, 90, 180, 270 degrees). Applying this group to a cube leaves its properties *invariant*, in the sense that an observer who did not witness the rotation would be unable to tell that any transformation has taken place.[5]

5. Joe Rosen. *Symmetry in Science.* (New York, NY: Springer-Verlag. 1995): chapter 2.

The importance of groups of transformations is that they can be used to classify geometric figures by their degree of symmetry: while a cube will remain invariant under the above set of rotations on any axis, it will not under a set containing rotations by, say, 45 degrees. A sphere, on the other hand, remains invariant under rotations by any number of degrees. The larger the group of transformations leaving an object unchanged the more symmetry the object is said to possess (relative to that transformation). If we imagine an event that would change a sphere into a cube, it would illustrate a *symmetry-breaking event*, since the original group of transformations would be made smaller. In other words, the event would cause the object to lose symmetry or to become less bland. A sequence of events in which this blandness is progressively lost (a symmetry-breaking cascade) would represent, in turn, a process of *progressive differentiation*, a process in which an originally undifferentiated object progressively acquires more and more detail.

Felix Klein, one of the most important nineteenth-century mathematicians, realized that not only geometrical figures but geometries themselves can be classified by their invariants under transformations. Euclidean and non-Euclidean metric geometries, for example, form spaces whose properties remain unaltered by a group containing rotations, translations and reflections. In other words, lengths, angles and shapes are invariant under this group of transformations. In projective spaces, on the other hand, those properties do not remain invariant but others do, such as linearity, collinearity and the property of being a conic section. Moreover, the group of transformations that leave the latter invariant is a *larger set*, including rotations, translations and reflections, but also projections (roughly, like shining light on a piece of film) and sections (the equivalent of intercepting those light rays on a screen). It was this realization, that the group characterizing metric spaces is a *subgroup* of the one characterizing projective spaces, that established the logical priority of the latter. Klein went on to classify all geometries known to him and realized that they form a hierarchy in which, as we move up from Euclidean geometry, fewer and fewer properties remain invariant (and groups include more and more transformations), and vice versa: as we move down, the geometric spaces become increasingly less bland or more detailed.

At the top of Klein's complex classification we have projective geometry, then, as more invariants are added we get affine geometry and, finally, Euclidean geometry. As we move up the hierarchy more and more geometric figures become equivalent to one another, forming *a lesser number of distinct classes*. Thus, while in Euclidean geometry two conic sections (the family of curves containing circles, ellipses, parabolas and hyperbolas) are equivalent if they are both of the same type (both circles or both parabolas) and have the same size, in affine geometry they need only be of the same type (regardless of size) to be equivalent, while in projective geometry all conic sections, without further qualification, are the same. (This becomes clear if one visualizes a circle drawn on a piece of film; when projected its size will change, and if the screen is tilted relative to the projector, it will become an ellipse or some other non-circular shape.)[6] Although Klein did not include topology or differential geometry above the projective level, these newer geometries were added later on. The newcomers continue this progression: in topological spaces, for example, not only all conic sections are the same, but all closed figures (e.g. a square and a circle) are one and the same figure. In a sense, we witness a progressive differentiation of space as we move down the hierarchy, with new distinct classes of geometric figures emerging one broken symmetry at a time.

Although the creators of these classifications saw in them a purely logical construction, in which theorems valid at one level are automatically valid at the levels below it, Deleuze views them as morphogenetic, as if metric spaces were literally *born* from non-metric ones through a loss of symmetry.[7] The morphogenetic processes that generate the wild variety of forms that surrounds us, from the embryological processes that generate tissues and organs to the meteorological processes that give rise to hurricanes and wind patterns, operate through one or another form of intensive *difference*. Indeed, the weather maps that have become standard on television, with their zones of high and low

6. David A. Brannan, Matthew F. Esplen and Jeremy J. Gray. *Geometry* (Cambridge, UK: Cambridge University Press, 1999): 364.

7. One way to illustrate the difference between Deleuze's morphogenetic and Russell's logical approaches is to return to one-dimensional spaces or series and to contrast their respective analyses of the theory of irrational numbers of Dedekind. Arguing that there were gaps in the compact series of rational numbers, Dedekind introduced the notion of a 'cut', a way of segmenting a dense series into two mutually excluding parts. His idea was to define the concept of number in terms of such cuts performed on purely ordinal continua. For Russell this was all unnecessary (since all he needed was to establish logical priority) but Deleuze sees in the cut a veritable symmetry-breaking event, which yields cardinal series out of ordinal ones. As he writes, 'in this sense, it is the cut which constitutes the next genus of number, the ideal cause of continuity or the pure element of quantitativity'. Gilles Deleuze. *Difference and Repetition* (New York, NY: Columbia University Press, 1994): 172.

ACT AND INTENSE

pressure, and their sharp hot and cold fronts, are perfect illustrations of an intensive map of differences (quite unlike an extensive map of coastlines and mountain ranges). And so are the maps of developing embryos and their intensive zones of chemical concentration, guiding the migration of cells from one part to another of the emerging body and directing the transformation of cells from one type to another. This fundamental role of differences is the first point of philosophical contact. To return to the distinction with which I opened this essay: while in cardinal series judgments of exact numerical identity of two series can be made, in ordinal series only rigorous judgments of greater or lesser *differences* can be made. Deleuze, whose ambition was always to create the first philosophical system based exclusively on positive differences, made a great deal out of this link. (The concept of 'positive difference' must be contrasted with the idea of difference as mere lack of similarity, an idea which introduces difference in a negative way, as an absence or deficit of resemblance.)[8]

Since spontaneous progressive differentiation is a natural way to explore the abstract space of possible forms, it can also be used by architects and engineers to generate detailed design starting from a more or less bland initial state. The ever closer linkage between the intensive and the topological may be glimpsed from material processes which act as 'form-finding' processes. The simplest of these processes are those in which an original intensive difference cancels itself out, allowing the process to reach a *minimum* in the intensity of some parameter. Thus, soap film will spontaneously find the form with the minimum of surface tension. Without any constraints (such as those exerted by a frame made of wire or rope), the form that emerges is a sphere or bubble. Adding constraints can break the symmetry of this sphere and yield a wide variety of other minimal surfaces. The question may be raised as to how soap film 'finds' or, indeed, 'computes' its way to a spherical bubble. One answer is that, within the space of possible forms, one of them (a sphere) seems to be favoured energetically. But a more enlightening answer is that the space of possibilities is pre-structured in such a way that a particular form attracts the difference-cancelling process towards a given outcome. Since the outcome is not always a sphere but whatever form happens to minimize surface tension given the constraints, the attracting form cannot be a sphere or any other metric shape. Mathematically, the space of possibilities is referred to as 'phase' or 'state' space (a space of all possible states for a system) and the shape that acts as attractor is a *singular point* in that space. As it happens, that singular point is always a *topological invariant* of the state space (itself typically a differential manifold). It is in this sense that material processes that possess morphogenetic power, the power to find or produce a given form, are always driven intensively and guided topologically.

Singular points, as mathematical entities, were first studied in the eighteenth century by Leonard Euler via his famous calculus of variations. One of the first variational problems to be tackled was the so-called 'catenary problem', which can be characterized by the question: what form will a chain find if allowed to hang freely while both its ends are constrained. Euler framed the problem in terms of the potential energy of the gravitational forces acting

8. Referring to negative differences (lack of similarity) as diversity he writes:

> Difference is not diversity. Diversity is given, but difference is that by which the given is given ... Difference is not phenomenon but the nuomenon closest to the phenomenon ... Every phenomenon refers to an inequality by which it is conditioned ... Everything which happens and everything which appears is correlated with orders of differences: differences of level, temperature, pressure, tension, potential, difference of intensity.

Gilles Deleuze. *Difference and Repetition*: 222.

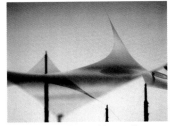

Frei Otto's experiment with soap film for calculating minimal surfaces. Frei Otto and Bodo Rasch. *Finding Form* (Fellbach: Axel Menges. 1995): 44.

on the chain. He realized, and proved mathematically, that of all the geometrically possible forms the one realized by actual chains is the one that minimizes this potential, that is, that the chain will be at equilibrium when its centre of gravity occupies the lowest position.[9] In the Western world it was the architect Antoni Gaudí who, at the turn of the twentieth century, first saw the potential of hanging chains or ropes for the discovery of the form for the arches of his Sagrada Familia church. But chain models can be used for more complex design tasks than arches or vaults:

> Chain networks showing significantly more complex forms than freely suspended individual chains can be constructed from small pieces of chain or short bars fastened together flexibly. Freely suspended networks of this kind open up the gigantic formal world of the 'heavy tents', as the so-called gravity suspended roofs can also be named. They can be seen in the temple and pagoda roofs of the Far East, where they were originally made as flexible bamboo lattices. Today roofs of this kind are made of rope nets with a wooden or lightweight concrete roof.[10]

The quote refers to work done since the 1950s at the Institute for Lightweight Structures (IL) in Stuttgart under the guidance of the architect– engineer Frei Otto. He is perhaps best known for his use of soap film as a membrane-forming liquid capable of finding minimal surfaces on its own. Form-finding for tent designs can also be performed with thin rubber films, knitted or woven fabrics, and thread or wire nets, but soap film is perhaps a better illustration of this technique since, as discussed above, we know more about the intensive aspects of the process and the topological form that guides it. Soap film models are literally 'analogue computers' with which the shape of a large variety of tent forms – simple sails as well as pointed, arched, humped and wave tents – can be calculated. Frei Otto's project went beyond architecture narrowly conceived and into the investigation of methods to observe nature 'processually and integrally'.[11] This led, for instance, to a new understanding of the architecture of biological cells 'on the basis of new perceptions about membrane and net construction supported by internal pressure'.[12] Since many non-biological natural forms use the same design principles, this insight has blurred the borders of the organic and the inorganic, bringing abiotic self-organizing processes to the fore right next to genetic information. The idea that genes contain a blueprint of the final organism, for example, is subverted once we realize that genetic information depends on the physics of form-finding processes to get the job done. Genes can manipulate intensive quantities only via their products (enzymes) and facilitate or inhibit symmetry-breaking events, but not dictate the final form in detail.

A vivid illustration of symmetry-breaking as a form-finding machine is the wool-thread machines that Otto and his team used for the purpose of computing transportation routes with minimal detours. In one version, the machine consists of a circular frame with wool threads (representing traffic routes) joining every point in the circumference to every other point. The apparatus is then submerged in water and lifted carefully to allow the surface

9. Ibid: 74–76.

Antoni Gaudí with his suspension model of the Sagrada Familia. Frei Otto and Bodo Rasch. *Finding Form* (Fellbach: Axel Menges, 1995): 154.

10. Frei Otto and Bodo Rasch. *Finding Form* (Fellbach: Axel Menges, 1995): 62.

11. Frei Otto. 'Natural Constructions, a Subject for the Future.' In Frei Otto and Bodo Rasch. *Finding Form*: 17.

12. Ibid: 18.

Frei Otto's IL team reconstructed Gaudí's suspension model to gain new insights in analogue computing for structural findings. Frei Otto and Bodo Rasch. *Finding Form*: 154.

tension of the water to bundle the paths together into intricate and beautiful designs. The complex bundling is made possible by giving the threads an overlength, which is then used up as the threads are made taut by the surface tension. In its original form, prior to being dipped, the apparatus has the symmetries of a circle, in particular, its properties remain invariant under all rotations in the plane. (Or rather, it approximates this rotational symmetry, since in reality not all points of the frame can be connected to every other point.) Once it emerges from the water, on the other hand, all rotational symmetry has been lost: the pattern of mergings, crossings and holes is now unique, and any rotation of the circular frame will be noticeable by an observer. Lars Spuybroek continues to adapt those machines for design purposes and finds inspiration in their anexact and intense materiality. And although one could conceivably simulate this machine digitally, turning atoms into bits, there is something about the analogue material process itself that fascinates Spuybroek. As he writes:

> The organizational and informational stage is material, not immaterial, as is so often put forth. It is the material *potential*, the material's distributed intelligence that sets the machine in motion, a transfer of water-turbulence to wool-curvature. Then it is the stickiness, the hairiness and the curvability of the wool thread, together with the cohesive forces on the water surface that bring it to a halt and inform the end result. It is simply impossible to do this in ink. It is an intensive technique within an extensive system, and though the quantities (surface area, number of houses, etc.) are given beforehand, the quality emerges through the interaction and multiplication of different parameters. Generally, the intensive is a deformational property (like heating), but here it also becomes a transformational property (like boiling): the threads restructure and reorganize to 'find form'. The system as a whole passes a critical threshold. The degrees of freedom of deformation, which are like extensive movements within an internal structure, become intensive, qualitative changes of that structure.[13]

An important feature of this apparatus is that, unlike the hanging chain and the soap film, which have a unique and global equilibrium (a unique minimum acting as attractor), it has *multiple equilibria*, one of the defining properties of complex systems. Although the system of threads does come to a resting point after being dipped, this stable configuration is not in any sense unique, indeed it would be hard to repeat the exact same arrangement of crossings, mergings and gaps. Thus, even though the original use of the apparatus was to help discover optimized path systems, it does not really optimize at all, if by that one means finding a unique global optimum. It finds a local optimum among many possible alternative local optima. This implies the other defining property of complexity: *path dependence*. It simply means that history matters. While in systems with a unique global optimum each path is in fact different (each chain or soap bubble will reach equilibrium in a different way), the history of the way the system reached the optimum may be ignored given that all histories have

Rubber-lacquer analogue model for the project *Soft Office*, see p. 221.

13. See p. 354. Lars Spuybroek. 'The Structure of Vagueness.'

MATERIALITY: ANE

the same 'destiny'. But with multiple equilibria history cannot be ignored, since what local optima are available to a system and where a system can go from a local optimum are now a function of what happens to a system on its way there.

Philosophically this change makes all the difference in the world. With single equilibria one can still think of the found form as perfect or optimal in some transcendent way. Indeed, the original discoverers of these simple singularities (Euler, Maupertuis) thought they had found proof of the existence of a rational God: if every phenomenon of spontaneous morphogenesis can be thought as optimizing, and if there is only one way of doing this, does this not show the existence of a divine plan? Unfortunately, postulating an optimizing God defeats the very philosophical advantage of the discovery of topological invariants acting as attractors. An intense and anexact materiality is one that does not need a creator with a plan to generate form, it is capable of generating it (or finding it) itself. It is not an inert materiality that can acquire form only if commanded to do so by a *transcendent* being, but an active materiality drawing its morphogenetic powers from a reservoir of *immanent* resources (multiple topological invariants of different kinds). Our form-finding machines should reflect this new anti-theology (and anti-teleology) and the re-enchantment of the material world that follows from it.

Chronolog

Lars Spuybroek – born 1959, Rotterdam, the Netherlands

Lars Spuybroek is the principal of NOX. Since the early 1990s he has been involved in researching the relationship between architecture and media, often more specifically between architecture and computing. He is Professor of Digital Design Techniques at the University and GhK of Kassel and also a visiting professor at Columbia University, Bartlett School of Architecture, Technical University Delft, and other academic institutions throughout Europe. Since 1992, Spuybroek has given numerous lectures around the world.

PROJECTS	INSTALLATIONS & EXHIBITIONS

1991

Dark Sections (NOX A, Actiones in Distans – study)

Traction Avant (solo exhibition) Tilburg, the Netherlands

Fahrenheit 451 (Europan II, Breda – competition entry)

1992

Fossile Towers (NOX B, Biotech – study)
VBC (conversion for the video broadcasting company, Amsterdam)
Baroque Army (furniture, including Patriot Coach for Gen. Schwarzkopf – study)
Harlem Shuffle (housing for the elderly, Haarlem, the Netherlands – competition entry)

Kracht van Heden (group exhibition, Stichting Fonds voor Beeldende Kunsten, Vormgeving en Bouwkunst) Amsterdam
Fire and Forget (group exhibition, V2_Organisation) Den Bosch, the Netherlands

1993

1001 PK (conversion editor's office/house, Amsterdam)
CENTROPA ('sign of the future': housing refugees in Graz, Austria –
   competition entry)
Full Moon (night resort: dance hall, night-clubs, pool, sleeping
   capsules, etc. – study)

P_R (group exhibition, Salle de Bains) Rotterdam
Armed Response (installation for the V2_Organisation) Den Bosch

 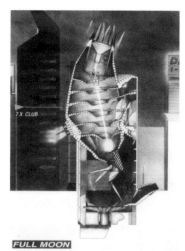

Soft City (video for VPRO television, broadcast on national
   television and at several international festivals, a.o. Ars
   Electronica 94)

1994

Excessive Force (entrance installation for the V2_Organisation,
   Rotterdam – study)
The Laboratories (study)
H₂Oexpo (water pavilion for the Ministry of Water Management
   and Delta Expo bv, on the island 'Neeltje Jans', Zeeland, the
   Netherlands) completed 1997

Heavenly Bodies (installation Galerie Peeters) Eindhoven
Day One (workshop Sculpture City, RAM Galerie) Rotterdam

1996

Soft Site (projection/installation for the V2_Organisation
   Rotterdam, presented at DEAF96 on the Internet and at the
   Netherlands Architecture Institute NAI) Rotterdam

1997

EDIT SP(L)INE (interactive installation at *H₂Oexpo*)
blowout (toilet block for Delta Expo bv, Zeeland, the Netherlands)

NINE + One (group exhibition '10 Young Dutch Architects', NAI)
   Rotterdam, Los Angeles, New York, São Paulo, Vienna, Berlin,
   Padua, 1997–98

FOAM HOME (housing project for the KAN area near Nijmegen,
the Netherlands – for the UnderCover Foundation, study)
"beachness" (a seaside hotel and boulevard, Noordwijk, the
Netherlands – commissioned by the Dutch Design Institute,
study)
V2_Engine (interactive facade for the V2_Organisation,
Rotterdam – study)

NOX sixty minutes (solo exhibition/video installation, NAI)
Rotterdam
transArchitectures02/03 (group exhibition, IFA) Paris, New York,
Graz, Los Angeles, Florence, Bordeaux, Monte Carlo, Brussels,
Rotterdam, Vienna, 1997–98

Arquitectura Virtual (Centro Cultural de Belem) Lisbon, 1997–98

1998

Tommy (psychotropic vase for Cor Unum, Den Bosch)
OffTheRoad/103.8 Mhz (housing and noise barrier, Eindhoven, the
Netherlands – for the StadBeeld Committee, study)
V2_Lab (renovation, international lab for unstable media for the
V2_Organisation, Rotterdam)
Flying Attic (exhibition installation for the UnderCover Foundation,
Arnhem, the Netherlands)
The New Man of Cacharel (perfume bottle for Cacharel/Droog
Design, Amsterdam – study)

NearDeathHotel, (wallpaper installation, Walker Art Center,
Minneapolis and MCA [with Francesco Bonami]) Chicago

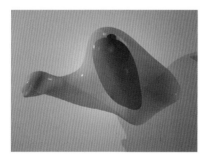

Goes goes (a company centre for A. Sinke bv, Goes, the
Netherlands – study)
Cheers! (a glass for Kristin Feireiss, 10 years, NAI)

Terra Incognita – architects as designers (group exhibition)
[Tommy] Museum Het Kruithuis, Den Bosch, Galerie BINNEN,
Amsterdam

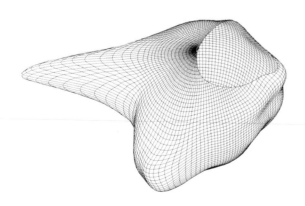

D-tower (a tower, a questionnaire and a website, for the city of Doetinchem, the Netherlands – in collaboration with artist Q. S. Serafijn) completed 2004

The Future Is Now (expo.01 Biel, for UBS, Switzerland [in collaboration with Harm Lux and Mike Tyler] – study)

1999

OffTheRoad_5speed (non-standard prefab housing, Eindhoven – for housing corporation TRUDO, research commission)

FACES (exhibition design for 'Whereishere', Bonnefanten Museum, Maastricht [with Lewis Blackwell]) completed 2000

Rotower (media tower and artists-in-residence hotel, Rotterdam [with artist Q. S. Serafijn] – study)

wetGRID (housing 250 paintings for 'Vision Machine', Musée des Beaux Arts, Nantes, France) completed 2000

The Weight of the Image (a 'slice' of stadium for Euro2000/NAI, Rotterdam – study for Kristin Feireiss)

DOMUS (cover *DOMUS* 820)

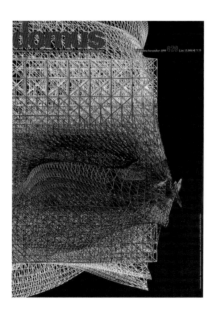

De Gothic Stijl (exhibition design for 'the virtual house of De Stijl', Netherlands Architecture Institute, Rotterdam) completed 2000

2000

Son-O-House, a house where sounds live (public artwork including house and sound installation, for the City of Son en Breugel, the Netherlands [with composer Edwin van der Heide]) completed 2004.

PRAGUE (clothing store for Louis Dijksman, Rotterdam – study)

Galerie der Forschung (expo centre for the Österreichische Akademie der Wissenschaften, Vienna – invited competition)

DeepSurface – the unvisual image (installation/exhibition and catalogue, EXEDRA gallery) Hilversum, the Netherlands

ArchiLab 1999 (group exhibition [12 Tommies] Centre Région FRAC) Orléans, France

SYNWORLD (group exhibition, Architektur Zentrum Wien) Vienna

Fractions (group exhibition, collections FRAC) Beijing and Tsinghua

MIR-Art in Space (group exhibition) Bolzano

Zeichenbau (group exhibition, Künstlerhaus) Vienna

RAUMstationen (group exhibition, Bauhaus) Weimar, Germany, November–December

NOX room (group exhibition, La Biennale di Venezia, Italian pavilion) Venice, June–October

CAVE (holiday house for the Weegels family, Drente, the Netherlands – study)

four projects, (group exhibition in 'Die Natur der Dinge', [project]) Düsseldorf, April–June
Artisti e architetti (group exhibition, Palazzo delle Papesse) Siena, Italy, July–October
NOX individuations (group exhibition 'Individualisation', Architectuur Centrum) Eindhoven

2001

Soft Office (shops, interactive playground and headquarters office for Anne Wood/Ragdoll television productions, Stratford-upon-Avon, United Kingdom)
maisonFOLIE (multipurpose hall, studios and exhibition spaces, media library, day care, artists' communal space, offices and a soup restaurant, Lille, France – invited competition, first prize) completed 2004
ParisBRAIN (a transurban scheme for the area west of La Défense, Paris – for Els Hoek/Institut Neérlandais, study)
La Tana di Alice (Alice in Wonderland pavilion in 'Pinopoli', Collodi/Italy – for Roberto Masiero/Carlo Collodi Foundation)
ObliqueWTC (a proposal for the new World Trade Center – for the Max Protetch Gallery, New York)
Spacecave (psychotropic pavilion – for Reverend Hans Visser, Rotterdam – study)

Blobs, Folds & Boxes (group exhibition, Carnegie Museum of Art, The Heinz Architecture Gallery) Pittsburgh
NOX introduces the FLURB© (solo exhibition, Aedes Galerie West) Berlin, April–May

ArchiLab 2001, NOX.exe (group exhibition, Centre Région FRAC) Orléans, France, May–June
Research Architecture (group exhibition, Rubelle and Norman Schafler Gallery, Pratt Institute) New York, February–March
Post.Rotterdam – NOX.exe (group exhibition) Porto, May–July
NOX FLURBS© (solo exhibition, Vormgevingsgalerie VIVID) Rotterdam, September–November

NOX screening (group exhibition, ExperimentaDesign2001) Lisbon, September–October

Expériences d'urbanisme – visions des Pays-Bas (installation in a group exhibition, Institut Neérlandais) Paris, November–December

2002

FEDUROK (popular music centre CRMA, two concert halls, bars, library, sound studios and offices; for the City of Nancy, France – invited competition, second prize)

A New World Trade Center (group exhibition, Max Protetch Gallery, New York) January–February

Re-imagining Ground Zero, National Building Museum, April–June, Washington; Cube Gallery, Manchester, 2002–03; Deutsches Architektur Museum, Frankfurt, 2003; Architekturmuseet, Stockholm, 2003

NOX FLURBS© (solo exhibition, Tel Aviv Museum of Art) Tel Aviv, February–May

10 NOX projects (group exhibition [tape] Fonds BKVB, 'Commitment', Las Palmas) Rotterdam

Archilab 2002, *ParisBRAIN* (group exhibition, Centre Région FRAC) Orléans, France, May–June; (deSingel International Arts Centre) Antwerp, 2002

10 NOX projects (group exhibition [tape] Cetinje Biennial, Montenegro) Yugoslavia, June–September

Re-imagining Ground Zero (group exhibition, La Biennale di Venezia, American pavilion) Venice, June–October

10 NOX projects, tape, in: *Digital Spaces* (group exhibition, XIII Bienal de Arquitectura) Santiago de Chile

ParisBRAIN (installation in group exhibition, Centro Cultural Conde Duque) Madrid, October–February

Latent Utopias – Experiments within Contemporary Architecture (group exhibition [NOX: porosity – large models of five projects] Steirischer Herbst/Graz Cultural Capital 2003) Graz, Austria, October–March 2003

2003

ECB (European Central Bank, headquarters offices including libraries, restaurants, landscaping, parking and sports facilities; for ECB and the City of Frankfurt, Germany – invited competition)

Pompidou Two (a second Centre Pompidou for the City of Metz, France [with Andrew Benjamin] invited competition)

La Tana di Alice/Amici dei Pinocchio (group exhibition, La Biennale di Venezia, Arsenale) Venice, June–November

Zoomorphic (group exhibition, Victoria & Albert Museum) London, September–December

Non-Standard Architecture (group exhibition [NOX: large models of five projects], Centre Pompidou) Paris, December–March 2004

BOOKS & MAGAZINES

NOX A, Actiones in distans (1991, ed. 1001, Amsterdam) 160 pp
NOX B, Biotech (1992, ed. 1001, Amsterdam) 160 pp
NOX C, Chloroform (1993, ed. 1001, Amsterdam) 160 pp
NOX D, Djihad (1995, ed. 1001, Amsterdam) 160 pp

NOX (which was then Lars Spuybroek with Maurice Nio) produced four magazines themed on the intersection of technology and society.

FORUM 38, #1/2: COMFORT/COMFORT (A et A, Amsterdam, 1995) 105 pp
FORUM 38, #3: HET PUBLIEKE/THE PUBLIC (A et A, Amsterdam, 1996) 72 pp
FORUM 39, #4: MASSA/MASS (A et A, Amsterdam, 1997) 250 pp

Forum (which changes its editorial board every five years) was then produced by Lars Spuybroek, Jurjen Zeinstra, Roelof Mulder, Winy Maas and Wim Nijenhuis. We planned four issues, but before producing the last one on Fear we were fired by the management.

Deep Surface, with a foreword by Bart Lootsma (Rotterdam, 1999) 64 pp

The Weight of the Image, teaching digital design techniques with Bob Lang (Rotterdam: NAi Publishers, 2001) 72 pp

WRITINGS

'De zwarte secties', *NOX A*, 1991: 106–11.
'Jap Tek Anima', *de Architect*, November 1992.
'De Remu formatie' (with Maurice Nio), *de Architect*, February 1994.
'Phantombody/Phantomhouse', *FORUM 38 #1/2*.
'Cybernetic Circus', *de Architect*, special issue 49.
'De Strategie van de Vorm' (with Maurice Nio), *de Architect*, special issue 57.
'X and Y and Z, a manual' (with Maurice Nio), *ARCHIS*, November 1995.
'SoftSite', *DEAF96* (Rotterdam: V2_Organisation and NAi Publishers, 1996).
'Motor Geometry' *TechnoMorphica* (Rotterdam: V2_Organisation, 1997): 143–66; also in *AD Hypersurface*; *Profile* 133; *ARCH+* 138; *SPACE* 9902; and *2A+P*.
'The Motorization of Reality', *ARCHIS*, November 1998 and *A+U* 349.
'Where space gets lost', interview by Andreas Ruby, *The Art of the Accident* (Rotterdam: V2_Organisation and NAi Publishers, 1998).
'WetGRID – the soft machine of vision', interview by Arielle Pélenc. *Vision Machine* – catalogue of the exhibition (Nantes, 2000): 152–67; also in *ARCHIS*, August 2000; *Archicrée*; *Concept*; *Léonardo*.
'The Primacy of Experience' (as 'The Structure of Experience'), *Anymore* (MIT Press, 2000); also 'die Struktur der Erfahrung', *tanzdrama*, 2000; and 'das Primat der Erfahrung', *Raumstationen*, 2001.
'Informational Form', interview by Im Sik Cho, *ANC/Architecture and Culture* #0109; also in *Sarai READER 02: The Cities of Everyday Life* (New Delhi, India: Sarai – The New Media Initiative): 243.
'Machining architecture', *The Weight of the Image* (Rotterdam: NAi Publishers, 2001).
'The Structure of Vagueness', *transUrbanism* (Rotterdam: V2_Publishing/NAi Publishers, 2002): 64–87.
'Africa Comes First – Lars Spuybroek meets Rem Koolhaas', *transUrbanism* (Rotterdam: V2_Publishing/NAi Publishers, 2002): 160–93.
'The Structure of Vagueness', revised version. *Architectures Non Standard* – catalogue of the exhibition (Paris: Centre Pompidou, 2003): 126–29.

BIBLIOGRAPHY

'Gebouwen met een huid van de nacht', Desirée Meulenbroek, *Het Nieuwsblad*, 11 July 1991.
'Fatale Strategieën', Bart Lootsma, *de Architect*, November 1992.
'Lars Spuybroek', Hans van Dijk, *Kracht van Heden catalogues*, 1993: 263–68.

1995
'Turbo-architectuur', Helmut de Hoogh, *Blvd*, October 1995.
'Vloeibare en geanimeerde barok,' Hans van Dijk, *ARCHIS*, November 1995.

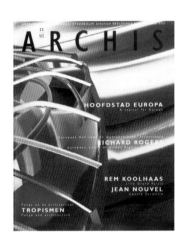

1996
'Vloeiend gebogen staal', Mark Bakker, *BouwWereld* #17.
Bart Lootsma, *l'architecture d'aujourd'hui* #306.
'Het Barbapapa-bouwen', Ineke Schwartz, *Elsevier* #43.
'The hype is over', Volker Grassmuck, *ICC*, September 1996.

1997
'Digital Territories', Pauline van Mourik Broekman, *MUTE* #7.
'Vloeiende vorm, statische techniek', Ed Melet, *de Architect*, March 1997.
'Het gevoel van water', Marina de Vries, *Het Parool*, 17 April 1997.
'Oervormen architectuur …', Ids Haagsma/Hilde de Haan, *de Volkskrant*, 31 May 1997.
'Natte cakewalk', Egbert Koster, *Het financieele dagblad*, 7–9 June 1997.
'Van beton tot pixels', M. van den Broek, *Bulletin* 7.
'Architektur als Medium', Andres Janser,

Archithese, March 1997: 38–39.
'Nueve mas uno', Domingo Merino, *Arquitectura Viva* 54: 37.
'Virtuele glimworm', Lex Veldhoen, *De Morgen*, 31 July 1997.
'Zoektocht naar materialen en constructies', J. v.d. Windt, *Bouwen met Staal* 137: 14–19.
'Vloeibare utopie stolt zichtbaar', Robbert Roos, *Trouw*, 23 August 1997.

'Waterpaviljoen mag niet op water lijken', Bernard Hulsman, *NRC Handelsblad*, 5 September 1997.
'Frederick Kiesler, Rethinking the Endless', Richter Verlag, *Witte de With – Cahier* #6: 93–104.
'A Testing Ground for Interactivity', Ineke Schwartz, *ARCHIS*, September 1997: 8–11.
'Risky Architecture', Hans van Dijk, *ARCHIS*, September 1997: 34–35.
'NOX/Aquatic pavilion', Bart Lootsma, *DOMUS* 796: 28–33.
Nine + One, Ten Young Dutch Architectural Offices (Rotterdam: NAi Publishers, 1997): 76–84.
'Potpalmen in Noordwijk', *de Volkskrant/ de Voorkant*, 4 November 1997.
'Das bearbeitete Territorium', Urs Primas, *Werk, Bauen+Wohnen*, October 1997.
'Any Architects out There in Cyberspace?', Odile Fillion, *DOMUS* 797: 96–99.
Job de Kruiff, *Leidsch Dagblad*, 8 November 1997.
'Motorische Geometrie/Flüssige Form', *ARCH+* 138: 67–75.
'Pavillon de l'eau', Florence Michel, *Architcréé* 279: 56–59.
'Licht ruggengraat', Tineke Aarts, *Bovenlicht 3* #2.

'De Molshoop en de Schelp', Olof Koekebakker, *ITEMS* 8: 22–27.

1998
'Hybride Compositie', Gerda ten Cate, *BOUW*, February 1998: 28–31.
'Pabellon de aqua dulce', *QUADERNS: Rethinking Mobility* 218: 4–14.
'arquitectura virtual: Lars Spuybroek – NOX', *Architécti* 39: 102–11.
'beachness', *BOUW*, 4/1998: 23–24.
'Structures narratives, Organisme numérique,' Marie-Claire Loiriers,

Techniques & Architecture 437: 76–79.
Jaarboek/Yearbook 97–98, Architecture in the Netherlands (Rotterdam: NAi Publishers): 42–47.
'Aquatecture', Catherine Lo, *WIRED Magazine* 6.05: 128–29.
AD Architectural Design Vol. 68: Hypersurface, ed. Stephen Perrella (Profile #133): 5–6, 48–55.
'Tunnelvision', Mark Hooper, *ARENA* #80: 26–27.
Kathy Battista and Florian Migsch, *The Netherlands: A Guide to Recent Architecture*: 202–07.
'En Route to a New Tectonics', Bart Lootsma, *DAIDALOS: Constructing Atmospheres* #68: 35–47.
'Golvend wonen in een geluidswal', Angelique Spaninks, *Eindhovens Dagblad, StadBeeld*, July 1998: 5.
'Seegurke', *AIT, Architektur/Innenarchitektur/Technischer Ausbau*, July–August 1998: 45–55.
'V2_Engine', *ARCHIS*, July 1998: 74–75.

'Cheers!', a Toast to the NAi (Rotterdam:
NAi Publishers, 1998): 72–77.
'frozen waves', Robert Thiemann, FRAME,
September–October 1998, no. 4:
30–33.

EDIT SP(L)INE, Leonardo Online,
November/December 1998: 50–51.
V2_Lab, ARCHIS, November 1998:
34–36.
'Wasserleuchten', Andreas Ruby, TAIN,
no. 6: 6–11.
AD Architectural Design Vol. 68: Architects
in Cyberspace II, ed. Neil Spiller (Profile
#136): 31–41.
'Everything flows', interview Renny
Ramakers with Lars Spuybroek on
ceramics, Terra Incognita – Architects as
Designers, ed. Het Kruithuis (Den Bosch,
the Netherlands, 1998): 50–61.
'Paradisi artificiali', INTERNI Magazine,
anno 2, no. 4: 27.
'water worlds', Connie van Cleef,
Architectural Review, vol. CCIV, no.
1222.
'Fluido e mutevole, V2_Lab', Maurizzio
Vitta, l'ARCA 132: 60–61.
'Vredig oorlogvoeren in golvend
landschap', Jos Bregman, ITEMS, August
1998: 36–38.

1999
'De wetten van het water', Chris
Reinewald, EOS #1/99: 38–40.
H₂Oexpo, The Virtual Dimension, ed. John
Beckman (Princeton Architectural Press,
1999): 264–67.
'Una "cosa" generata', Stefano Pavarini,
l'ARCA 133: 44–47.
blowout, V2_Lab, 'beachness', H₂Oexpo,
OffTheRoad_5speed, SoftSite, Tommy,
'MaNO7 Lars Spuybroek', SPACE 9902:
Mapping ARCHINET: 110–38.
'The Dutch Model', SD space design
9902: 99.
H₂Oexpo, OffTheRoad_5speed,

'beachness', 'NOX/The interactive
future', Architectura Viva 73 'NL 2000':
114–21.

'Weicher Monolith', Andreas Ruby,
Architektur Aktuell, 224–225: 64–73.
'NOX – SoftSite', Andreas Ruby,
DAIDALOS: The Need of Research,
no. 69/70: 122–25.
ArchiLab – Orleans 99, ed. M.-A. Brayer
and F. Migayrou: 170–77.

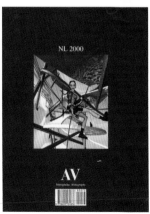

'Oficinas V2_Lab en Rotterdam', Diseño
Interior, no. 84: 116–23.
'Onde di energia', Maddalena Padovani,
Panorama INTERNI, April 99: 102–03.
Tracy Metz, Architectural Record, May
1999: 202–11.
OffTheRoad/103.8 MHz, Stad Beeld, ed.
Ton Verstegen (Rotterdam: NAi
Publishers, 1999): 58–67.
'Onde architettoniche/architectural
waves', interview by Marieke van Rooij,
CROSS #2: immersion(e): 52–69.
'Design after Mies, Lars Spuybroek/the
Cartesian split', ANY 24: 13.
INTERVIEW Magazine, August 1999:
52–53.
OffTheRoad_5speed, ARCH+ 147: 78–79.
'Lars Spuybroek, The Topological
Interstitial Field', Lier en Boog, vol. 14 –
Territorial Investigations: 139–44.
'Geometria Motoria', 2A+P – the Body:
58–63.
'Gute Formen funktionieren wie der
Herzmuskel', AUDI, A6 Limosine und
Avant – Katalog: 10–15.
FOAM HOME, Flying Attic, UnderCover,
ed. Frans Sturkenboom (SUN 1999):
50–55, 84–91.
H₂Oexpo, Catalog Fundacio Mies van der
Rohe (Barcelona, 1999): 110–13.
'beachness', blowout, 'Architettura
dissolta', Alessandro Gubitosi, l'ARCA
140: 72–77.
'NOX World', blowout, V2_Lab, H₂Oexpo,
with an introductory essay by Bart
Lootsma, A+U 349: 68–101.
D-tower, 'Twelve storeys and a thousand
stories', Hari Kunzru, The Daily
Telegraph, 14 October 1999: 8–9.
H₂Oexpo, Philip Jodidio, ConNAissance
des Arts, no. 565: 128–31.
'Maak verlangens los!', Lars Spuybroek
interviewed by Anna Tilroe, NRC
Handelsblad/Cultureel Supplement, 12
November 1999: 27.
DOMUS 820: cover and 124.
Peter Zellner, HybridSpace: New Forms in
Digital Architecture (London: Thames &
Hudson and New York, NY: Rizzoli,
1999): cover and 110–25.

H_2Oexpo, V2_Lab, Philip Jodidio, *Building a New Millennium – Architecture Today and Tomorrow* (Taschen Verlag, 1999): 396–403.
'NOX/Pabellón de exposición de agua', *Ecological Architecture*, ed. arco: 24–27.
OffTheRoad_103.8 MHz, V2_Lab, *deepSurface*, AD Hypersurface II, ed. Stephen Perrella: 52–59.
l'architecture d'aujourd'hui, no. 325: 94–95.
'studio de création V2_Lab', *AMC*, December 1999: 57–59.
Masayuki Fuchigami, *The Contemporary Architecture Guide*, vol. 2: 208.
Art and Architecture: New Affinities, Julia Schulz-Dornberg (Ed. GG): 45.
'Die Struktur der Erfahrung', Klaus Witzeling, *tanzdrama*, no. 51: 42–45.
D-tower, Cathy Ho, *Architecture*, December 1999: 59.
'Het utopisch gehalte van de Nederlandse architectuur', Robbert Roos, *BladNA*, no. 12, 1999: 10–11.

2000

OffTheRoad_5speed, DOMUS 822: 36–41 (also guest editor).
OffTheRoad_5speed, *Boekman Cahier*, no. 43, March 2000.
'Onbedoelde parodie op computerbarok', Bernard Hulsman, *NRC Handelsblad*, 31 March 2000.
'beachness', *Archithese* 3/00: *Hybrid Structures*: 38–41.
'Holländer im Höhenflug', Dirk Meyrhofer, *Architektur & Wohnen*, April/May 2000: 152–65.
10x10, eds. Kristin Feireiss et al. (London: Phaidon Press, 2000): 288–91.
Less Aesthetics, More Ethics, catalogue of the 7th Biennale di Venezia, 2000: 346–51.
'NOX 60 Minutes', interview by Yolanda Fernandez, *NEO 2*, June–August 2000: 148–55.
David Winner, *Brilliant Orange – The Neurotic Genius of Dutch Football* (Bloomsbury, 2000) chapter 10: curves: 67–71.
'"Vision Machine"/WetGRID: Lars Spuybroek on his exhibition design "Vision Machine",' *ARCHIS*, August 2000: 50–57.
OffTheRoad_5speed, AD Architectural Design vol. 70: *Contemporary Processes in Architecture*, ed. Ali Rahim, June 2000: 56–61.
SUPERDUTCH: New Architecture in the Netherlands, Bart Lootsma, ed. (London: Thames & Hudson; Amsterdam, the Netherlands: SUN; New York, NY: Princeton Architectural Press, 2000): 163–73.
'Het Kunstmatig landschap/The Artificial Landscape', Hans Ibelings, ed: 159–62.
'Idee, Forme, Spazi – *Vision Machine* 2000, Nantes', Stefano Pavarini, *l'ARCA*, no. 151: 36–39.
'Dutch architect Lars Spuybroek of NOX gets visionary in Nantes, France', Claire Downey, *Architectural Record*, September 2000: 67–69.
'Vision Machine/Grille Liquide', Arielle Pélenc, *Archicréé*, no. 294: 61–68.
'MATRIX', Jean-Max Colard, 'Les Inrockuptibles', 5–11 September 2000: 77–78.
'Destination Inconnu', Natacha Wolinski, *Beaux-Arts Magazine*, August 2000: 79–82.
'Arquitectura Liquida', *NEO 2*, October/December 2000: 101–09.
'Exhibition Machine (Detail)', *FRAME* 17: 10–11.
Maria Luisa Palumbo, *New Wombs, Electronic Bodies and Architectural Disorders* (Basel: Birkhauser IT-series 2000): 70–74.
Alicia Imperiale, *New Flatness, Surface Tension in Digital Architecture* (Basel: Birkhauser IT-series 2000): 80.
'De Blobs van Spuybroek', Tom de Vries, *Detail in architectuur*, November 2000: 36–39.
'Die Sanfte Machine der Wahrnehmung', *Leonardo Online*, November/December 2000, no. 6: 20–26.
Interview Arjen Mulder and Maaike Post with Lars Spuybroek, *Book for the Electronic Arts* (Rotterdam: V2_Organisation/de Balie, 2000): 122–30.
OffTheRoad_5speed, wetGRID, ZOO, no. 7: 324.
'Zoveel mensen, zoveel huizen, het individuele verlangen en de nieuwste architectuur volgens Lars Spuybroek', Angelique Spaninks, *Eindhovens Dagblad*, 30 November 2000: 8.
'liquid form (4)', Dick Raaijmakers, *Cahier 'M'*: 128–30.
D-tower, FRAME Virtual Interiors Annual 2000: 72–75.

2001

'de quelques mondes inventés par les architectes', Claude Parent, *303 – Arts, recherches et creations*: 18–25.
'High-tech geluidspaviljoen op Ekkersrijt', Angelique Spaninks, *Eindhovens Dagblad*, 31 January 2001: 17.
'Das Primat der Erfahrung', V2_Lab, *Raumstationen: Metamorfoses des Raumes im 20. Jahrhundert* (Wüstenrot Stiftung): 78–83.
ArchiLab – Orleans 01, ed. M.-A. Brayer and F. Migayrou: 174–75.
'Bewohnbare Mutanten', Johann Reidemeister, *Neue Züricher Zeitung*, 4 May 2001.
'Die Diagrammdebatte', Bart Lootsma, *Arch+* and Archilab 2001 catalogue.
NOX/Lars Spuybroek, *D-tower*, ZOO, no. 8: 223.
'Process: *wetGRID* – the soft machine of vision', *Architecture & Concept*, no. 24: 42–57.
'Process: *OffTheRoad_5speed*', *Architecture & Concept*, no. 25: 64–77.
'In einer Mulde des amorphen Raums', Insa Lüdtke, *Der Tagesspiegel*, 8 May 2001: 26.
'Design Machine', Pitupong Chaowakul, *Art4d*, no. 70, April 2001: 60–65.
'The Virtual House of De Stijl', Jean-Paul Baeten, *The Art of Architecture Exhibitions*, ed. Kristin Feireiss (Rotterdam: NAi Publishers, 2001): 98–104.
Post.Rotterdam, ed. Pedro Gadanho (Rotterdam: 010 Publishers, 2001): 80–85.
wetGRID exhibition design, *Crossing, #2 'exchanging roles'*: 64–67.
wetGRID, *D-tower*, A+U 370, 01: 07: 27–33.
H_2Oexpo, *OffTheRoad_5speed*, Andrew Watts, *Moderne Baukonstruktion* (Vienna and New York: Springer Verlag): 59, 213, 226.
'autour du corps' cover, *Archicréé* 299, July 2001.
'Lars Spuybroek, Die Struktur der Erfahrung', *Umzug ins Offene*, eds Tom Fecht and Dietmar Kamper (Vienna and New York: Springer Verlag): 258–63.
NOX: H_2Oexpo, V2_Lab, *OffTheRoad_5speed*, *D-tower*, *wetGRID*, *Galerie der Forschung*, *HOLOskin*, *Son-O-House*, *Soft Office*, ANC/Architecture and Culture, no. 0109: 52–117.

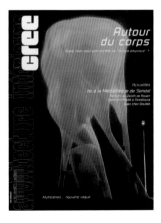

'Machine Effects', Bart Lootsma, *ANC/Architecture and Culture*, no. 0109: 54.

388

'Not Determinately Nothing', Brian Massumi, *ANC/Architecture and Culture*, no. 0109: 84–87.

Günther Feuerstein, *Biomorphic Architecture* (Stuttgart and London: Axel Menges, 2001): cover and 75–77.

James Steele, *Architecture and Computers* (London: Laurence King, 2001): 139–46.

Giuseppa di Cristina, *Architecture and Science* (London: Wiley-Academy, 2001): 164–77.

'Flurbs bieden kijkje in wondere wereld van Lars Spuybroek', *Rotterdams Dagblad*, 24 October 2001.

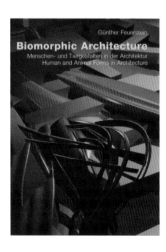

Peter Gössel/Gabriele Leuthäuser, *Architectuur van de 20e eeuw* (Cologne: Taschen, 2001): 391–94.

'NOX Flurbs', Edo Dijksterhuis, *ITEMS*,

September 2001: 17.

'Quartieri d'autore', Filippo Romeo, *Io Donna*, 10 November: 273–76.

'Lars Spuybroek utopista' on *ParisBRAIN*, Massimiliano Fuksas, *L'Espresso online*.

2002

'Rotterdam Rising', Kevin West, *W-magazine*, January 2002: 80–89.

'Lars Spuybroek, The Soft Machine of Vision', *Designing for a Digital World*, ed. Neil Leach (London: Wiley-Academy, 2002): 93–101.

'Twisted Towers', various publications on the New World Trade Center/oblique-WTC, *Wall Street Journal; Corriere della Sera; Bauzeitung; Süddeutsche Zeitung; die Presse, Cobouw; l'architecture d'aujourd'hui; Häuser; Technisch Weekblad; DOMUS; VPRO gids.*

'Un mondo liquido', Jeannette Plaut, *Ambientes Magazine*, no. 23/4: 38–45.

'V2 symposium transUrbanism', Olof Koekebakker, *ITEMS*, March–April 2002: 60–63.

NOX (transUrbanism), *D-tower, OffTheRoad_5speed, ARCHIS*, no. 1/2002: 76–77.

'Digital Handicraft' *ParisBRAIN*, Chris Scott, *FRAME*, March/April 2002: 34–35.

'NOX-Il limiti della contemporaneita'. Livio Sacchi, *Il Progetto*, no. 11, March 2002: 14–15.

NOX (*Soft Office, obliqueWTC* and *Tana di Alice*), *CA – Contemporary Architecture*, no. 42: 42–63.

Lars Spuybroek, *obliqueWTC. Sarai Reader 02: The Cities of Everyday Life* (New Delhi: Sarai – The New Media Initiative, 2002): 234–35.

Kari Jormakka, *Flying Dutchmen – Motion in Architecture* (Basel: Birkhauser IT-

series, 2002): 59–89.

The New Paradigm in Architecture, Charles Jencks (New Haven: Yale University Press, 2002): 221–25.

'The Structure of Vagueness', *ParisBRAIN, D-tower, transUrbanism*, ed. Joke Brouwer (Rotterdam: V2_Publishing/NAi Publishers, 2002): 65–87.

'Africa Comes First – Lars Spuybroek meets Rem Koolhaas', *transUrbanism*, ed. Joke Brouwer (Rotterdam:

V2_Publishing/NAi Publishers, 2002): 161–97.

OffTheRoad_5speed, Archilab's Future House – Radical Experiments in Architecture (London: Thames & Hudson, 2002): 174–76.

maison*FOLIE*, *Tana di Alice*, *ParisBRAIN*,
ArchiLab – Orleans 2002, ed. M.-A.
Brayer and F. Migayrou: 176–81.
Lars Spuybroek: *obliqueWTC*,
'Commitment', exhibition catalogue.
Water pavilion, Sutherland Lyall,
Masters of Structure (London: Laurence
King, 2003).
'New York, reser sig ur askan',
obliqueWTC Illustrerad Vetenskap: cover
and 22–27.
Soft Office, *A+U* 385 *New Skin*, 02: 10:
96–101.
A New World Trade Center, ed. Max
Protetch et. al. (Regan Books, 2002):
106–09.
'Das Kraken-Hochhaus', on *obliqueWTC*,
P. M. Wissenschaft Aktuell, December
2002: 32.

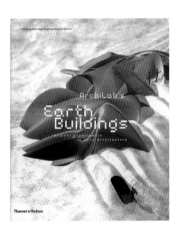

NOX/Lars Spuybroek: *Holoskin*, *Soft
Office*, Philip Jodidio, *Architecture Now 2*
(Cologne: Taschen, 2002): 386–97.
NOX: *Water Pavilion*, Aaron Betsky,
Landscrapers: Building with the Land
(London: Thames & Hudson, 2002):
42–45.

'Altijd weer de eeuwige vraag: wat stelt
het voor?', interview with Arnold
Zweers, *Apeldoornse Courant*, *Nacht
van de Architectuur*, 30 November
2002: 4.

2003

'Les Maisons-folies', *La Pierre d'Angle*,
no. 33: 12–13.
FEDUROK, maison*FOLIE*, *Son-O-House*,
D-tower, *L'Architecture
Méditerranéenne*, no. 59, June 2003:
114–20.
*The Metapolis Dictionary of Advanced
Architecture*, ed. ACTAR (Barcelona:
ACTAR, 2003).
*Innovations/New Arch 07: From
Experimentation to Realization*, ed.
Alexandra and Andreas Papadakis
(London: New Architecture Group,
2003): 102–05.
Zoomorphic, Hugh Aldersey-Williams
(London, Laurence King, 2003).
'Lars Spuybroek, le cyber cool', interview
by Guy-Claude Agboton, *IDEAT*, no. 27,
September–October 2003: 134–35.
Ecstacity, Nigel Coates (London:
Laurence King, 2003)
Non Standard Architecture, eds Frédéric
Migayrou/Zeynep Mennan, Centre
Pompidou, NOX: 126–29.

Acknowledgments

Work like this depends strongly on intense personal exchanges. Clearly it needs to be not only explained and defended on very different platforms, but also supported and stimulated in very different areas. The first to mention would be the research field, located not just at one university but at various schools, which has now grown into an invisible, global network of people that repeatedly meet at each other's reviews, each other's exhibitions and symposia. Thanks to my friends at Columbia University in New York I have been able to take a clearer direction: Hani Rashid, Lise Anne Couture, Sulan Kolatan, Bill Mac Donald, Greg Lynn, Karl Chu and Mark Wigley. I especially want to thank Bernard Tschumi for his support: lecturing and teaching at Columbia has been formative. Also at the AA DRL in London I have enjoyed the exchanges with Brett Steele, Patrik Schumacher and their students. Moreover, I would like to thank all of my own students, not only in New York, but also in Kassel, Germany, who have joined in the research and pushed it on to higher levels. Special thanks to my assistants for making everything work out: Ludovica Tramontin, Christian Troche, Leonore Daum, Gemma Koppen and Tao Zhu.

Between research and architecture there is a huge cultural field of (flying) curators who have invited me for exhibitions and become friends or even clients and who are often more obsessed than I am, so thank you to Frédéric Migayrou, Marie-Ange Brayer, Saskia Copper, Aad Krol, Meira Yagid, Harm Lux, Massimiliano Fuksas, Francesco Bonami, Ton Quik, Hans Menke, Jean-Paul Baeten and Els Hoek. And further to these, directors of cultural institutions, Kristin Feireiss and Ruud Brouwers, respectively of the Netherlands Architecture Institute and the Netherlands Architecture Fund, who have been of crucial help. And, within the same field, I'd like to thank artists Q. S. Serafijn, Hans Werlemann and Edwin van der Heide who have been co-authors of some of the projects at the intersection of art and architecture. It is in the nature of the work that the border between culture and clients is blurred; in that financially not always stable zone I want to thank especially: Arielle Pélenc, Alex Adriaansens, Ashok Bhalotra, Joep Baartmans, Jos Wilbrink, Ad van Etten, Paul van der Lee, Mark Penninkhof, Anne Wood, Roberto Masiero, Richard Castelli, Didier Fusillier, Martine Aubry – many projects have relied on your often silent help.

Special thanks go out to Rem Koolhaas for his support.

Somehow the memories of theoretical exchanges are set around dinner tables: Manuel DeLanda, Andrew Benjamin, Brian Massumi, Arjen Mulder, Detlef Mertins – thank you so much for helping me to develop the ideas for this book. In addition I'd like to thank Bart Lootsma, Anna Tilroe, Scott Lash, Lev Manovich and Derrick de Kerckhove for their comments throughout the years.

Special thanks to Kris Mun of my office and Lucas Dietrich of Thames & Hudson for your confidence and strong support during the making of the book.

Very special thanks go out to Joke Brouwer, my love, my critical eye and the graphic designer of this book. Without her none of this would have happened.

NOX Office:
Lars Spuybroek with **Joan Almekinders:** H_2Oexpo, "beachness", blowout, FOAM HOME, Flying Attic, V2_Lab, OffTheRoad_103.8 Mhz, OffTheRoad_5speed, deepSurface, Goes goes, wetGRID **Florian Boettcher:** Pompidou Two, D-Tower **Pitupong 'Jack' Chaowakul:** D-tower, Son-O-House, Galerie der Forschung **Antonio Correia:** obliqueWTC **Estelle Depaepe:** Maison Folie, Son-O-House **Bernhard Frodl:** Pompidou Two, D-tower **Peter Heymans:** H_2Oexpo, "beachness", V2_Lab, Goes goes **Kees Gajentaan:** "beachness" **Thomas Garnier:** FEDUROK **Josef Glas:** Son-O-House, ECB, Pompidou Two **Loic Gestin:** Maison Folie **Dominik Holzer:** wetGRID, De Gothic Stijl **Gemma Koppen:** deepSurface, OffTheRoad_5speed **Nicola Lammers:** Soft Office, Son-O-House **Dave Lee:** D-tower, Pompidou Two **Agustina Martire:** obliqueWTC **Ouafa Messaoudi:** Maison Folie **Kris Mun:** Maison Folie, Soft Office, Son-O-House, ParisBRAIN, obliqueWTC, FEDUROK, Pompidou Two **Maurice Nio:** Soft City, H_2Oexpo **Wolfgang Novak:** wetGRID, Galerie der Forschung **Norbert Palz:** Son-O-House, Galerie der Forschung, D-tower **Sven Pfeiffer:** wetGRID **Florent Rougement:** Maison Folie, Soft Office, ParisBRAIN, FEDUROK, Pompidou Two **Wouter Thijssen:** Son-O-House, Galerie der Forschung **Ludovica Tramontin:** Maison Folie, Soft Office, Son-O-House, La Tana di Alice, ParisBRAIN, FEDUROK, Pompidou Two **William Veerbeek:** H_2Oexpo **Remco Wilcke:** OffTheRoad_5speed, Galerie der Forschung, wetGRID, D-tower **Chris Seung-woo Yoo:** D-tower, Maison Folie, Soft Office, Son-O-House, obliqueWTC, ParisBRAIN, FEDUROK, ECB, Pompidou Two **Geri Stavreva:** D-tower, Son-O-House, Pompidou Two **Saskia Vandersee:** Soft Office **Christian Troche:** Pompidou Two **Hans Vermeulen:** FEDUROK

External Collaborations:
François Andrieux (Architecte d'Operation): Maison Folie **Artem Baguinski** (V2_Lab): D-tower **Simon de Bakker** (V2_Lab): D-tower **Jeroen Beckers** (programmer): SoftSite **Andrew Benjamin:** Pompidou Two **Eelco van den Berg** (programmer): SoftSite **Jeroen van den Berg** (programmer): SoftSite **Jean-Marcel Berthet** (OTE): Maison Folie **Lewis Blackwell:** FACES **Bert Bongers** (sensors/sound): deepSurface, EDIT SP(L)INE **Joke Brouwer** (designer): deepSurface **Michel Cova** (Ducks Scéno): Maison Folie, FEDUROK, Pompidou Two **Daniel Dekkers** (programming BLOB): EDIT SP(L)INE **Bruno Felix** (VPRO Television): Soft City **Asko Fromm** (Bollinger+Grohmann): Son-O-House **Xavier Fouquet:** wetGRID **Sylvain Gasté:** wetGRID **Manfred Grohmann** (Bollinger + Grohmann): Son-O-House, D-tower **Bob Lang** (ARUP-Group 4): Soft Office **Harm Lux:** The Future Is Now **Jo Mantelers** (programming WAVE): EDIT SP(L)INE **Bob den Otter** (programmer): SoftSite, **Walther Roelen** (programming RIPPLES): EDIT SP(L)INE **Q. S. Serafijn** (artist): D-tower, ROtower **Mike Tyler** (artist): The Future Is Now **Aad-Jan van der Helm** (programmer): SoftSite **Edwin van der Heide** (composer): EDIT SP(L)INE, Son-O-House **Meik van der Noordt** (V2_Lab): deepSurface **Pieter van Kemenade** (V2_Lab, webmaster): SoftSite **Floris van Manen** (software light): EDIT SP(L)INE **Laurens van Manen** (light): EDIT SP(L)INE **Matthijs van Manen** (hardware light): EDIT SP(L)INE **Marco Vermaas** (programming): Soft City **Victor Wentinck** (composer): EDIT SP(L)INE **Hans Werlemann** (photographer): De Gothic Stijl **Jan van der Windt** (Buro Zonneveld): H_2Oexpo **Gregor Zimmermann** (Bollinger+Grohmann): D-tower

Contributors

Andrew Benjamin is a philosopher, architectural theorist and professor of Critical Theory at Monash University, Melbourne, and a visiting professor at the University of Sydney. He is the author of *Architectural Philosophy* (Continuum, 2001) and *Disclosing Spaces. On Painting* (Clinamen, 2004) and has written widely on art theory, criticism and philosophy.

Manuel DeLanda teaches two seminars at Columbia University, School of Architecture: 'Philosophy of History: Theories of Self-Organization and Urban Dynamics' and 'Philosophy of Science: Thinking about Structures and Materials'. He is the author of *War in the Age of Intelligent Machines* (Zone Books, 1991), *A Thousand Years of Nonlinear History* (Zone Books, 1997) and *Intensive Science and Virtual Philosophy* (Continuum, 2002), as well as of many philosophical essays published in various journals and collections.

Brian Massumi teaches in the Communication Department of the Université de Montréal. He is the author of *Parables for the Virtual: Movement, Affect, Sensation* (Duke University Press, 2002), *A User's Guide to Capitalism and Schizophrenia: Deviations from Deleuze and Guattari* (MIT Press, 1992) and *First and Last Emperors: The Absolute State and the Body of the Despot* (with Kenneth Dean; Autonomedia, 1993); and editor of *A Shock to Thought: Expression After Deleuze and Guattari* (Routledge, 2002) and *The Politics of Everyday Fear* (University of Minnesota Press, 1993).

Detlef Mertins is an architect and historian known for his revisionist work on the history of twentieth-century architecture. He is Professor and Chair of the Architecture Department at the University of Pennsylvania. His publications include an extended introduction to the theory of design as *Gestaltung* for the English edition of Walter Curt Behrendt's *The Victory of the New Building Style* (Getty Trust Pubn, 1927). He is currently co-editing an English translation of the avant-garde journal *G: Material zur elementaren Gestaltung* (1923–26) and completing a monograph on Ludwig Mies van der Rohe.

Arjen Mulder is a biologist and media theorist. He has published several books of essays on the relationship between technical media, physical experiences and belief systems. His recent publications include *Book for the Electronic Arts* (with Maaike Post, V2_, 2000) and *Understanding Media Theory: Language, Image, Sound, Behavior* (V2_, 2004).

Photography Credits:
pp 2, 36, 97, 139, 227 cross-reference image (Eventstructure Research Group: Theo Botschuijver, Jeffrey Shaw, Sean Wellesley-Miller, photo by: Peter Boersma in 1969); pp 2 bottom left, 324 (Ernst Mach); pp 3, 187 cross-reference image (Gérard Degeorge); p. 25 top right (Peter Buteijn); p. 38 top (René de Wit); pp 42 bottom left, 66 bottom left, 247 second top right (Hans Namuth); pp 52–53 (Kaori Fujino); pp 54, 124, 164, 270, 356 cross-reference image (Ståle Skogstad); pp 90–91, 92, 93, 94 bottom (Christian Richters); p. 114 top centre (Englewood Colorado); pp 130 top right, bottom left, bottom right, 132 top, 133, 279 middle right (Paul Mellaart); p. 134 bottom four (Hans Werlemann); pp 135, 163, 310 cross-reference image (Markus Hilbich); p. 135 top right (http://www.smcm.edu/users/lnscheer/lecture%20web%20pages/208open/open.html); pp 146–47, 147, 148, 149 top, 152–53 front page, 154–55, 156–57, 157 top (Alain Guillard); p. 163 bottom middle (Achim Bednorz); p. 163 bottom right (Pablo de la Riestra); p. 208 top right (Aad Krol); p. 233 (Harry Noback); p. 246 top right (Edgar Cleijne); p. 247 bottom right (Victor E. Nieuwenhuys); p. 379 top right, bottom right (Jan Sprij).

Image Credits:
pp 3, 187, 202, 272 cross-reference image (original illustration from the first volume of Gottfried Semper's *Der Stil in den technischen und tektonischen Künsten*, 1860–63, p. 186, Fig. 4); pp 3, 55 cross-reference image (D'Arcy Thompson, *On Growth and Form*, Dover Publications, reprint 1992); p. 6, Richard Held and Alan Hein, *Perceptual and Motor Skills*, 8; p. 26 (van Manen); pp 42, 247 cross-reference image (Peter Wollen, ed. *On the Passage of a Few People Through a Rather Brief Moment in Time*, MIT Press, 1991); pp 42 bottom left, 66 bottom left, 247 second from top, 273 top left © ARS, NY and DACS, London 2004 (Jackson Pollock, *Autumn Rhythm*, 1950); pp 42 bottom right, 247 top © Asger Jorn/DACS 2004 (Guy Debord and Asger Jorn, *Mémoires*, 1959); p. 43 (http://www.v2.nl/DEAF/96/softsite); p. 96 bottom centre (Iannis Xenakis, *Metastasis*, 1954); p. 134 middle (Szépművészeti Múzeum, Budapest); p. 156 top left (IVAM Instituto Valenciano de Arte Moderno); p. 157

© ADAGP, Paris and DACS, London 2004 (Henri Michaux, mescaline drawing, 1969); p. 163 top left, top right (Gregor Zimmermann); pp 172, 173 (Q. S. Serafijn); p. 183 middle right, bottom right (Bollinger+Grohmann); p. 197 (Edwin van der Heide); p. 208 middle left (Jean Suquet); p. 208 bottom left © ADAGP, Paris and DACS, London 2004 (Marcel Duchamp, *Large Glass*, 1923); p. 234 (Original illustration from the first volume of Gottfried Semper's *Der Stil in den technischen und tektonischen Künsten*, 1860–63); pp 246–47 © DACS 2004 (Constant, *New Babylon/Ruhrgebiet*, 1963); p. 247 bottom © DACS 2004 (Constant, *Round Etching with Three Holes*, 1958); pp 260–61 bottom centre (Paul Virilio and Claude Parent, *Architecture Principe*, 1966); pp 268–69 top (Tao Zhu); pp 268–69 middle (Marcus Leinweber); pp 268–69 bottom (Matthias Schrader-Thiet); p. 269 top © DACS 2004 (Mies van der Rohe, Seagram Building, 1954–58); p. 271 (Hermann Finsterlin, architectural sketches, 1919); p. 272 right column (Hanna Stiller); pp 272–73 centre column (Matthias Theek); p. 273 left column (Geri Stavreva); p. 273 right column (Angelika Kauffmann); p. 290–91 centre (Ernst Haeckel, *Radiolarien*, Plate 7, 1862); p. 308 top (Jørn Utzon, scheme for shopping centre, from Kenneth Frampton's, *Studies in Tectonic Culture*, MIT Press, 2001, p. 270); p. 309 top left (Jørn Utzon, Sydney Opera House, from Kenneth Frampton's *Studies in Tectonic Culture*, p. 277); p. 309 top right (Jørn Utzon, Bagsvaerd Church, from Kenneth Frampton's, *Studies in Tectonic Culture*, p. 289); p. 326 © ADAGP, Paris and DACS 2004 (Frantisek Kupka, *Conte de pistils et d'étamines*, 1919–20).

From the *IL* Books:
pp 3, 141, 179, 218, 247, 270, 352 cross-reference image (*IL* Archive, K. Bach); p. 55 bottom right (*IL 33* p. 116, *IL* Archive); pp 67, 110, 220, 261, 314 cross-reference image (*IL* Archive, K. Bach); p. 160 left (*IL 9*, p. 30, *IL* Archive); p. 198 (*IL 9*, pp 92–94, *IL* Archive); pp 216–17 top centre, top right (*IL 35*, p. 298–41, *IL* Archive); p. 10, 260 top left (*IL 35*, p. 180, *IL* Archive); pp 280–81 top centre (*IL 33*, p. 175, *IL* Archive, K. Bach); p. 315 (*IL 35*, p. 180, *IL* Archive); p. 320 top right (*IL* Archive).

This book was made possible by financial support from The Netherlands Architecture Fund.

Design by Joke Brouwer

First published in the United Kingdom in 2004 by Thames & Hudson Ltd, 181A High Holborn, London WC1V 7QX

www.thamesandhudson.com

British Library Cataloguing-in-Publication Data
A catalogue record for this book is available from the British Library

ISBN 0-500-28519-5

Printed and bound in China by C & C Offset Printing Co Ltd